Research Methods for Clinical
and Health Psychology

Research Methods for Clinical and Health Psychology

Edited by
David F. Marks and Lucy Yardley

SAGE Publications
London • Thousand Oaks • New Delhi

SAGE Publications Ltd
6 Bonhill Street
London EC2A 4PU

SAGE Publications Inc
2455 Teller Road
Thousand Oaks, California 91320

SAGE Publications India Pvt Ltd
B-42, Panchsheel Enclave
Post Box 4109
New Delhi – 100 017

British Library Cataloguing in Publication data

A catalogue record for this book is available from the British Library

ISBN 0 7619 7190 4
ISBN 0 7619 7191 2 (pbk)

Library of Congress Control Number: 2002112769

Typeset by Mayhew Typesetting, Rhayader, Powys
Printed and bound in Great Britain by TJ International, Padstow, Cornwall

We dedicate this book to our students,
past, present and future.

CONTENTS

LIST OF CONTRIBUTORS

Claire Ballinger is a Lecturer at the University of Southampton.

Paul Camic is Professor at Columbia College.

Kerry Chamberlain is a Reader in Health Psychology, Massey University, New Zealand.

David Clark-Carter is a Reader in Psychology, Staffordshire University.

Hélène Joffe is Senior Lecturer, University College, London.

David F. Marks is Professor and Head of Department of Psychology, City University, London.

Michael Murray is Professor of Social and Health Psychology, Memorial University, Canada.

Sheila Payne is Professor, University of Sheffield.

Nichola Rumsey is Research Director, Centre for Appearance Research, University of West England.

Cathenne M. Sykes is Project Manager, CHD Partnership, King's College Hospital, London.

Sue Wilkinson is Ruth Wynn Woodward Endowed Professor, Simon Fraser University, Canade.

Lucy Yardley is Professor and Head of Department of Psychology, Southampton University.

PREFACE AND ACKNOWLEDGEMENTS

This book is designed as an introduction to research methods, primarily for clinical and health psychologists. It should also be useful to students in other fields of applied psychology such as counselling and occupational psychology, and to students of other health care disciplines such as medicine, nursing, occupational therapy, speech therapy and physiotherapy, or in the kindred fields of social work, sociology, anthropology, social geography and social history. Our aim is to give the reader a flavour of the excitement and the pitfalls of carrying out research, and a basic appreciation of a range of methods commonly used in clinical and health psychology.

The book incorporates a number of features intended to assist the novice researcher. The objectives of each chapter are set out at the beginning, the key features of the research methods are summarised in a set of 'Method boxes', and extended examples of how to apply a variety of research methods are also provided. **Key terms** are highlighted in **bold type**. Definitions of key terms are printed in the Glossary at the end of the book. The definitions are designed to be helpful to readers unfamiliar with these terms – experts will, naturally, be able to debate and contest each definition! Each chapter concludes with a chapter summary and a small list of recommended reading that may be consulted for a more in-depth treatment of the methods described.

In this book we have sought to combine the advantages of drawing on specialist input for each chapter while maintaining coherence across chapters. As editors we have co-authored each chapter to ensure that the book as a whole provides coherent coverage of research methods, with continuity of style and terminology, and no duplication or inconsistency. At the same time, so that each chapter benefits from the authority and experience of experts, we have brought together a team of twelve specialists in particular methods and techniques. In addition to their academic training, all these authors have carried out research in a variety of health care settings and reported their studies in high quality peer-reviewed journals. We acknowledge with appreciation our collaborators' efforts to create a text that is well informed, readable and concise. Specifically, we thank our co-authors for their central contributions to the following topics: Nichola Rumsey – carrying out research (Chapter 2); Sue Wilkinson – focus groups (Chaper 3); Hélène Joffe – interviews (Chapter 3) and content and thematic analysis (Chapter 4); Kerry Chamberlain – grounded theory (Chapter 5); Paul Camic – case studies (Chapter 5); Michael Murray – narrative analysis

(Chapter 6); Claire Ballinger – participant observation (Chapter 7); Sheila Payne – action research (Chapter 7); David Clark-Carter – survey, experimental and quasi-experimental design and analysis (Chapters 9 and 10); Catherine Marie Sykes – systematic reviews (Chapter 11).

We would like to acknowledge the comments of two anonymous referees – you know who you are, and we thank you, even if we did not take all of your advice. We also acknowledge the inspirational work on evidence integration at the NHS Centre for Reviews and Dissemination that informed the first section of Chapter 11. Last, but certainly not least, we thank our respective partners for their forbearance while we worked unsociable hours on the manuscript, often to the neglect of our domestic duties.

David F. Marks and Lucy Yardley

1 INTRODUCTION TO RESEARCH METHODS IN CLINICAL AND HEALTH PSYCHOLOGY

Lucy Yardley and David F. Marks

AIMS OF THIS CHAPTER

(i) To consider what readers can expect to gain from this book.

(ii) To discuss the aims and purposes of research, in relation to different theories of how knowledge can be obtained.

(iii) To introduce the context of research in health and clinical psychology.

(iv) To discuss procedures for establishing the validity of research.

WHAT CAN YOU GAIN FROM THIS BOOK?

One genuine frog is worth a bucketful of toads. Anon

What's that? Frogs and toads, indeed! What have they got to do with a book on research methods? Well, read on – by the end of this chapter you will see.

This book is an introduction to methods for carrying out research in clinical and health psychology. It introduces the kinds of study designs and methods that are in common usage across the health sciences and which are of particular relevance to psychologists and social scientists. We aim to give readers sufficient understanding of the nature of psychological inquiry in these fields to be able to understand how and why a variety of different research approaches and methods can be used, and to ask sensible and searching questions about the best ways of doing things before, during and after a research project. This broad overview of the process of carrying out research will enable you to critically appraise published research, to evaluate the potential and limitations of a variety of qualitative and quantitative research methods, and to identify those that you may wish to use for particular research purposes.

Of course, it is not possible to provide exhaustive details of all the specific methods in a single textbook, and so we have provided references and recommendations for further reading that will help you to become more expert in any particular method that you may wish to use. We encourage the reader to apply the methods described here creatively to the particular unique setting in which she or he is planning a project. Obviously it is also impossible to list a complete set of features that will apply to all settings, times and places. Policies, circumstances and contexts vary enormously across settings and across time, and readers will need to adapt the research methods to each new situation.

This chapter provides the context for the following chapters on specific aspects of research, by examining some fundamental questions regarding the aims and validity of research in general, and considering the context of research in clinical and health psychology.

WHAT SHOULD BE THE AIMS AND METHODS OF RESEARCH?

Although this question might at first seem almost superfluous, it is actually the starting-point for some fundamental and long-lasting debates about **ontology** (what there is to be known, that is, what 'reality' is) and **epistemology** (how knowledge can be obtained). A range of positions has been taken in this debate, ranging from **realism** and positivism at one end of the spectrum to **constructivism** and idealism at the other.

The realism/constructivism debate

The modern realist perspective can be traced back to the philosophy of Descartes, who proposed that we have direct knowledge of subjective, mental reality ('I think, therefore I am'), but must derive our knowledge of objective, physical reality through observation (see Yardley, 1999). Subjectivity is viewed as pure, rational thought, internal to the individual, and separate from the body. The rational mind is viewed as the vehicle with which we can seek to understand and control a mechanical, physical world (which includes our own bodies). Consequently, the task for research is to attempt to obtain accurate information about objective physical reality. This can be achieved by maximising the precision of our observations through quantification, and ensuring that error and **bias** are eliminated from our observations – for example, by isolating the variables we are studying in order to be able to identify cause–effect relationships more clearly. Subjective distortions of reality may also be introduced by us as researchers and, in psychology, by human 'subjects' or 'participants', and these potential sources of bias must be minimised also.

In the classic positivist **hypothetico-deductive method**, observations can then be used to empirically test our mental models of the generalisable causal laws that govern reality, using objective methods of analysis such as statistics to ensure that these analyses are not influenced by subjective expectations or values. Having ascertained the causal laws that govern the physical world we can intervene to achieve desired objectives. This approach to research provided an extremely useful initial foundation for modern science and medicine, and proved so successful that it was also adopted by the emerging discipline of psychology. Consequently, for most psychologists this is the most familiar approach to obtaining knowledge through research.

Despite the practical utility of the scientific method, **post-modern** critics of the realist perspective have suggested that eliminating subjectivity from our knowledge of the world is actually impossible to achieve (Gergen, 1985; House & McDonald, 1998). The constructivist argument is that since we can only gain knowledge through the human medium of our minds and bodies, *all* our knowledge of both 'self' and 'body/world' is inevitably mediated, constrained and thus *constructed* by our thoughts and activities. Moreover, constructivists do not view the construction of meaning as a private, subjective matter, but as an essentially social process, since our habitual ways of thinking and acting are fundamentally shaped by social interaction, language and culture. From this perspective, differences in perceptions and interpretations of 'reality' are not error, since different ways of living and thinking create different experiences of the world and different systems of meaning. This does not mean that the 'objective reality' of science is incorrect – in the context of the activities of predicting and controlling physical phenomena (including physical health) it is the most valid and useful way we currently have of understanding the world. However, it is not the *only* valid and useful way of understanding the world. For example, religion, politics, art and personal experience all offer different but equally valid perspectives.

At this point, a common realist response is to invoke the 'death and furniture' argument – to bang the table to prove it is objectively real not socially constructed, and to object that events such as death have a physical reality that cannot be construed in any other way (Edwards, Ashmore & Potter, 1995). However, death is actually a good example of an event that psychologists *must* consider from multiple points of view if they are to acknowledge and understand the psychological experience of health and illness. Without doubt, the physical dimension of death is best explained in scientific terms – although it should be noted that as our knowledge and practice of medical science has changed, so has the definition and indeed the physical reality of death; people whose heart had stopped would have been incontrovertibly 'dead' two centuries ago, but now death can be postponed until brain activity ceases (and two centuries into the future who knows at what point death will be considered to be irreversible?). Consequently, for the practical purpose of preventing death the medical scientific definition of reality is undeniably the most relevant. However, death cannot ultimately be prevented by science – and the non-scientific views of reality and interpretations of death may be much more relevant to understanding and shaping the experience for the living, dying and bereaved. These include all the religious, cultural, philosophical and personal beliefs that can help us to accept and find positive meaning in the inevitability of dying, and offer a way of integrating it into our lives.

Since constructivists believe that human culture and activities profoundly shape our experience and knowledge of 'reality', the aim of constructivist research is to understand the different meanings by which people in different contexts make sense of the world and of their lives, and the social processes whereby these meanings are created. Consequently, rather than isolating variables from their context and regarding human interpretations as 'bias' which obscures objective reality, constructivists deliberately seek to investigate how context and interpretation (including those of the researcher) influence our experience and understanding of the world. This can be achieved by collecting contextualised data, often in real-world settings and in the natural language of participants, and encouraging reflection on the social and subjective processes influencing the interpretations that are constructed. The aim is not to identify universally applicable laws but to develop insights which are meaningful and useful to particular groups of people, such as patients, participants in a study, or people in similar situations, health care workers, and/or other researchers.

Despite the passion with which researchers sometimes argue for one or other pole of the realism/constructivism divide, the ontology on which each position is founded can never actually be proven correct or incorrect, but must remain a matter of faith; since we cannot extricate our knowledge from our subjective perceptions and thought processes we will never know with complete certainty whether there is an 'objective' reality out there or not (Potter, 1996). Moreover, as the next section explains, the divergence in ontology and epistemology between realists and constructivists need not become a barrier to maximising and integrating the insights and benefits that can be derived from different approaches to research.

Beyond the realism/constructivism divide

In practice, few researchers are extreme realists or extreme constructivists, and there are many intermediate positions that can be adopted (see Guba & Lincoln, 1998). For example, the **post-positivist** view is that although an objective reality exists, and we should seek to understand it, we can never gain perfect knowledge of it. While this view is entirely compatible with the scientific method, rather than seeking to establish the 'truth' through experimentation, the aim of post-positivist research is to test, falsify and thereby improve our imperfect models of reality, using a variety of methods. Similarly, many researchers are happy to concede that indeed there may be an independent external reality which constrains and shapes people's lives, but that it remains vitally important for researchers to take into account and investigate the way in which human experience (including the process and outcome of research) is also shaped by subjective interpretation and social interaction.

Moreover, although the different aims and assumptions of realist and constructivist researchers clearly tend to steer them towards different methodologies, there is no rigid mapping between ontology/epistemology and method. A qualitative grounded theory analysis of interviews with patients might be undertaken by a realist who wanted to uncover their rationale for accepting or rejecting a particular treatment, or by a constructivist who wanted to explore how the treatment was perceived and depicted by the patients. In each case the method used and data obtained would be similar, but the focus of the analysis and the interpretation would be slightly different; the realist would be interested in patients' statements as a reflection of the underlying beliefs which caused them to behave in a particular way, whereas the constructivist might be interested in the accounts as an illustration of the range of socio-cultural meanings whereby patients made sense of the treatment in relation to their wider values and identities.

If the choice of method is based on the purpose of the research, rather than on epistemological assumptions about how to obtain valid knowledge, then it becomes possible to combine different methods in order to gain diverse forms of knowledge that can provide complementary insights (House, 1994). The insights gained using different approaches will not necessarily be congruent or converging; rather, the insights from one perspective can be used to challenge, modify or elaborate the understandings reached with a different approach. Eisner (2003) has pointed out that every perspective and every method reveals some things and conceals others; consequently the question the researcher should ask is not which method is 'best' in any absolute sense, but rather 'what can we learn from each perspective?' This attitude to research is consistent with the **pragmatist** view (Hickman & Alexander, 1998; Tashakkori & Teddie, 1998), that common-sense, scientific and moral judgements are *all* purposive, constructive activities which share the same fundamental test of validity as any other form of human inquiry: 'What happens if . . .?' From the pragmatist perspective *all* human inquiry involves the interpretation, intentions and values which constructivists regard as paramount – but must also necessarily be grounded in the empirical, embodied experience which realists regard as fundamental.

With respect to our basic understanding of the experience of health and illness, **qualitative methods** are generally most suitable for inquiring into subjective meanings and their socio-cultural context, as these are not causes or mechanisms which can be scientifically proven, but malleable, negotiable interpretations which people offer themselves and others to make sense of their feelings and actions. In this respect, qualitative data could be considered analogous to a video diary, which provides rich, personal information about what it is like for a certain person to be in a certain place. Data derived from **quantitative methods** is more like a map; it provides precise and economical information that is essential in order to discover the location and distance of a place relative to other places. Maps do not convey the information needed to know what a place is like, and so we need video diaries to understand subjective experience (for example, the personal and socio-cultural meanings and implications of 'stress'). However, we also need maps in order to locate precisely experiences relative to other similar experiences (for example, to determine whether a person's stress is greater than at a different time-point, or than that of other people), and to link them with other dimensions of experience (for example, to determine whether stress causes or is caused by changes in physiological functioning). Similarly, different methods can serve different but complementary purposes with respect to applied research in health care. Case studies can provide a sound foundation for informing health-related practice (Fishman, 1999), but planners and policy-makers may require quantitative data on prevalence and cost-effectiveness in order to be persuaded and to persuade others of the utility of planned health care provision, and to manage such provision effectively on a large scale.

Integrating the results of research which has employed such different perspectives and methods requires an appreciation that it is perfectly possible for realist analyses of quantitative data and constructivist analyses of qualitative data to yield different but equally important kinds of 'truth' (see Box 1.1). For example, if a healing relationship produces a 'placebo' effect, patients' first-hand accounts of the interactive process which enhanced subjective wellbeing may be as important to effective health care as the hard quantitative evidence that physiological status remained unchanged. Another example is the biological approach to the understanding of psychosis. The psychopharmacological treatments that have evolved from this approach are making a major contribution to patient wellbeing. Yet the understanding of the experiences of patients requires methods that are tuned to the **phenomenology** of altered conscious experience. Since health and clinical psychology are applied disciplines that must be able to contribute to multidisciplinary research, it is vital to adopt a theoretical framework (such as pragmatism) that can embrace and integrate qualitative research into subjective experience and socio-cultural meanings and quantitative research into psychophysiology and evidence-based medicine.

Research methods can be viewed, not as recipes for mechanical knowledge production, but more as creative or adventurous means of inquiry (Willig, 2001). Using qualitative or quantitative methods does not make one a particular kind of psychologist, nor does a particular kind of psychologist necessarily use qualitative or quantitative methods. The critical issue is not the method used, but the theory, beliefs, values and political positioning, which underpin **praxis**, the translation of theory into action. The next section of this chapter outlines some of the different theoretical and practical contexts in which clinical and health psychologists carry out their research.

Box 1.1 *Hypothetical example of how the topic of 'adherence' to single or multiple dose medication might be approached from different perspectives*

The research question

Medication to reduce chronic high blood pressure should ideally be prescribed to be taken four times a day, as this will maintain blood levels of the medication near the required level throughout the day. However, patients may be less likely to adhere to this prescription than to a single slow-release dose of medication, which they may be less likely to forget to take and which will interfere less with their daily routine and identity as a basically healthy person. How should the prescription of this medication be managed in the best interests of the patient?

Positivist/biomedical approach

Design: Give patients instructions to take medication in one or four doses a day, quantify blood levels of medication, compare levels when prescribed in one or four doses.
Rationale: Experimentally manipulate prescription to test effect on objective physiological status.
Knowledge gained: Objective, practical information about which method of prescribing is more effective in achieving optimal blood levels of medication.

Post-positivist/biopsychosocial approach

Design: As above, but supplemented with questionnaire measures of self-reported adherence, intentions, recall of instructions, perceived costs/benefits of medication, etc.
Rationale: As above, but also relate information about objective physiological status to quantitative measures of subjective factors (reported behaviour, recall, beliefs, intentions) which may mediate relationship between prescription and physiological status.
Knowledge gained: As above, but supplemented by information which may identify intervening psychological variables potentially amenable to modification (for example, recall, beliefs, intentions).

Interpretive/humanist approach

Design: Interview participants to find out how prescription of single and multiple daily doses of medication is perceived by people in different circumstances, how lifestyle is affected, understanding of 'adherence', reasons given for non-adherence.
Rationale: Acquire insight into the various meanings ascribed to single and multiple daily prescriptions in the context of different people's identities, daily lives, beliefs about medication, etc.
Knowledge gained: Understanding of the different perspectives of different patients; the influence on these of culture, identity, practical and social context; discrepancies between the assumptions and perspectives of researchers, health professionals and patients.

Constructivist/critical approach

Design: Record dialogue in consultations, analyse how the ideal of 'adherence' is constructed as the only rational choice, the way rhetorical strategies are used to promote acceptance of prescription, how alternative discourses are suppressed or assimilated.

Rationale: Examine the socio-cultural functions of the normative discourses, possibilities for alternative discourses, ways in which power is negotiated in relation to prescription.

Knowledge gained: Understanding of the socio-cultural implications of the identities and discursive strategies available to doctors and patients, and how these can be deployed to promote or resist particular forms of prescription.

THE RESEARCH CONTEXT OF HEALTH AND CLINICAL PSYCHOLOGY

Clinical psychology has its origins in the 1940s when psychological techniques were being used to assist battle-fatigued personnel in the Second World War, more recently termed 'Post Traumatic Stress Disorder' (Napier, 1995). The requirements of the military services have had an important influence on the development of clinical psychology; for example, the use of mental tests and measurement for selection of military personnel, and the use of neuropsychological techniques for screening and rehabilitation of war veterans, the victims of torture and other forms of violence. Educational and clinical psychologists share similar concerns in understanding the developmental and family influences on wellbeing. **Health psychology** emerged in the 1970s and 1980s when different discourses about health were developing, one leaning towards the idea that individuals are responsible for their own health through the choices that are made or dictated by so-called 'lifestyles', others resting on biological determinants, and yet others on relevant socio-political factors (Matarazzo, 1982; Marks et al., 2000; 2002b).

While clinical psychology and health psychology have different historical roots and specialised interests, physical and mental health can be regarded as two complementary aspects of health and illness. In many countries the training pathways have common generic components, and there are strong overlaps between the interests of clinical and health psychologists in their work with patients in the health care system. It is therefore not surprising that a similar set of research methods are used by both groups and also by other specialists including nurses, doctors and paramedical staff. The aims and methods of research in clinical psychology and health psychology depend on the context and the general orientation to undertaking research.

Most clinical psychologists work in the health care system, although they may also work in private practice, carry out assessments for the criminal courts, and work in academic and research settings. Others specialise in forensic work involving correctional services in prisons and correctional facilities of various kinds. Clinical psychologists often work in multidisciplinary teams of health care professionals consisting of doctors, nurses, social workers, occupational therapists, speech therapists and physiotherapists. The principal service users are referred by general practitioners (GPs) or family physicians. An important function of the clinical psychologist is critical thinking using an evidence-based approach to evaluation and intervention. Clinical psychologists are seen as 'scientist-practitioners' with the ability to design and carry out applied research and to carry out critical evaluation of research activity. Clinical psychologists also develop and evaluate new interventions using psychological theory. According to the American Psychological Association (APA) website:

> Researchers study the theory and practice of Clinical Psychology, and through their publications, document the empirical base of Clinical Psychology . . . Clinical Psychologists also engage in program development, evaluate Clinical Psychology service delivery systems, and analyze, develop, and implement public policy on all areas relevant to the field of Clinical Psychology. (American Psychological Association, 2002)

From the above description it can be seen that clinical psychology as a discipline is not wedded to any one model, theory or method, but uses what works best on the basis of the evidence base collated from experience including various methods of assessment using questionnaires and interviews, randomised controlled trials and observational studies of the effectiveness of therapies, and qualitative evidence on patient experience. Clinical psychology uses a variety of models including the scientist-practitioner model, the reflective practitioner model and the evidence-based practitioner. These models have been debated within the profession for many years and each has influenced various aspects of the clinical psychologist's role (Parry & Watts, 1995; Barker, Pistrang & Elliott, 1994).

In health psychology, contrasting approaches to understanding health and illness have sprung up in a relatively short period, reflecting different priorities and values about the nature of psychology and health, and therefore the theory and practice of psychology. While these different approaches are overlapping and evolving, it is possible to distinguish at least four ways of working that offer theory, research and recommendations for practice. While tensions exist between the different value systems and assumptions of these four approaches, each complements the others, and there is a potential for a powerful coalition of psychologists for health. Each approach is discussed in turn below.

Clinical health psychology grew out of biomedicine and clinical psychology with a perspective that is broadly realist but also interpretative, seeking to relate psychological variables to biomedical conditions in order to understand, predict and control health processes, outcomes or **quality of life (QoL)**. Clinical health psychology is the best established and most mainstream of the four health psychology areas as represented by the majority of textbooks, journals and academic programmes. It has been very successful at making psychological inroads into the health care system and the medical curriculum and is the principal reason for the existence of health psychology today as a vibrant new field. The principal characteristics of clinical health psychology are summarised in Table 1 (column 2).

Public health psychology (see Table 1.1, column 3) is an approach allied to epidemiology and health promotion. It is broadly realist but also interpretive, seeking to identify and manipulate psychological variables predicting mental and physical health and health promoting behaviours in the general population. Like clinical health psychology, public health psychology is practised within the health care system but working towards health promotion and prevention rather than treatment of illness. Public health is a multifaceted, multidisciplinary activity and public health psychology recognises the expertise of other disciplines, especially in health promotion, communications and epidemiology. It has the potential to enhance the effectiveness of public health through the application and evaluation of theories of behaviour change. However, this does not simply mean targeting the beliefs and behaviour of individuals – promoting public health also means engaging with social processes, such as advocacy, negotiation, community building and social capital.

Community psychology (see Table 1.1, column 4) is allied to critical theory, and tends to be constructivist and pragmatic in nature. It may be defined as:

> Advancing theory, research and social action to promote positive well-being, increase empowerment, and prevent the development of problems of communities, groups and individuals. (Society for Community Research and Action, 2001)

Community psychology involves working in coalition with members of vulnerable communities and groups, mainly outside the health care system. It sees health as wellbeing in its broadest sense, including not only mental and physical health, but also positive psychosocial aspects, such as resilience. Community psychology is represented by Division 27 of the APA, the Society for Community Research and Action (SCRA). Membership of the SCRA includes not only psychologists but also people from related disciplines such as psychiatry, social work, sociology, anthropology, public health and political science, including teachers, researchers and activists. Community psychology is concerned with healthy psychosocial development within an ecological perspective.

Critical psychology is allied to critical theory and other social sciences. It tends to be constructivist, seeking to analyse and critique assumptions and discourse associated with health and illness, including that of health professionals and researchers, in order to promote awareness of socio-political functions and consequences of these. Critical psychology aims to analyse

Table 1.1 Characteristics of clinical, public, community and critical health psychology (adapted from Marks, 2002a, 2002b)

Characteristic	Clinical health psychology	Public health psychology	Community psychology	Critical psychology
Definition	'The aggregate of the specific educational, scientific, and professional contributions of the discipline of psychology to the promotion and maintenance of health, the prevention and treatment of illness, the identification of etiologic and diagnostic correlates of health and illness and related dysfunctions, and the analysis and improvement of the health care system and health policy'. (Matarazzo, 1982)	The application of psychological theory, research and technologies towards the improvement of the health of the population	'Advancing theory, research and social action to promote positive well-being, increase empowerment, and prevent the development of problems of communities, groups and individuals'. (Society for Community Research and Action, 2001)	The analysis of how power, economics and macro-social processes influence health, health care, and social issues, and the study of the implications for the theory and praxis of health work
Theory/ philosophy	Biopsychosocial model. Health and illness are: 'the product of a combination of factors including biological characteristics (e.g., genetic predisposition), behavioural factors (e.g., lifestyle, stress, health beliefs), and social conditions (e.g., cultural influences, family relationships, social support)'. (APA, 2001a)	No single theory and philosophy. Supportive role in public health promotion which uses legal and fiscal instruments combined with preventive measures to bring about health improvements. Working towards general theories, for example, health literacy improves health	Social and economic model: 'Change strategies are needed at both the individual and systems levels for effective competence promotion and problem prevention.' (Society for Community Research and Action, 2001). Acknowledges the interdependence of individuals and communities. Shares some of the aims of public health psychology, for example, improving health literacy	Critical psychology: analysis of society and the values, assumptions and practices of psychologists, health care professionals, and of all those whom they aim to serve. Shares some of the aims of community health psychology, but with universal rather than local constituency

continues overleaf

Table 1.1 (cont.)

Characteristic	Clinical health psychology	Public health psychology	Community psychology	Critical psychology
Values	Increasing or maintaining the autonomy of the individual through ethical intervention	Mapping accurately the health of the public as a basis for policy and health promotion, communication and interventions	Creating or increasing autonomy of disadvantaged and oppressed people through social action	Understanding the political nature of all human existence; freedom of thought; compassion for others
Context	Patients in the health care system, i.e. hospitals, clinics, health centres	Schools, work sites, the media	Families, communities and populations within their social, cultural and historical context	Social structures, economics, government and commerce
Focus	Physical illness and dysfunction	Health promotion and disease prevention	Physical and mental health promotion	Power
Target groups	Patients with specific disorders	Population groups who are most vulnerable to health problems	Healthy but vulnerable or exploited persons and groups	Varies according to the context: from the entire global population to the health of an individual
Objective	To enhance the effectiveness of treatments	To improve the health of the entire population: reducing morbidity, disability and avoidable mortality	Empowerment and social change	Equality of opportunities and resources for health

Orientation	Health service delivery	Communication and intervention	Bottom-up, working with or alongside	Analysis, argument, critique
Skills	Assessment, therapy, consultancy and research	Statistical evaluation, knowledge of health policy, epidemiological methods	Participatory and facilitative, working with communities, community development	Theoretical analysis, critical thinking, social and political action, advocacy, leadership
Discourse and buzz words	'Evidence-based practice', 'Effectiveness', 'Outcomes', 'Randomised controlled trials'	'Responsibility', 'Behaviour change', 'Risk', 'Outcomes', 'Randomised controlled trials'	'Freedom', 'Empowering', 'Giving voice to', 'Diversity', 'Community development', 'Capacity building', 'Social capital', 'Sense of community', 'Inequalities', 'Coalitions'	'Power', 'Rights', 'Exploitation', 'Oppression', 'Neo-Liberalism', 'Justice', 'Dignity', 'Respect'
Research methodology	Efficacy and effectiveness trials, quantitative and quasi-experimental methods	Epidemiological methods, large-scale trials, multivariate statistics, evaluation	Participant action research, coalitions between researchers, practitioners and communities, multiple methodologies	Critical analysis combined with any of the methods used in the other three approaches

how **power**, economics and macro-social processes influence or structure health, health care, health psychology and society at large (see Table 1.1, column 5).

While critical psychology cannot offer a positive programme of action for health care psychologists, it fulfils an essential reflective function, asking fundamental questions about the rationale, purpose and consequences of the conceptualisations and activities of clinical and health psychology, and championing the cause of neglected or oppressed sections of society.

From this brief overview, it will be evident that clinical and health psychologists work in a wide range of contexts, and approach physical and mental health from many different perspectives. It is for this reason that it is necessary for clinical and health psychologists to have a basic appreciation of a variety of research methods suitable for different purposes. For example, an understanding of the correct design, conduct and analysis of clinical trials and meta-analyses is needed in order to critically evaluate the evidence base for therapeutic interventions (see Chapters 2, 10 and 11). Familiarity with questionnaire development and validation is needed in order to select suitable outcome measures for such research (see Chapters 8 and 9). And there is growing recognition in the field of medicine and health that qualitative methods are a valuable tool for studying lived experiences of health care interventions from the different perspectives of patients and health professionals (see Chapters 3 to 7). Each of these equally important and related objectives requires a quite different approach to research, which asks different types of questions and generates different kinds of information. The following section considers how the validity of such different approaches to research can be assessed and enhanced.

HOW CAN THE VALIDITY OF CLINICAL AND HEALTH PSYCHOLOGY RESEARCH BE MAXIMISED?

It will be clear from the preceding sections that the approach to health and clinical psychology that we are advocating is to employ a variety of research methods that are suitable for different purposes. Employing a wide range of methods has clear advantages with respect to maximising the **validity** of research, because each method can only provide limited knowledge, whereas a combination of approaches may allow the researcher to elaborate, supplement, correct or modify the limited insights gained from each single method.

To return to the example of adherence given in Box 1.1, if the investigation of adherence to the two methods of prescribing was restricted to the objective experimental data, the researcher might learn that prescribing the single dose of medication resulted in better blood levels of medication, but would not know for certain why this was, or how the effectiveness of the theoretically superior multiple dose method might be improved. By adding questionnaire measures of behaviour, recall and beliefs the researcher might discover that blood medication levels were linked to reported levels of adherence, and demonstrate that these were reliably predicted by reported concern about the side-effects of the medication. However, the researcher would still have only a limited understanding of why and which people reported concern about side-effects. The interview data might then enhance the researcher's understanding of the link between beliefs about side-effects and lower adherence to multiple doses. For example, the interviews might reveal that people believed that four doses must be stronger and therefore potentially more harmful than a single dose, and that having to take multiple daily doses interfered with their social identity as an essentially healthy person. Comparisons between interviewees might uncover greater concern about taking medication and risk of non-adherence in those to whom a healthy identity was particularly important, such as younger, working, male patients. Finally, the analysis of discourse in the consultation might reveal that invoking concern about side-effects could serve as a rhetorical device employed by patients to justify non-adherence and resistance to medical authority regarding management of their health.

In summary, only by using *all* of these methods could the researcher obtain the vital evidence needed to optimise health care, that is, that a) the multiple dose was not as medically effective as it theoretically should be; b) this was caused by non-adherence associated with expressed concern about side-effects; c) these concerns were greatest in younger, working, male patients (who arguably had most to lose by non-adherence to potentially life-saving medication); but d) simple education and reassurance about the strength and potential risks of multiple doses might offer only a partial solution to the problem, since the apparent concern about taking multiple doses was linked to the damaging effects of doing so on identity, and was used as a justification for resisting a 'sick' identity.

Despite the clear advantages of using multiple methods to research health problems, there are also potential pitfalls. It is essential that the methods be combined in a manner that both respects and utilises their *different* purposes and potentials. For example, the purpose of qualitative research is to carry out intensive, in-depth analysis of rich data to derive an understanding of a particular situation or context that may give rise to theoretical principles with relevance to similar situations or contexts. The purpose of quantitative research is to reliably identify factors and relationships in a sample that can be assumed to be true of the whole population from which the sample was drawn. It is therefore essential for quantitative research, but wholly inappropriate for qualitative research, to gather data from a large, statistically representative population sample; conversely, 'intensity' sampling of typical cases and 'purposive' sampling of atypical cases could increase the validity of the qualitative research but totally undermine the validity of the quantitative research. Similarly, inconsistency in responses may undermine the validity of a quantitative study by reducing the reliability of measurement, and would therefore need to be reduced (for example, by eliminating inconsistent items), whereas in qualitative studies the meaning of such variability might be a central focus of the research. It is therefore essential when combining methods to have a sound grounding in each method, and an appreciation of the very different forms of validity and procedures for establishing validity that are relevant to each method.

The common procedures for establishing the validity of quantitative research are generally familiar to psychologists. Clarity about the hypotheses tested and constructs measured is required. It is necessary to ensure that the **power** of the study is sufficient to detect the 'effect' one is investigating, by enhancing the strength of the effect studied (for example, by comparing samples which differ greatly on the variable of interest, or employing a highly effective intervention) and minimising random error (for example, by maximising the precision and reliability of the measures used, excluding or controlling for sources of variance other than those of interest, and employing a sufficiently large sample). Steps should be taken to ensure objectivity, such as minimising potential bias due to the expectations of the researcher or the participants (for example, by using objective measures or double blind clinical trial designs). The method should be specified in such detail that it could be replicated, including the statistical analysis of data. In addition, it may be desirable to demonstrate ecological validity – to show that despite these tight constraints necessitated by the experimental method, the findings correspond to outcomes and relationships in naturally occurring situations; for example, that treatment efficacy effects found in clinical trials under ideal conditions (with expert therapists and highly motivated, carefully selected patients) can also be demonstrated in pragmatic trials in the normal clinical context.

Common procedures available for establishing the validity of qualitative research are generally less familiar to psychologists. Realist qualitative research may employ procedures to check **inter-rater reliability** (see Chapter 4) in order to show that the categories assigned to segments of text can be reliably applied by more than one person, and hence have a degree of objectivity. Non-realist qualitative research does not take inter-rater agreement as a sign that objectivity has been achieved, but sometimes also employs various procedures for comparing how more than one person categorises the text, as a useful method of exploring alternative interpretations, and refining the meanings of the categories used to make sense of the data. A good paper-trail from the raw data to the final interpretation demonstrates that the interpretation is well grounded in the empirical data and documents the way in which the process of analysis influenced the findings of the research; this involves linking the definitions of the categories developed to a record of the researchers' thought processes and decisions which contributed to these definitions, and the segments of raw data corresponding to each category (see for example discussion of coding frames in Chapter 4 and memos in Chapter 5). Researchers who wish to show that their interpretations correspond to those of the participants may feed the results of their analysis back to participants for comment, although it should be noted that participants may be unable or unwilling to comment on complex analyses, and may have individual views that are inconsistent with the overview provided by the research (Barbour, 2001). Deliberately seeking and analysing 'deviant cases', or instances which seem to contradict or depart from the interpretation presented, is an excellent way of avoiding selective attention to patterns in the data that are consistent with the researcher's preconceptions, and over-generalisation from these cases. In addition, the researcher can use **triangulation** of data or analyses as a means of approaching the topic from different perspectives in order to see whether these converge or throw up interesting differences related to the context examined or the method used. For example, the data may be gathered from different people (for example, doctors, patients, other family members), at different times and places, by different investigators, or using different methods and theoretical approaches (as advocated above).

As will be obvious from the brief review of methods of establishing validity given above, it is not possible to draw up a definitive list of procedures that will be applicable for all approaches and methods. Although useful checklists of ways of demonstrating the validity of qualitative studies have been published, it is acknowledged that they should only be regarded as providing indicative guidance and not as setting out prescriptive, comprehensive criteria (Barbour, 2001; Blaxter, 2000); moreover, these criteria are not applicable to quantitative methods. Nevertheless, there are broad principles that can be applied to *all* research (Yardley, 2000), although the ways in which these principles are satisfied will differ widely between the various quantitative and qualitative methods. These principles, and some of the ways in which they can be applied, are briefly outlined below.

Sensitivity to context

All research should obviously demonstrate sensitivity to the theoretical context of the topic studied, and previous relevant empirical literature, in order to extend our understanding beyond what has already been suggested or established. Research which is undertaken in ignorance of existing theory and findings risks 'reinventing the wheel', or simply unconsciously replicating what is already known – or worse still, may fail to take into account important factors and processes which have already been shown to be relevant. Further, all research should be clearly sensitive to the empirical data collected, that is, the analysis should examine which interpretation(s) is consistent or inconsistent with the data, or as Kvale (2003) puts it, the object of the research must be allowed to object. If data are simply used to illustrate an argument rather than to examine its empirical validity then the 'study' may be an excellent and valuable exposition of theory but does not constitute truly empirical research. In addition, research which focuses on socio-cultural processes should demonstrate a reflexive awareness of the operation of these in the process of research: for instance, the effects on the outcome of the research of the context and aims of the research; the different assumptions, values and viewpoints of the researchers and the participants; the relationship and dialogue between them, and related ethical issues.

Commitment and rigour

The quality of all research is related to the rigour and commitment with which the researcher engages with the topic. This can be demonstrated by means of the competence and skill with which the method used is applied, and by the depth and/or breadth of the analysis. For example, just as high quality quantitative research should be carried out with a sample size adequate to provide a powerful test of the hypothesis, high quality qualitative analyses should go beyond superficial or commonsense description of what has been said or done.

Transparency and coherence

All research reports should provide sufficient detail of the methods and analyses employed to allow the reader to evaluate their merits and limitations, to be satisfied that the research has been thoughtfully, meticulously and appropriately carried out, and to form a judgement as to whether the data truly support the conclusions drawn. While this form of 'transparency' should be characteristic of the method and results sections of all studies, constructivist researchers will often add a further layer of reflexive transparency concerning the way the aims, context and process of the research may have influenced its outcome (see 'sensitivity to context' above). The quality of all research is also affected by the clarity and power with which the descriptions and arguments are communicated, as well as their internal consistency; as noted above, it is essential to maintain coherence between the aims of the research method and the means that are employed to ensure and demonstrate that the conclusions are valid.

Impact and importance

Research cannot have any value unless it matters to someone for some reason! Its value may be at an abstract level, for example, opening up new ways of looking at an issue, which may in turn suggest new understanding and further useful lines of research. Research can have socio-cultural value, providing evidence relevant to arguments about what policy is preferable or what factors are responsible for various outcomes. Finally, research may have practical value for a range of different people and purposes, from providing health care professionals with information about the mechanisms that mediate illness, prevention or cure, to providing sections of the community with a means of voicing their viewpoint and achieving greater insight into and control over their situation.

HOW TO MAKE THE BEST USE OF THIS BOOK

In the light of the discussion above, there can be no golden or guaranteed method for producing good quality research in any area of psychological or social inquiry. We have argued for a diversity of methods to fit the diversity of possible questions, perspectives and problems that arise in the study of health and clinical issues. This book is therefore not a 'cookbook' for carrying out research. There are no menus or recipes. This book is a source of ideas about the nature of psychological inquiry, the various approaches that are available, and the pragmatic analysis of a theory, question or problem. Try to match your chosen method(s) with the research question(s) that you are asking, but first of all be clear about the question. Then be clear about the advantages and disadvantages of the methods that might yield evidence relevant to your question. Finally, use the method(s) you choose with all of the rigour that you can bring to bear.

In the end there can be no substitute for the greatest method of all, thinking about what you are doing. This book is designed with this purpose in mind. A plea to all student researchers is therefore: by all means be enthusiastic about your research, but never risk your or others' wellbeing or safety by leaping before you look. Think carefully about the implications of your research – be ethical, prudent, joyful and wise. If that sounds a bit like a recipe for life as well as for research it is probably not very surprising – there are some similarities. In both life and love, thinking things through before acting is a sensible policy, as much as it is in carrying out a research project. Doing good research is not as easy as might at first sight appear, and is never a mechanical process. For every valid study there are several 'no-hopers' – there are just so many ways that a study can be done badly compared to the ways of doing it well. There are a lot of tadpoles in the pond but relatively few become fully grown. (At last, we come back to the frogs again!) This means that an awful amount of time, energy and resources are wasted on research of poor quality.

We'd like to think that this book can help in some small way to lower the ratio. That way you may at least kiss a few more frogs and avoid the toads that look the part but can never deliver a prince, or princess – or a cool piece of research that tells you exactly what you want to know with elegance and style. This book is about the best ways of finding a frog. And remember, one genuine frog is worth a bucketful of toads![1]

---

[1] We have nothing against toads as such. They are wonderful creatures with a charm all of their own. In fact one of the author's childhood pets was a toad. But frogs are something special to behold, especially when you are looking for one.

REVISION QUESTIONS

1 What is meant by the terms 'ontology' and 'epistemology'?
2 Describe 'social constructionism'.
3 What objections do social constructionists have to positivism?
4 What is 'pragmatism'?
5 What is meant by the validity of research? List some of the ways in which you might demonstrate the validity of a) a quantitative study, and b) a qualitative study.

2 GETTING STARTED: THE PRACTICALITIES OF DOING RESEARCH

Nichola Rumsey and David F. Marks

AIMS OF THIS CHAPTER

In this chapter we describe the practical 'nitty-gritty' of doing research and **consultancy** in health care settings. In particular, we address issues related to five aspects of carrying out research or consultancy:

(i)   Working with colleagues.
(ii) Obtaining funding.
(iii) Obtaining ethical approval.
(iv) Managing a project.
(v)   Reporting results and dissemination.

WORKING WITH COLLEAGUES

Research, teaching, training and consultancy frequently involve working both with other psychologists and professionals from other disciplines. Colleagues may enter the working relationship with different sets of values, adhering to different ethical or professional codes and research practices, necessitating a negotiated agreement concerning joint working.

The number of collaborations and working relationships a psychologist may be involved in at any one time can be considerable. Multiple roles may bring conflict; for example, the conflicting demands of being both a practitioner and researcher, or acting as a consultant and an employee and working for a variety of clients, who could be individuals, groups or organisations, patients, health care staff, managers or policy-makers. In all of this there will be challenges about drawing boundaries and managing finite amounts of time and energy. Good communication skills are of key importance in managing the challenges inherent in all of these situations.

Team working

Your work may lead you to become a temporary or 'permanent' member of a variety of teams; for example, teams of researchers, care providers, consultants, evaluators, or a combination of these. For each group, it is important to clarify your status. Is the group of your own formation, or have you been asked to join an already existing group, for example, as a consultant or as a trainer contributing your own particular knowledge and skills? Are you perceived by others as a leader, organiser, or as an 'agent' of the person who was instrumental in arranging your membership of the group. For example, a consultant might ask you to collect data in a clinic, but may not have informed any other members of the team. Might the position of the person who asked you to join the team oblige you to weight your view, or can you act freely and independently? How does your agenda fit in with the priorities of others in the group? It will be helpful to clarify your role (for example, as researcher, trainee, trainer, evaluator, observer, consultant), the timescale of your involvement, and the agenda and objectives of others within the group at an early stage. If you cannot perceive or negotiate your role, you probably do not have a useful place in the group and may well be wasting your and everyone else's time.

Each person should have a clear function in relation to the project. However, some functions may need to be shared, and roles should be 'understudied' in case of absence or other difficulty. Ideally, the successful completion of the project should never depend upon the continued involvement of any one individual, but in practice this is hard to realise. Downie and Calman (1998) warn that research projects can alter relationships within a team and may divide loyalties. Whenever possible, decisions concerning the project should be made collectively. Ongoing, regular communication with all those involved is vital for the life and progress of the project.

Organising research

It is often necessary to 'sell' a proposed piece of work to colleagues and other members of staff. Persuasion may be needed at several different levels in the organisational hierarchy, and the message will need to be tailored to appeal to each audience. It is sensible to go through the following three stages: firstly, to explain the rationale for the proposed project; secondly, to listen and respond to the reactions of others to the initial ideas; thirdly, to present and defend a more detailed proposal and, lastly, to get agreement and commitment (Robson, 2002).

Even if the aims of the project have been agreed, there are likely to be different agendas for the people engaged in the work. Differences in opinion and conflicts of values and interests are inevitable throughout the life of a project. The protocol for the research may require participants to change their working routines. These changes may be considered irksome or in some cases even morally wrong by some of the people involved, especially if there are team members who do not fully share or own the vision and aims of the project, or who do not feel fully involved. There may be conflicting priorities within the team, for example, in response to time pressures; some health care workers may feel that it is more important to offer high quality standard care than to collect a full set of data. It may be necessary to compromise the research design or the choice of measures in order to maintain the goodwill of colleagues and to provide the best conditions for participants. Once again, communication and interpersonal skills are absolutely crucial.

Acting as an advisor or consultant to a project

The task of advisor or consultant is to 'give away', trade or sell one's knowledge, skills and experience. This may be in an informal or more formal capacity and does not necessarily involve payment. One's participation may be a favour, for the goodwill that will be generated, or it may be paid for in kind. In order to avoid the dangers of misuse and misapplication inherent in the giving and receiving of advice, it is important to seek an early clarification of your status and to agree this status with all members of the group. Do your 'clients' have sufficient knowledge, skills and experience to use the advice appropriately? Are they sufficiently committed to the proposed activity or is the choice to seek advice merely tokenism? In relation to research advice, a whole series of issues needs to be explored with a view to ensuring that the research sophistication of the group is sufficient to carry the project through successfully. These issues include the research agenda, possible methodologies, likely methods of reporting, informed consent and confidentiality.

Tension between the values of those involved in a project may be more acute in the case of paid consultation. There may be issues concerning the topic of the proposed project, the methods to be employed or the ways in which the results might be used. Research workers cannot morally detach themselves from the design or results of research in which they have been involved (Downie & Calman, 1998). Advisors and consultants must take full responsibility for the implications of both the process of the research and the outcome. This may necessitate withdrawal from a project at an early stage.

When acting as an advisor or consultant, one's involvement is going to be time limited. Some thought and discussion should be given to the likely time commitment and to the point at which withdrawal is appropriate. There needs to be a set of boundaries that are respected by all parties. The aim should be to produce a self-sustaining team of researchers or practitioners who are self-motivated and powered from within. To act as an effective manager of change, a psychologist will need a sophisticated understanding of the change process and the likely barriers to change that will be erected, both from within a team and from outside it.

OBTAINING FUNDING

Funding is essential

Health and clinical psychologists generate a significant proportion of the research in the field of psychology, perhaps about one-fifth of the total. However, research is an expensive activity and there is no recipe that will automatically result in funding. This means that you, your supervisor or your research team will need to invest considerable efforts in securing the necessary resources for your project or accept that you may not be able to carry out the work – at least, not beyond a preliminary or pilot stage. Normally, in colleges and universities, doing research is a requirement of any academic post. For example, in the United Kingdom, university departments are rated for the quality of the research that they do in a national Research Assessment Exercise. The ratings of research quality are made by a panel of experts from across the psychology discipline. Of key significance to the national and international reputation of a department is the amount of research funding that it has obtained over a five-year period. Therefore applying for research funding is a core activity for health and clinical psychologists in academic or research posts. Research grants also generate additional posts in the form of research assistantships, fellowships, doctoral studentships and post-doctoral grants and research bursaries.

Not all research projects require special funding. The primary asset for some projects is *staff time*. Since research is part of any academic's job description, the time involved in carrying out research is available up to a reasonable level free of any specific charge to the research project. The institutions involved will also normally allow staff members to carry out printing, photocopying and computing and use existing equipment for the purpose of research. Consequently pilot projects are often carried out using existing infrastructure and resources. However, when extra staff, computers or other equipment are needed, or if the printing, photocopying and postage costs are going to be high, specific sources of funding will need to be identified and a funding application made. Depending on the nature of the employment contract that a psychologist has, the preliminary 'leg work' usually has to be undertaken in addition to normal activities. Researchers have to make an early assessment of whether their motivation is sufficient to carry them through the conflict, drudgery and slog involved in the vast majority of projects (Robson, 2002). Almost always it is the best policy to play to your strengths and develop projects that use the expertise that you, your supervisor or team members have already developed to some degree. In this case it is less likely that you will be frustrated or surprised by barriers and problems that may lie hidden behind the well-constructed plan that you have prepared for your project. A sensible rule of thumb for all planning exercises is to work out how long it will take to complete everything you have to do and then double it. Otherwise you can expect to be working at evenings and weekends 'like there is no tomorrow'. It is a common experience to discover that the submission deadline for a research proposal is only a few days away, in which case 'tomorrow will be too late'.

Sources of funding

Once the focus for the research has been carefully chosen, the next step is to identify the most promising sources of funding. Alternatively, it is possible to turn this process around, identifying potential sources of funding and then tailoring your pet project to fit the source's priorities. Whichever way around your idea develops, competition for support from the major funders is always going to be fierce. To increase the chances of financing a project it is worth thinking broadly about different possible sources. In addition to large public sector funders (for example, government departments, research councils and international bodies such as the European Commission) and major charities, local sources of funding may also be available, such as Hospital Trust funds, local government departments, benefactors and private companies. The possibility of obtaining funds from charities specifically concerned with the focus of your proposed research is worth considering, as is sponsorship by pharmaceutical companies.

Each potential funder will have its own agenda and set of priorities, which may include negotiating tangible signs of their sponsorship and possibly also defining the form of dissemination of your findings. The quid pro quo for accepting funding from a source may well be an enforced restriction on publication of the research findings. This is an issue that must be negotiated at the time the funding is being agreed and accepted. There is always a strong preference on the researcher's part for no strings to be attached to the findings, but if one is carrying out a project funded by local or central government, or for commercial organisations that will have a stake in positive rather than negative reports, this will seldom be the case. The researcher and the funding body both have an interest in clarifying publication rights before the funding is allocated and the project begins. Then the decision about whether to accept funding must be based on ethical and pragmatic considerations. If one holds out for no restrictions, one could lose the funding altogether. Yet if one accepts the restrictions, one's ability to disseminate the research findings may be severely limited and subject to the approval of the sponsoring body. Nobody can decide this issue except for the research team members, taking into consideration the full context of the organisations, values, ethics and politics that come into play.

If a major funding body is to be approached, a useful first step is to trawl brochures and websites in order to establish the current funding agenda of each body, the amount of funding available, the preferred beneficiaries of the research and the kinds of applicants the funders are seeking to encourage. Do they, for example, entertain bids from academics, practitioners, charities or user groups? Might the bid be enhanced by a team of applicants that includes the favoured elements? Usually the answer to the latter question is 'yes' and you will be wise to include such people in your team. Applying for research funding, like research itself, is a pragmatic exercise that combines interpersonal skills, ethical awareness, political nous, scientific method, logic, intuition and sheer dogged determination, not necessarily in that order.

Developing a research proposal

Once target sources of funding have been identified, a detailed proposal should be developed according to the guidelines offered by the funding body. Many funders ask for an initial outline submission to ensure that the proposed research falls within their remit or terms of reference. Typically, a research officer employed by the funding body considers this initial submission. If the outline is approved, applicants are invited to submit a detailed proposal. This proposal may be sent out to **referees** for review, with the subsequent funding decision made by a committee in the light of the reviewers' comments. It is helpful to establish the detail of this process in order to tailor the application appropriately. Some grant-giving bodies consult external referees, others do not. Which circumstances apply? If reviewers are consulted, how many reviews will be sought? Do applicants have a chance to suggest potential reviewers? What is the likely expertise of the reviewers and the members of the committee making the funding decisions? What is the timescale for the final decision on funding?

In order to develop a proposal that is worthy of funding, many detailed decisions about the proposed research must be made at this early stage. Do not underestimate how much effort and time is involved in this process! A suitable project team should be assembled and consulted concerning the details of the project and the proposal. Many funding bodies favour the inclusion of a statistician, a practitioner and an applicant with experience of successfully achieving and administering grants. The latter is invaluable in terms of support when the going gets tough at this and any subsequent stage of the project. It is also useful to solicit advice from others who have previously applied, whether successfully or unsuccessfully, to the particular funding body.

Funders often provide detailed application forms for completion. These forms vary and they can sometimes be idiosyncratic and fiddly to complete. Having Acrobat Reader on your computer will be essential. In a few cases, typewriters may have to be used because the forms are not yet available electronically, although this practice is becoming a rarity these days. Better still, you can retype the funding body's forms in word-processor format, checking first that this will be acceptable to the funder. Common elements include a summary of the proposal, the aims and anticipated outcomes/ benefits, a detailed justification for the resources requested together with a budget statement, curriculum vitae and signatures from all applicants, and additional signatures from representatives of the host institution(s). Applicants are often given the opportunity to submit the bulk of the research proposal using their own chosen format, with the requirement that certain elements (for example, timescale, milestones and ethical considerations) are included. There are usually space or word limits on funding applications.

When working on the detail of the structure and content of the application, it is worth considering Robson's (2002) advice that a good proposal is well organised, clearly expressed, understandable and appealing from the perspective of an intelligent (and quite possibly disinterested) layperson. Imagine the reviewers posing a series of questions. Is the context of the research clear? What is the problem or issue to be investigated? Is there a pressing need for research at this point in time? Are the aims and objectives achievable? Is the research question well articulated, informed by relevant theory and located in the literature? Are the proposed design and methodology appropriate? How will participants be recruited and is the sample size justified? Is the proposal ethical? How will the research be monitored and progress checked? What are the important milestones? How will the interests of the various **stakeholders** be represented? Are the likely outcomes/benefits clearly articulated and persuasive, and is the research worth any possible upheaval? Are the requested resources sufficient? Does the research represent value for money? How will the results be presented and disseminated?

In addition to the detail required by the funding body, many institutions now require that all applications are subject to internal scrutiny. This may be limited to the head of department or specialty, who may be required to approve the nature of the research and to confirm that facilities are available to carry out the work, and a representative from the relevant finance department to confirm that the budget calculations are correct and that sufficient funds to cover resources (for example, the use of facilities, staff time) are included in the bid. In some institutions, the application may additionally require a 'round' of signatures including the chief executive, head of section, faculty, department or school, a representative from the research support unit, the institution's finance director and a representative from the executive of any collaborating organisations. All this takes time, and may well result in further frustrating delays while changes are made to the application.

Pricing and timing

In bringing the project planning to its final conclusion, the aim will be to design a study or set of studies that can be completed within a fixed timescale and for an agreed price. In these respects a research project is no different from hiring a builder to make an extension to your house. Just like a builder, the researcher needs to calculate estimates that are achievable and make reliable predictions of what will happen in reality without the need to cut corners or work through the night to get the work finished on time. If the estimates are wrong, your team members will become overloaded and disgruntled and your paymaster unimpressed at your lack of reliability and management skills. If your first project fails, they will be disinclined to entrust you with another.

There are two tools that are very useful in the planning and budgeting of projects. The first is **cash flow analysis**. In cash flow analysis income and expenditure are plotted on a monthly basis for the lifetime of the project. The computer package Excel is well suited to this purpose. You need to identify all sources of expenditure and plan what these will be month by month over the course of the project. You will also need to ensure that all employment costs are included, that salaries are on the appropriate scale points, that you allow for recruitment costs, salary increases, national insurance, superannuation, payments of any part-time staff or participants, the cost of equipment, consumables, printing, postage, travel and institutional overheads, if the sponsor allows you to charge for these.

When all of the necessary items have been included you will be able to obtain the total price for the project and also break this down into annual or quarterly amounts. This information will be needed in some form by the grant-giving body, which may negotiate the figures with you with the aim of reducing some of the costs.

The second is the **Gantt diagram**, another useful tool for planning projects. Like cash flow analysis, it uses a spatial arrangement to represent time across the course of the project, plotting activities that need to be carried out at different stages in their logical order with time estimates and deadlines for each one. Box 2.1 contains a simple example of a Gantt diagram prepared for a two-year research project consisting of three studies.

Box 2.1   *A Gantt diagram for a two-year project that includes three studies*

The activities that need to be completed are placed in a sequence of two- or three-month blocks. In a more complex case, several overlapping activities may be plotted across time blocks, in different lines or rows of the diagram. For example, parts of the report writing could be started before the data analysis is completed, or study 1 could be designed while the research assistant is being recruited.

	Jan Feb Mar	Apr May Jun	Jul Aug Sep	Oct Nov	Dec
Yr 1	Recruit and train research assistant	Design and pilot study 1	Collect data for study 1	Analyse data for study 1	Write intermediate report
Yr 2	Design and run study 2	Analyse data for study 2	Design and run study 3	Analyse data for study 3	Write final report

MANAGING A RESEARCH PROJECT

Unlike the role of advisor or consultant which often demands a high level of input in the initial stages of a project tailing off into a watching brief as work progresses, managing a research project requires a consistently large investment of time and effort from start to finish. After the considerable effort involved in producing the initial proposal, gaining ethical approval and launching the research, it may be tempting to take more of a back seat as data collection progresses. However, for most projects, responsibilities change rather than reduce, and many issues require attention at all stages (Ovreteit, 1997).

In the early stages

Pilot the proposed methodology and allow all those involved in the research time to adapt to new ways of working and to express any concerns. Ask participants about the experience of being involved in the research, and be prepared to tweak the protocol in response to feedback. Check on estimates of the number of participants, particularly if the research is taking place in a health care setting. If you are undertaking quantitative research, you will need to carefully estimate the number of participants that you need to recruit into your study using **power analysis**. This is a method for calculating the sample size that is necessary to give you an acceptable chance (90 per cent or more) of finding an effect if an effect is really there (see Chapter 10).

The need to have a high powered study must be balanced against the time constraints and problems that will be encountered in recruiting your participants. Clinicians are prone to overestimation of the numbers of patients presenting with a particular problem or condition. This combined with patients' reluctance to participate in research can create serious problems so allow plenty of time to collect your data. Essentially, make a realistic estimate of a number of weeks or months, then double it.

During the project

Be prepared to regularly monitor the concerns and issues of all those involved in the research process. Check on progress towards milestones (for example, is recruitment of participants proceeding as expected?). Involve those parties who are interested in the outcomes of the research in appropriate ways; offer interim reports whenever possible. Explore the fate of previous projects and make a note of any useful information which may affect whether the results are implemented. Seek advice on how best to influence decision-makers and prepare the likely channels for dissemination.

Finally, when the dust settles, it is helpful to stand back at the end of the process, to adopt a self-critical stance and to assess the experience gained during the research. What lessons have been learned for future studies and for one's own professional development? How could the process be improved next time?

OBTAINING ETHICAL APPROVAL

Ethical issues should be considered at every stage of the planning process. Issues that should be addressed early in the proceedings include whether all those involved or impacted by the research or consultancy know what they are letting themselves in for, and whether they have the possibility of opting out. How will the results be used? Will those who are able to act upon the findings be 'good guys' or 'bad guys' (Robson, 2002)? How will the participants find out about the results? It is also important to discover at an early stage how and when formal ethical approval for the proposal will be sought.

Some funding agencies require ethical approval to be obtained before an application is submitted. Others are content that funding can be offered subject to ethical approval being achieved before the research begins. Either way, obtaining ethical approval from non-psychologists means that you must satisfy an **ethical committee** composed of people from different backgrounds, often including the general public, that the benefits posed by your research to the participants and to other members of society outweigh the risks and costs, that you have minimised any potential harm, and that you have ensured that participants are provided with the information and time they need to give genuine informed consent to take part. Applicants will also be required to demonstrate that the research is methodologically sound (as it is unethical, as well as wasteful, to carry out poor quality research), feasible, and will not have a negative impact on the context in which it is carried out (for example, take up too much time or resources of busy health professionals). This is likely to involve providing extensive detail of the proposed measures and procedures, methods of recruitment (including the advertisements and letters you will employ to contact patients or other participants), how data will be safeguarded and confidentiality will be preserved. Often supporting evidence may be necessary, such as the signatures of clinicians, managers and/or data protection officers who must approve and accommodate your research, providing insurance, space and access to patients. The process is likely to be lengthy and can cause considerable delay to the anticipated start date for a project. Once again, the uninitiated would be advised to double the amount of time they anticipate the process will take!

Conflicting values

Because of its focus on the health care practices of people, research in health and clinical psychology is riddled with decisions, choices and practices requiring justification in moral and ethical terms. There really is no such thing as a 'value free' researcher. Psychologists should critically evaluate whether their own values, those of the stakeholders, or those of the discipline of health psychology are unreasonably imposed on the client or participant. The research questions and measurement tools may be value laden and/or more relevant to some sections of the population than others. A research paradigm or theory may lay emphasis on the current preoccupations of psychologists, health care providers or policy-makers. For example, the desirability of changing health behaviours in a particular way, the public taking responsibility for their own health behaviour, or providing patients with detailed information about their condition may seem worthy to the researcher, but may be counter to the beliefs and values of the participants. There is a particular need to be sensitive to cultural variations and to be aware that ways of working which may seem self-evident in one culture may be at odds with another (Francis, 1999).

Researchers must consider whether the investigation is likely to improve the current situation or whether it could lead to an exacerbation of existing problems. If the investigation indicates that change is desirable, is that change in fact possible, or will one's involvement merely serve to increase the dissatisfaction and disillusionment of those involved?

Inclusion/exclusion criteria

Careful decision-making is called for when deciding who should be included in a study and who should be excluded. Once again, a series of questions may be helpful. Do all members of the study population have an equal chance of participating? What about the less articulate or vociferous and those typically excluded from health care research because of complicating factors: the young, the elderly, illiterate people, those for whom English is not a first language, those with multiple presenting problems? Are these decisions driven by the needs of potential participants, or by research questions and methodology favoured by the researchers? It is a requirement of all health research in the United States that the participants include people from ethnic minorities, or if not, that this decision is explained and justified. This is a sound principle for health research everywhere. It ensures that the sample will contain people from groups that have hitherto been neglected or forgotten.

Informed consent

Despite a general consensus that informed consent is necessary and desirable before participating in research, Ward (1995) offers a reminder that the concept raises a 'sigh of despair' among some health care professionals who perceive the whole process as a tedious ritual necessary to defend themselves from patients with unrealistic expectations and from predatory lawyers. In the turmoil of preparing proposals and applications for ethical approval, psychologists might be forgiven their own occasional sigh of despair. However, Lansdown (1998) in discussing the use of informed consent for children reminds us that 'Informed consent . . . is more than just a legal obligation . . . it also has a moral basis fundamental to human relationships; the recognition of individual autonomy, dignity and the capacity for self-determination'. Evidence from psychological research on patient consent indicates that the majority do not understand and do not remember what they have consented to do (Ley, 1988).

In their efforts to cover every eventuality, many ethical committees have now produced detailed and lengthy proformas for patient information and for informed consent. Some potential participants will welcome these; others may be bewildered or irritated and will ask for an oral summary. In some cases, researchers may be required to produce their own patient information and informed consent sheets. Careful thought needs to be given to how the information will be framed. What verbal and nonverbal messages will be offered to participants? Detailed consent forms may be seen as unnecessarily legalistic and 'binding' and once the participant has agreed to take part, she or he may find it difficult to withdraw. Despite reassurances to the contrary, participants may feel that they have to commit to the whole project because otherwise their care will be compromised, they will be thought of in a negative light, they will be breaking an agreement (informed consent) or letting the researchers/staff down. Many people receiving health care are motivated to help out of gratitude to staff and because they wish to contribute to improvements in health care for others. It is important not to abuse, take for granted or take advantage of their goodwill by making light of the more onerous aspects of participating in the research, or by downplaying any opt-out clause.

Confidentiality

Seasoned researchers will know that it is one thing to commit to maintaining **confidentiality** as part of a funding proposal, yet another to maintain high standards in the course of the research and in the reporting of results. Although now it may be second nature for researchers to devise methods of coding data omitting unnecessary identifying characteristics, other issues remain. For example, most researchers when faced with a decision whether or not to collect a particular piece of information will gather it 'just in case'. However, as Downie and Calman (1998) point out, it is not acceptable to collect as much information as possible 'for the sake of it' but, on the contrary, researchers should decide which information is strictly necessary for analysis at a later date.

Researching as a member of a team can raise additional issues of confidentiality as there may be conflicting views concerning the amount and type of information necessary and how this material should be used. What happens if information comes to light during the research that is relevant to the care of a participant and you feel the care team should know about it?

Downie and Calman (1998) suggest agreeing a set of **confidentiality rules** within the team designed to optimise the anonymity of the participants. What types of information have to be shared and with whom? Who must, should, could, shouldn't know?

Concluding comments to this section

The process of obtaining funding and ethical approval can be daunting for the inexperienced. Navigation through the various 'hoops' requires considerable effort and commitment akin to a complex initiation rite. However, once the successful applicant has passed these tests, she/he can be reasonably confident that the research is ethical, worthwhile and well conceived. There will also tend be a snowball effect, as the applicant's confidence grows stronger and a track record of successful funding is established. On the other hand, the unsuccessful applicant will almost certainly be disappointed and, if the process appears unfair, feel aggrieved. Some applicants feel that the process is akin to a lottery. Hopefully, however, the researcher will not become bitter and broken by the gruelling experience. As the gap between the submission of the proposal and the final verdict on funding is frequently lengthy, the intervening time can usually be used to identify other funding sources and to plan how subsequent proposals can be tailored to the requirements of other funding bodies. If the outcome of the first application is a rejection, any feedback from the reviewers can be swiftly taken into account when making the next submission. The golden rule to not to give up, but to apply, apply and apply again.

REPORTING RESULTS AND DISSEMINATION

Providing information to participants

Most researchers subscribe to the ideal that, whenever possible, the results of research involving the general public should be offered to the participants. However, the reality may be different. Francis (1999) notes that, for a variety of reasons, some research is never written up. Reports are often prepared under time pressure at the end of a funding period, and priority may be given to final submissions to funding bodies or sponsors and articles for fellow academics. When information *is* made available to participants, great care should be taken in relation to the content and framing of that information. What if the results conclude that care is substandard? Will this raise unnecessary fears in patients, many of whom may previously have been content with the care provided and some of whom may still be receiving treatment? Suppose the results relate to risk factors for disease and the results conclude that behaviour change is desirable to reduce risk, how will this impact on the participants?

Marteau and Lerman (2001) posed a series of questions in relation to people who may be offered information about their genetic susceptibility to potentially preventable diseases. How should the risk information be framed? Will offering the information be enough to encourage them to change aspects of their behaviour? Research suggests that more help will be required and it may well be that information alone merely serves to increase distress.

Finally, Francis (1999) noted that psychologists should resist the temptation to stray beyond the actual findings of the research and to provide a 'grand finale' to a project by offering unsubstantiated opinions, advice or conclusions.

Disseminating results to stakeholders

The research manager has a responsibility to ensure that the results of research reach all stakeholders in the project. Different groups are likely to be concerned with the content of the reports and how the information is presented. Sponsors and funders will have a view of how they would like to feature in the reports. Participants and colleagues may also be concerned with how they are represented. A strategy should be developed to disseminate the findings to relevant people in the most effective way at the most appropriate time. Ask the questions 'who is this particular report for?' and 'what am I seeking to achieve in reporting to them?' and invest time in mastering appropriate report writing styles. Recognise that different channels and methods of presentation will be necessary to target participants, decision-makers, practitioners and academics. For example, how can information be presented for practitioners in ways that allow them to act on the findings? Be prepared for the fact that due to long time lags between deadlines for the submission of abstracts and actual conferences, and between the submission of manuscripts and eventual publication, efforts to disseminate information are likely to be necessary for a considerable period of time after the project has been completed. Your funding body, on the other hand, will require a full report as the project is drawing to a close. Further discussion of dissemination may be found in Chapter 11 (pp. 193–6).

In writing reports of research, Robson (2002) suggests that a clear distinction be made between findings, interpretations, judgements and recommendations. It is particularly important to clarify which findings are directly informed by the research, and which are subject to speculation. It is also useful to consider what kinds of evidence will appeal to the various interested parties. Whenever possible, the wording and content of recommendations should be negotiated with the people who are likely to make use of them, as interested parties will be more likely to act on findings they 'own' than those foisted on them by an outside researcher (Robson 2002).

Box 2.2   *A clinical study in a hospital setting with a multidisciplinary research team (Manyande et al., 1995)*

The five basic research processes described in this chapter can be illustrated by an example of a multidisciplinary clinical study. The study was concerned with the preoperative rehearsal of active coping imagery in preparing patients for abdominal surgery. The five processes are briefly described in turn.

Working with colleagues

The study was part of a series carried out over several years with a team that changed over time. The setting was St Mark's Hospital, London, specialising in abdominal and bowel surgery. This study required very careful planning, co-ordination and communication across a team of nine people across five different areas of health care and three institutions. The procedures required careful vetting for the ethical issues involved and the study would have been impossible but for the collaboration of a clinical psychologist, a health psychologist, two nurse researchers, three surgeons and two anaesthetists working as a team. The research study was part of a PhD project carried out by Anne Manyande at University College London under Peter Salmon's supervision. DM was consulted concerning the design of the intervention that consisted of active imagery rehearsal of the subjective, sensory and somatic effects of the anaesthetic and surgical procedures associated with the operation.

Obtaining funding

No special research funds were sought specifically for this project, which was made possible by the provision of staff and facilities in the participating organisations. Careful planning was necessary to ensure that all parties were able to devote the agreed time and resources for the duration of the study.

Obtaining ethical approval

Ethical approval was sought from the relevant NHS Trust. The reason for using an active imagery technique for rehearsing the effects of the procedures on the body was ethically justified. The rationale stemmed from the theory of Janis (1958) who hypothesised a U-shaped association between fear before an operation and outcome. Janis' U-shaped curve suggests that both low and high levels of anxiety are associated with a worse outcome, while medium levels of fear are associated with the best recovery. However, more recent research suggested a linear relationship not a U-curve, with the lowest levels of anxiety predicting the best outcomes, with the ability to surrender control possibly being more adaptive than a controlling style (Johnston, 1986). This conflict left the issue of whether active rehearsal of bodily sensations would have a positive or a negative influence on outcomes unresolved. Hence the need for the study. All participants were required to give their fully informed consent. The study design was a randomised controlled trial with a control treatment consisting of cognitive information about the quality of the hospital and the staff.

Managing the project

The project required careful management on the part of the research team leader, Peter Salmon. Among the many necessary tasks was to obtain agreement of the study design and to ensure that the study was well controlled. Key issues in managing the project were agreeing to the number of conditions that would be included and the number of participants that would need to be recruited and allocated to each condition. One of the major risks to the successful completion of the study was the difficulty in recruiting a sufficient number of participants to yield a statistically powerful study. Ideally, a third condition, consisting of audio-taped relaxation training, shown in an earlier study to be associated with increased circulating cortisol and adrenaline levels (Manyande et al., 1992), would have been included. This would have enabled a comparison of relaxation, active imagery and information preparation in a single trial. However, the research team leader knew that this would be impossible to achieve in the time available because of the slow recruitment resulting from the exclusion criteria and other factors. This was proven by actual experience because only 51 participants were recruited, an insufficient number if distributed over 3, rather than 2, experimental conditions. Other important issues revolved around the recruitment procedures carried out by nursing staff on the ward, ensuring that these were carried out in a systematic, consistent and ethical manner.

Reporting results and dissemination

The results of the study were fed back to the major stakeholders. The study was published in a leading peer-reviewed journal, *Psychosomatic Medicine*. The abstract briefly summarised the study in the following words:

> In a controlled trial of abdominal surgery patients, we . . . tested the effects of a preoperative preparation that used guided imagery, not to reduce anxiety, but to increase patients' feelings of being able to cope with surgical stress; 26 imagery patients were compared with 25 controls who received, instead, background information about the hospital. The results showed that state-anxiety was similar in each group, but *imagery patients experienced less postoperative pain* than did the controls, were *less distressed by it, felt that they coped with it better,* and *requested less analgesia.* Hormone levels measured in peripheral venous blood did not differ on the afternoon of admission, before preparation. *Cortisol levels were, however, lower in imagery patients than in controls immediately before and after surgery. Noradrenaline levels were greater* on these occasions in imagery patients than controls. (Manyande et al., 1995; italics added to highlight key points)

Since publication, two other clinical studies used similar active imagery techniques with equally positive effects. At the University of Innsbruck, Doering et al. (2000) used a videotape preparation of patients before hip replacement surgery. This study involved 13 members of 4 departments: psychological medicine and psychotherapy, orthopaedics, anaesthesia and general intensive care, and psychiatry (8 MDs, 3 PhDs, and 2 MSs!). Reduced stress and lowered analgesic medication after surgery occurred in patients prepared with the videotape.

At Mount Sinai Hospital in Toronto, Esplen and Garfinkel (1998) used a guided imagery treatment to promote self-soothing in bulimia nervosa. A

randomised controlled trial compared patients receiving six weeks of individual guided imagery therapy with a control group of untreated bulimia
nervosa patients. The imagery group showed a substantial reduction in
bingeing and purging, improvements on measures of aloneness and the
ability of self-comforting.

The three studies suggest that active mental rehearsal is a helpful preparatory tool prior to surgery or as a part of psychotherapy.

Although all those involved in a successful research project are generally
fired up by the findings, researchers must be realistic about the lack of
impact their work usually has. Several writers have reached the somewhat
depressing conclusion that in the face of resistance to change and inno-
vation, research has relatively little influence on practice. In spite of a lot of
rhetoric about evidence-based practice, implementation of research findings is disappointingly slow. Investing in the involvement and ownership
of the research by relevant practitioners from inception to completion,
helping practitioners decide how to act upon the findings and subsequently
working with them to help them change their routines seem likely to be
the most effective strategies to counter this phenomenon (Ovreteit, 1997).
However, all these strategies require continued effort well beyond the
completion of the project.

SUMMARY

Five key processes in research and consultancy have been described. Firstly,
the role of working with colleagues and developing a strong team, who
share a common vision and plan for the project. Secondly, how to approach
the obtaining of funding. Thirdly, obtaining ethical approval. Fourthly, the
management of the project. Fifthly, the importance of dissemination. We
have highlighted the importance of careful planning, good communications
with all involved, taking into account the needs and the rights of the participants, and of the funding body, and the consequential responsibilities
that fall on researchers to carry out research that is well-conceived, meaningful and ethical. These principles were illustrated with a clinical research
project involving a large multidisciplinary research team on a new method
for preparing patients for surgery.

RECOMMENDED READING

Francis, R. (1999). *Ethics for psychologists: A handbook.* Leicester: BPS Books.
Robson, C. (2002). *Real world research* (2nd edn) Oxford: Blackwell.

REVISION QUESTIONS

1   In addition to the careful use of research methods, what else must a researcher be able to do?
2   What differences are there between 'research' and 'consultancy'?
3   Who are the 'stakeholders' in a research project?
4   What are the main issues that need to be addressed in obtaining ethical approval for a research study?
5   List as many methods for disseminating the results of a research project as you can think of.

---

3 QUALITATIVE DATA COLLECTION: INTERVIEWS AND FOCUS GROUPS

Sue Wilkinson, Hélène Joffe and Lucy Yardley

AIMS OF THIS CHAPTER

(i)   To outline the rationale for qualitative data collection.
(ii) To describe how to collect data by carrying out interviews.
(iii) To describe how to collect data from focus groups.
(iv) To consider briefly other methods for collecting qualitative data.

THE RATIONALE FOR QUALITATIVE DATA COLLECTION

The purpose of qualitative research is to gain an appreciation of how people's experiences are shaped by their subjective and socio-cultural perspective: the different viewpoints of people in different circumstances; the ways that people actively make sense of their experiences; and the psychological, socio-cultural and linguistic factors and processes which influence this process of creating meaning (see Chapter 1). For these purposes, it is necessary to use a method of collecting data that permits the participants to express themselves in ways that are not constrained and dictated by the researcher (as in the case of questionnaires, which restrict the participants to a limited range of responses to the questions considered important by the researcher). Interviews and focus groups have become the most widely used methods of eliciting the viewpoint of participants for qualitative analysis. The accounts and arguments elicited by these methods have the potential to provide unexpected insights into factors which may not previously have been considered relevant, valuable details of the personal and social context which impact upon the meaning attributed to experiences, and an understanding of how the socio-cultural resource of language itself contributes to meaning-making.

This chapter provides an introduction to the advantages and techniques of obtaining qualitative data through interviewing and **focus groups**. Many practical and ethical considerations are common to both methods; for example, at one level both require good basic interviewing skills, effective recording and **transcription** procedures, and attention to issues of inter-personal relations and **confidentiality**. However, focus groups are not simply group interviews, and so while both halves of this chapter cover topics which are relevant to both data collection methods, each section also notes the rather different merits and methods of one-to-one interviews and focus group research. Moreover, each section illustrates a different epistemological approach to qualitative data collection. Talk can be viewed either as a more or less accurate expression of the inner thoughts and feelings of the individual, or as a social process of creating meanings and identities which serve social functions (see Chapters 1 and 6). In this chapter we illustrate the former approach in the context of interviewing, and the latter in relation to conducting focus groups. While there is a good rationale for this mapping of epistemology and method, since interviews are typically focused on individuals whereas focus groups encourage social interaction, this mapping is by no means obligatory; interviews can be and have been used to examine the social construction of meaning, and focus groups are often used to collectively explore a range of personal views and experiences.

INTERVIEWS

> In a qualitative research interview the aim is to discover the interviewee's own framework of meanings and the research task is to avoid imposing the researcher's structures and assumptions as far as possible. The researcher needs to remain open to the possibility that the concepts and variables that emerge may be very different from those that might have been predicted at the outset. (Britten, 1995: 251)

Since interviews are time-consuming and costly (as the researcher must be present for the full duration of the interview, interviews must be transcribed, a non-standardised coding scheme must often be devised), if interviews are to be used their advantages must be maximised. This section will identify the different types of interview, the advantages of interviewing, what characterises a skilled interviewer, the range of questions that can be asked and to what effect, as well as examining the common pitfalls in interviewing.

Types of interview

There are a number of different types of interview.

The structured interview utilises a structured **interview schedule**, containing a fixed set of questions. Most have fixed choice answers, which are coded in a standardised way. Structured interviews are sometimes accompanied by a written questionnaire, which elicits demographic information. Britten (1995) gives an example of the type of question asked in the structured interview: is your health excellent, good, fair or poor? In general, qualitative studies may utilise a few questions of this type, but would not be characterised by them.

The **semi-structured interview** is based upon an interview guide with typically five to eight broad questions, plus probes to supplement them if respondents have difficulty in elaborating their perspectives. For example, following on from a question such as 'What experiences of therapy have you had?' one might use probes such as 'Can you tell me more about that?' or 'What was the experience like for you?' (Riessman, 1993). The same questions are administered to all respondents. This allows the researcher to compare across interviews while simultaneously permitting each respondent to move into uncharted territory, and have their particular line of thought pursued. The order of questions may vary, and the probes cannot be standardised since they try to pursue what the particular respondent says.

The depth interview covers one or two key issues in great detail and the interviewee's perspective shapes what the interviewer follows up. It avoids all *a priori* categorisation that may impose upon the naturalistic worldview of the interviewee. It is sometimes termed an '**ethnographic** interview' (see Fontana & Frey, 1998). This type of interview overlaps with the narrative interview.

Advantages of interviewing

There is a vast disparity between the structured as opposed to the semi-structured and depth interviews. Consequently, they confer different advantages. Structured interviews are very similar to questionnaires but are administered in person, which can be necessary when respondents have difficulty reading or writing (for example, due to age, linguistic background, cognitive impairment or physical disability). They are used for eliciting data that will be quantitatively coded, as well as limited qualitative data in cases where questions permit open-ended answers. However, note that self-administered, anonymous questionnaires may be more acceptable to respondents than structured interviews when asking about sensitive issues, since it may be awkward to talk about certain topics face-to-face (Arksley & Knight, 1999).

Semi-structured and depth interviews offer advantages unique to wholly qualitative research. The statements that follow apply to both. First and foremost, such interviews facilitate insight into how a respondent spontaneously structures an issue in a way that highly directive methods, which are accompanied by predefined response categories, cannot. Responses to **open-ended questions** reflect an individual's personal reaction to the phenomenon under investigation, rather than one elicited by way of a forced choice between predefined options.

A further advantage of open-ended measures is that they do not force consistency on people's thinking. According to Billig (1987), there is an inter-personal motive to be consistent: this wards off criticism that you are contradicting yourself in the eyes of others. Psychologists, like lay people, have tended to promote the idea that people's attitudes and beliefs are rational, stable and consistent (an assumption which underpins the procedures used to develop reliable and valid questionnaire measures of attitudes). Yet 'thinking is like a quiet internal argument' (Billig, 1987: 118). Thinking is not consistent, but people have a tendency to make it *appear* to be so in order to be persuasive. Contradictory views co-exist and must be accepted as such. Qualitative research reveals that the attitudes which psychologists tap are ambiguous and complex, because: 'attitudes are not neat bundles of responses, awaiting the opinion-sampler's clipboard, but they represent unfinished business in the continual controversies of social life' (Billig, 1987: 225). People's commonsense contains contrary elements, which pose dilemmas for them. The interview can throw light on these.

Not only can lay ideas contain inconsistencies, they often contain elements that would not appear rational. In discussion of certain topics, in particular, people may be motivated by more emotional issues. When talking about AIDS, for instance, fear may motivate the desire to portray the threat as a risk for others rather than oneself, for example by attributing it to 'alien' practices and identities such as foreigners or people engaging in unusual sexual practices (see Joffe, 1999). According to Hollway and Jefferson (1997), interviews (especially depth interviews) have the ability to follow emotional rather than rational pathways of thought. During an interview in which researchers choose not to impose their structure on the story to be told, respondents provide a narrative that is created by way of unconscious, emotive associations rather than conscious logic.

In summary, more interventionist methods not only prevent a spontaneous set of associations from coming to light, they often cue respondents to think rationally rather than emotionally. This corroborates Haddock, Zanna and Esses' (1993) finding that highly directive questions, accompanied by predefined response categories, may be particularly problematic for tapping 'affective evaluations'. They force people into response choices, which do not necessarily map onto their feelings. A growing body of the mainstream psychological literature points to the primacy of affect in cognitive evaluations (see Finucane et al., 2000).

Countering the argument that the interview taps a naturalistic worldview and feelings is the concern that the issue of **self-presentation** can pose difficulties for the interview method. Although this is a problem for other methods too, the desire to make a particular impression (such as that of consistency) in the eyes of another/others may blight the interview. The strategies used to enhance positive impression formation in relation to an interviewer can affect the content of what is said. For instance, if interviewees do not want to show prejudice in a society where the social institutions indicate that prejudices are unacceptable, they tend to cover up by way of the content of their language (Billig, 1985). The presence of such self-presentation is difficult to assess. How can one discern whether a non-prejudiced response is a 'cover up' or an expression of a non-prejudiced way of thinking? The answer must lie in the nuance; Billig asserts that the most prevalent form of contemporary prejudice lies in its denial, in the form of 'I am not prejudiced, but . . .'. An example is a statement in an interview for a study on representations of the Ebola virus:

> I wouldn't say that all Africans are ignorant and all westerners are intelligent and informed, but [I] imagine that there are a lot of people whose understanding and ability to grasp the process of medical information is limited by their education. (British male broadsheet reader – Joffe & Haarhoff, 2002)

Perhaps the less structured the method, the more likely it is that such complexities are revealed – but only if the researcher is attuned to the nuance of the detail.

What characterises skilled interview technique?

What skills are required for eliciting rich data? Both the interviewer's attitude and the atmosphere created are involved. Many of the skills learned by counsellors are developed to facilitate individuals in giving an account of an experience or of some broader issue in their lives. Such skills facilitate interviewees in pursuing a subjective journey concerning the research object. Thus the following four elements are vital for the skilled interview and draw on the counselling literature.

Being a good listener A strong interest in interviewees must be conveyed such that they feel that their perspectives are fascinating. This is facilitated by the interviewer being a good listener, which involves keeping quiet as much as possible so as not to impose on the talking space of the interviewee. Good interviewers demonstrate that they are attending by careful placement of chairs (perpendicular is best), leaning forward, not crossing arms or legs, and eye contact that is consistent and interested but not staring or overintrusive.

Being empathic not judgemental An empathic atmosphere must be created since people will not want to talk if they feel judged. To facilitate this it is often useful to suggest, at the beginning of an interview, that there are no right or wrong answers. Respondents can be told that it is their worldview that is being explored. Even what may seem like encouraging statements such as 'that's good – tell me more' imply a judgemental quality that is best avoided, and may influence the interviewee to present their account in a certain way.

Allowing the respondent's worldview to come to the fore People should be encouraged to express themselves in their own words. By responding in a way that picks up the interviewee's own wording, a naturalistic pathway through their worldview can be established. If interviewees appear to be contemplating their own line of thought, the researcher's own silence can leave them the space to formulate their contemplation in words. Learning not to cut in too soon when the interviewee is silent is vital but can be surprisingly difficult – silences may seem awkward, but can be filled by non-verbal encouragement such as nodding. In addition, reflecting, mirroring, paraphrasing or summarising *exactly* what the respondent says can maintain the flow of the conversation without the researcher imposing his or her own understanding. For example, if the interviewee pauses after referring to their experience of cancer as 'stressful', the interviewer could signal interest and prompt confirmation and further elaboration by saying, 'So you find your illness stressful?'. However, if the interviewer instead said, 'So you feel anxious about your illness?' this could distort the interview. The minor but important change from describing the illness as stressful to describing the interviewee as anxious (which imposes a psychological diagnosis on their experience) might either be accepted by the interviewee (out of politeness or deference, to avoid contradicting the interviewer) or might lead them to deny the subjective stress they felt, for fear of seeming psychologically weak or defective.

Allowing exploration of feelings   The interviewer is not merely concerned with what the interviewee thinks and their rational, socially acceptable explanations. There is also interest in how interviewees *feel* about the issue under investigation. Therefore an atmosphere that encourages exploration of feelings must be shaped. The interviewer needs to respond in a way that encourages exploration of feelings, which involves reflecting not just on the content but on the feelings that emerge. There may be direct cues, such as a tear welling in the eye or nervous laughter, or this may require empathy. In the latter case, the interviewer would need to tune into how they might feel in the situation that is being described by the interviewee, and to reflect upon this. However, interviewers must be careful not to impose their own viewpoint, by jumping to conclusions about how the interviewee might feel.

What characterises an effective interview?

For semi-structured and depth interviews, the aim is to ask questions that elicit an account rather than a 'yes' or 'no' answer. These can range from accounts of the knowledge that the interviewee has about a phenomenon, such as the Ebola virus; attitudes and opinions in relation to an entity, such as a recent health campaign; their experiences of something like an illness or treatment; or their beliefs and representations, feelings and values relating to an issue, such as healthy eating.

   In terms of the procedure of the interview, the interviewee can be best relaxed by beginning with the least sensitive, easy-to-answer questions. Once the contact and empathic environment have been established, more sensitive material can be elicited. It is useful for the interviewer to state, at the start, not only that there are no right or wrong answers but also that if questions about the study arise in the respondent's mind, they can be discussed after the interview. This prevents the flow of the material being interrupted by questions from the respondent about the underlying goal of the research, or about the interviewer's role/status in the research process. Although all questions should be covered in every interview, there is usually no need to keep to a pre-defined order; often it is better to follow up the respondent's ideas using both the phrasing and ordering used by them. Some guidelines are given below for constructing questions that will encourage extended, revealing answers:

1   Use open rather than closed questions, that is, use questions which *cannot* be answered in a few words. Asking 'Did you find treatment helpful?' may simply elicit 'Yes', 'Fairly' or 'No'. In fact, it is a **leading question** which should be avoided, in particular, since it will probably elicit the answer 'Yes'!
2   Avoid 'Why' questions. Often people have difficulty pinpointing or revealing their personal motives, and so when confronted with the need to explain why they do, feel or believe something they may offer socially desirable rationalisations, or even intellectualised or sociological accounts of their situation.
3   Instead of asking abstract questions, ask about concrete events that have happened to the interviewee. Word your questions so as to elicit stories, for example, 'Tell me all about your first experience of therapy'. The story and details chosen, the manner in which it is told, which points are emphasised and which morals are drawn will all provide rich information about motives, beliefs and feelings.

In summary, good qualitative material is usually best elicited without a 'head on' approach (for example, 'What do you believe about . . .?') but rather, emerges, when asked questions such as 'Could you talk about healthy eating in your community?'. Questions which directly address your hypotheses or concerns can be bewildering to respondents, overly influence what they say, and intimidate them into short, defensive answers. However, you will find all the answers to the questions that inspired your research by analysing the rich data generated by these more open-ended methods.

Hollway and Jefferson (1997, 2000) have developed this open-ended question technique into a quasi-clinical interview method, which aims to be theoretically driven rather than to take respondents' accounts at face value. Their method probes people's stories without expecting respondents to be able to understand their own actions, motivations and feelings. When left to flow, people's narratives can be thought of as similar to 'free association' in psychoanalysis, revealing unconscious paths of association, rather than conscious logic. These pathways are defined by emotional motivations, as opposed to rational intentions, such as unconscious attempts to avoid or master anxiety. Hence free association may allow access to concerns that define people's meaning frames that would not be visible using more traditional methods (see also Kvale, 2003).

Inter-personal, practical and ethical issues

When agreement is sought to do the interview, the interviewee should be asked if they consent to the interview being recorded. Always test the recorder before each interview to ensure that a good recording will be obtained. If possible, do this in the absence of the interviewee so that the obtrusiveness of the recorder is diminished, and interviewees do not become overly self-conscious about being recorded. Self-consciousness can be a problem during the interview, since it may increase the tendency for people to distance themselves from acts/ideas which they regard (or think the interviewer will regard) as unacceptable. The interviewer's task is to facilitate the answering of questions in a way that reaches the worldview of participants, without their loss of face.

It is important to be aware that the class, race, gender, age and social status of the interviewer may have an impact on the interviewee. For example, young people may be reluctant to openly discuss their sexual behaviour with someone their parents' age – and vice versa! Similarly, patients are more likely to feel able to reveal personal views of treatment to someone who is not a health professional, and is not viewed as closely associated with their care team. Consequently, it may be advisable to carry out interviews in patients' homes rather than in a room at a hospital, and to recruit participants independently rather than through their doctor. However, a good interviewer may be able to overcome such potential barriers by an open and friendly manner, and by emphasising confidentiality and impartiality.

Precisely because the aim of the open-ended interview is to facilitate an 'opening up' in respondents, interviewers need to be careful about the ethics of the interview. Usually ethical approval has been sought for a set of questions and researchers should not veer beyond the areas of investigation approved by such committees. Arksley and Knight (1999) point out that there is very little literature on how best to handle displays of emotion in such contexts. They advocate the strategy proposed by Kitson et al. (1996) which states that one should acknowledge emotional displays (for example, tears) by maintaining eye contact and legitimate the respondent's distress by gestures such as offering tissues. They also propose that one should allow them to delve into the issue by way of statements such as 'It may help to talk about it', rather than changing the subject abruptly. Finally, they advise that the interviewer sit quietly until the respondent calms down, and not assume that the interview continues. The decision on this should be jointly negotiated between interviewer and interviewee. However, in cases where the interviewer is not a trained clinical psychologist, counsellor or psychotherapist, such strategies may be inappropriate. In contrast to the strategies proposed, a more ethical response might be for interviewers to rely on their sense of when they may be entering territory that is not appropriate, for them to make an empathic response such as 'It must be tough for you', and move back to less emotive territory (Kvale, 2003).

Maintaining confidentiality can pose problems when analysing and writing up qualitative research. Audiotapes and videotapes should normally be kept securely (for example, in a locked cabinet) to prevent voice or facial identification of participants, and erased once the study has been completed. Transcripts should not include names and locations. Nevertheless, some accounts may still contain details that would identify the interviewee to people who knew him or her – and these might be the people who are most interested in seeking out the final report of the research. Consequently, informed consent should be obtained explicitly to publish verbatim quotes from the interviews in research reports, and sometimes it may be necessary to omit uniquely identifying and sensitive passages from the report (Morse, 1998).

Box 3.1   *Key features of interviewing*

- Whereas structured interviews (and questionnaires) employ questions which restrict participants to a limited topic and range of responses, semi-structured and depth interviews allow participants to freely express their views and feelings about a subject.
- A good semi-structured or depth interview schedule is based on a small number of open questions which elicit lengthy personal accounts rather than brief or abstract explanations.
- Good interviewing technique involves conveying empathy and interest, and avoiding making evaluative or leading comments.
- Use a good quality microphone, and before starting an interview always test your recording equipment, and make sure that the interviewee is happy for verbatim quotes to be used in your report.
- Be aware of and try to minimise the potential influence on the interview of the relative social positions of the researcher and the interviewee.

FOCUS GROUPS

Although focus groups were first used in the 1940s (by sociologist Robert Merton and his colleagues), they have only been employed in health research for the last 20 years or so, and in health and clinical psychology for less than 10 years. Health researchers pioneered the use of focus groups in social action research, particularly family planning and health education, and the method subsequently became popular in the field of HIV/AIDS research, as well as in more 'experiential' studies of health and illness (see Wilkinson, 1998a, for a review).

Focus group data can be collected within a variety of different theoretical frameworks – and the framework selected will, of course, determine the way in which the data will be analysed (see Chapters 4 to 6 for different ways of analysing qualitative data). The theoretical assumption which underpins the following account of focus group research is that meaning-making is a collective, or socially shared, activity. It is based on the premise that meanings are constructed in interaction with others, in specific social contexts, rather than generated by individuals in splendid isolation. Viewed in this way, the collection of focus group data opens the process of meaning-making to scrutiny. Conducting a focus group provides the researcher with the opportunity to observe the processes through which meanings are constructed and negotiated, within the social context of the focus group itself. This is a very different approach from one which sees meanings (ideas, beliefs, opinions, etc.) as individual subjective phenomena, and the task of the researcher as eliciting these meanings. However, it is equally possible to approach focus group research from the latter premise (in which case, focus groups may be seen as facilitating the expression of individual ideas, beliefs, opinions, etc., through interaction with others).

Conducting focus groups

Essentially, focus group methodology involves engaging a small number of people in an informal group discussion (or discussions), 'focused' on a particular topic or set of issues. This is most commonly presented to them (either orally or in written form) as a set of questions, known as a focus group 'schedule' – although sometimes as a film clip, a collection of images, a card-sorting task, a game to play, or a vignette to discuss. The researcher generally acts as a **moderator** for the group: posing the questions (or directing the other activities), keeping the discussion flowing, and encouraging group members to participate fully.

Focus group participants (usually 4 to 8) may be pre-existing clusters of people (such as family members, friends or work colleagues) or they may be drawn together specifically for the research. Focus group projects often bring together a group of people with a shared experience, specifically to talk about that experience: for example, women diagnosed with breast cancer; partners or carers of stroke victims; providers and/or users of a counselling service. Discussions between group participants are usually audio-taped (sometimes video-taped), transcribed and subjected to conventional techniques of qualitative analysis. Hence, focus groups are distinctive primarily for the method of data *collection* (that is, informal group discussion), rather than for any particular method of data *analysis*.

Although focus groups are sometimes referred to as 'group interviews', the moderator does *not* ask questions of each group member in turn – but, rather, facilitates group discussion, actively encouraging group members to interact *with each other*. This interaction between research participants is a key feature of focus group research – and the one which most clearly distinguishes it from one-to-one interviews. Compared with interviews, focus groups are much more 'naturalistic' (that is, closer to everyday conversation), in that they typically include a range of features such as story-telling, joking, arguing, boasting, teasing, persuasion, challenge and disagreement.

The dynamic quality of the group interaction is a striking feature of focus group data. Here is an example of an interaction between three women in a focus group, drawn from the research of one of the authors on breast cancer. 'Barbara', who has only very recently undergone breast surgery (mastectomy), is asking 'Anne' and 'Carol' (who both had surgery some time ago) about their experiences of wearing a prosthesis (artificial breast). Anne responds with an unexpected offer:

> Anne: Would you like to see my prosthesis? The *size* of it?
> Barbara: [Laughs] Well, mine's only really tiny. [Laughs]
> Anne: Excuse me [Pulls out breast prosthesis and passes it around the table] Feel the weight.
> Carol: [Gasps]
> Anne: You don't, you don't feel it though, once it's . . .
> Carol: My friend's, though, isn't as, it doesn't seem as *heavy* as that.
> Anne: [To Barbara] Pick it up. Look at it.
> Barbara: No, I've had . . .
> Carol: [Cuts in] It's *very heavy*.
> Several: [Raucous laughter, voices indistinct]
> Carol: It's ra- [Collapses into laughter]
> Several: [More laughter]
> Carol: It's *rather heavy*, isn't it?
> Anne: You can imagine *my* scar.
> Barbara: Do you want to see my scar?
> Several: [More raucous laughter and clamorous voices overlapping] Look at *my* scar. Look at *my* scar.

Focus group data like these offer the possibility of analysing how people make *collective* sense of their individual experiences and beliefs. In this extract we see Barbara learning a socially acceptable attitude to prostheses and mastectomy scars for women with breast cancer. Through the focus group interaction she learns that prostheses and surgical scars are something which can be shown to and explicitly discussed with others, something about which women post-mastectomy can laugh, joke and even brag! The possibility of analysing interactions like this for what they reveal about collective (rather than individual) sense-making is one of the key advantages of focus groups.

Another advantage is the flexibility of the method: focus groups can be used in large- and small-scale projects; within the psychology laboratory or out in the field; to study the social world or to attempt to change it – in

action research projects (see Wilkinson, 1998b for a review). Focus groups can also be used as a stand-alone qualitative method, or combined with quantitative techniques as part of a multi-method project. One popular strategy is to use focus groups to explore the language and concepts of a particular group of people (for example, teenage gangs, black gay men, working-class mothers) in order to compile an appropriately worded and relevant questionnaire. Another is to follow-up in more depth and detail an interesting finding from a large-scale survey. A good way to get a sense of this flexibility and variety is to look at one of the recent edited collections of focus group research projects: for example, Barbour & Kitzinger (1999), Morgan (1993).

Doing focus group research

There is more to doing focus group research than may first be apparent. For any focus group to provide the best possible data, there are two key requirements: an effective moderator and a well-prepared session. Ideally, the moderator should have basic interviewing skills, some knowledge of group dynamics, and some experience of running group discussions. Although some of the skills involved in moderating a focus group are similar to those involved in one-to-one interviews (for example, establishing rapport, effective use of prompts and probes, sensitivity to non-verbal cues), the number of research participants involved in a focus group requires more in terms of active 'people management'. The shy participant must be encouraged to speak, the talkative one discouraged at times, and instances of discomfiture and/or disagreement must be handled with care. More information about techniques of people management may be found in Krueger (1994).

Proper preparation for, and efficient planning of, the focus group session itself is just as essential as moderator skills for obtaining high-quality data. A well-run focus group session might *look* effortless, but it almost certainly is not; a surprising amount of preparatory work is needed before, during and after the session itself. Here are the main steps.

Design and ethics   First, you will need to decide on the broad parameters of your project: the overall timescale; how many focus groups you will run; what kind of focus groups they will be; the number and type of participants you will have (and how you will recruit them); and how you will record, transcribe and analyse your data. You should also consider ethical issues. Focus group research, like any other psychological research, must be conducted in accordance with the ethical guidelines of the relevant professional body and with the informed consent of participants. Confidentiality is a particular issue within focus groups – and 'ground rules' should be set requiring all participants to respect and preserve the confidentiality of others. The interactional nature of focus group research also raises some specific ethical issues. For example, very occasionally a participant may be visibly worried or distressed by the experiences or opinions being aired; an argument may 'turn nasty'; or several focus group members may collude to silence or intimidate a particular individual. It is important to handle such a situation immediately, within the group – and it may also be necessary to address it further with the individual(s) involved once the group has finished.

Materials   You will need to prepare a focus group schedule at least, and perhaps also written or pictorial materials. In devising a schedule, make sure that it is likely to engage the participants, that it uses appropriate vocabulary, that the questions flow logically, that it provides the opportunity for a variety of viewpoints to be expressed, and that it allows participants to raise points which may not have occurred to the researcher. Try out all the materials you intend to use, to ensure they are intelligible, legible, visible and the right length. If you are intending to use slides or video clips, make sure that the appropriate projectors are readily available, and that you know how to operate them. Have back-ups available in case of equipment failure. Write out your introduction to the session (include a brief description of the project, the procedure to be followed, and the 'ground rules' for the focus group); and your closing comments (include a summary of the session, any necessary debriefing, and a reiteration of thanks).

People and place   Getting people to turn up at a focus group session is much harder than you might think! Always over-recruit by about 50 per cent (that is, recruit nine participants for a six-person group) – however much enthusiasm/commitment participants express, some of them *always* fail to turn up on the day, for one reason or another. Make sure they have clear directions for finding the venue, and (particularly if you recruit some time in advance of the session), issue several reminders, including – most crucially – a phone call the day before the focus group itself. Your decisions about venue will need to take into account both participant comfort and the recording environment (although sometimes there is little choice). If possible, select a relatively comfortable, quiet room where you won't be disturbed or under time pressure to finish. Participants should be seated in a circle – either in easy chairs or around a table (your choice may be dependent on what participants will be asked to do, but these two options have a very different 'feel').

Preparation   It is ideal to have an assistant on the day, especially for larger focus groups. Whether or not this is possible, think through how you will handle: arrivals and departures (including late arrivals and early departures); refreshments; dealing with unforeseen queries or problems; and taking notes and/or operating the recording equipment while moderating the group. Note that Murphy's law ('if anything can go wrong, it will') holds as much for focus groups as other types of research – but seems to apply particularly to recording equipment! This should be checked and double-checked before every group. While highly specialised recording equipment is unnecessary, it is essential to use an omni-directional, flat microphone, in order to produce a recording clear enough for transcription. These can be purchased relatively inexpensively at large high street electrical retailers. If you do not have an assistant to list the sequence of speakers (see below) then you may wish to make a video-recording of the focus group, as it can be very difficult to identify which individual is speaking from an audiotape (but note that the sound quality of the video may not be good enough for transcription). Video-recording is especially useful if you are interested in examining body-behavioural aspects of interactions. You will also need (all or most of) the following: refreshments (water; tea or coffee; possibly simple food); writing materials (paper and pens); informed consent forms; paper tissues; name badges or cards; spare tapes and batteries. Set up the room well in advance, if possible, and check the recording equipment (again) just before using it.

The session itself   At the *beginning* of the session you need to do the following (not necessarily in this exact order): attend to participants' comfort (refreshments, toilets, any special needs); offer thanks, a welcome and introductions; complete consent forms; reiterate issues of confidentiality; complete name badges; outline purpose of study and procedure to be followed; set ground rules for the group; provide an opportunity to ask questions. You then move into the discussion itself. You should aim to create an atmosphere in which participants can relax, talk freely and enjoy themselves. Although it may take a while to 'warm up', once it gets going, a good focus group discussion will appear almost to run itself. The discussion will flow well – and it will seem to move seamlessly through the schedule – sometimes even without the moderator needing to ask the questions. Although your main energies should be directed towards effective moderation of the group discussion, it is also desirable to keep notes of the main discussion points, and of any events which may not be captured on audiotape. An assistant will be able to take more comprehensive notes, which could include a systematic list of the sequence of speakers (this helps in transcription, especially with larger groups). The following activities are needed at the *end* of the focus group (again not necessarily in this exact order): reiterate thanks; reiterate confidentiality; give a further opportunity for questions; provide further possible sources of information (as appropriate); debrief (as appropriate, including a check that participants have had a good experience); offer appropriate farewells and/or information about any follow-ups.

After the session   Be sure to make back-up copies of all notes and tapes (which should be clearly labelled). Try to transcribe the data as soon as possible after the end of the focus group, while it is still fresh in your mind. Specialised transcribing equipment is not necessary, but it will aid the process. Transcribing will take *much* longer than you expect! Focus group data are harder to transcribe than one-to-one interview data, because of overlapping talk (although the degree of detail and accuracy with which you need to transcribe this will depend on whether it is a feature of your planned analysis). Transcription is really the first stage of data analysis and a careful, detailed transcription will facilitate the next steps in analysis.

Focus group research does take a lot of planning and preparation, but it is also great fun (for both researcher and participants) and it typically provides lively and compelling data. Focus groups are not, however, as sometimes assumed, 'a method for all seasons' – rather, like any other qualitative method, they are more suited to some kinds of research questions than others. Focus groups are a good choice of method when the purpose of the research is to elicit people's own understandings, opinions or views, or to explore how these are advanced, elaborated and negotiated in a social context. In particular, as I have shown, they offer insights into the processes of collective sense-making which are not easily available via any other research method. Focus groups are less appropriate if the purpose of the research is to categorise or compare types of individual and the views they hold, or to measure attitudes, opinions or beliefs (although they are sometimes used in this way).

Box 3.2　Key features of focus groups

- The aim of the focus group method of data collection is to bring people together for a group discussion of a topic.
- Focus groups can reveal the ways in which people collectively make sense of their experiences and beliefs through social interaction.
- The moderator of the focus group must have the knowledge and skills required to manage the group interaction (for example, by preventing intimidation of quieter group members by more assertive individuals).
- When transcribing focus group data it can be very difficult to distinguish who is saying what; it may help to video-tape the discussion, or have an assistant who records the order in which people speak.

ALTERNATIVE METHODS OF OBTAINING QUALITATIVE DATA

Interviews and focus groups were selected for detailed coverage because they are extremely popular and efficient methods of eliciting qualitative data. However, it must be noted that the methods described above are by no means the only methods of obtaining good qualitative data. For example, discourse analysis frequently takes excerpts of naturally occurring dialogue as its data source. Where interview-based methods are used in discourse analytic research, they tend to be conducted in a rather different manner from that described here. Instead of creating space for the uninterrupted flow of the interviewee's narrative, the aim is to encourage a more natural, conversational exchange of views in which interviewees are induced to display the conversational strategies available for justifying a particular identity or position (Potter, 2003). In this style of interviewing, the researcher takes a much more active part in the dialogue, and may even engage in argument.

Written texts can also serve as a rich source of material. Texts such as newspaper reports or web pages accessed on the internet can be systematically sampled to gain insights into contemporary cultural representations of a topic or issue. Alternatively, researchers interested in the subjective opinions or experiences of participants may request them to provide written material for qualitative analysis, such as written replies to open-ended questions, or written diaries of their experiences and thoughts. These methods of qualitative data collection can have particular advantages in specific situations. Asking a patient to keep a diary can be a valuable means of obtaining **prospective** longitudinal data about personal experiences and changes over an extended time period (for example, while undertaking therapy), whereas these might not be accurately recalled in a **retrospective** interview, while repeated interviews might be too impractical or intrusive. Similarly, if a target population is too geographically dispersed to access easily in person and/or a topic is too sensitive to discuss face-to-face then an alternative to interviews is to obtain written answers to open-ended questions administered by post or the internet. However, it is important to be aware that many people find writing difficult or tedious, and so it is common to find that written answers are brief and lacking in detail, while strong incentives may be needed to encourage people to keep a diary reliably.

Another style of interviewing (sometimes known as protocol analysis or cognitive interviewing) involves asking participants to give a verbal description of their thought processes while, or immediately after, they carry out some task. This technique has been employed to explore the cognitive processes involved in various tasks (Green & Gilhooly, 1996), but can also be used to shed light on the internal assumptions, beliefs and debates underlying a wide range of behaviours, such as participants' pattern of responses in an experiment, patients' decisions as to which treatment option to choose, or health professionals' private thoughts underlying their communications with patients. Of course, this method assumes that interviewees are able and willing to access and accurately report their thought processes, and that the process of verbalising them does not affect either their behaviour or their thought processes. Since these assumptions may not always be valid, it is important to remember that qualitative material need not be linguistic. In Chapter 1, qualitative research was likened to a video diary – and it can indeed be based on video material, photographs or live observation. The advantages of these types of data are that data collection does not require the participants to be able to accurately describe their experiences (see Chapter 7).

SUMMARY

Qualitative data are a potentially rich source of information concerning how people's experiences are structured by their subjective and socio-cultural perspectives and environmental circumstances. The data enable the investigator to explore how people actively make sense of their lived experience and how that experience is interpreted through linguistic, cultural and historical means of expression. Two primary methods for eliciting such data are the interview and the focus group. These together with dialogues, reports, texts, diaries and narratives provide a valuable source of data for analysis in health and clinical psychology.

RECOMMENDED READING

Interviewing

Arksley, H. & Knight, P. (1999). *Interviewing for social scientists*. London: Sage.
Hollway, W. & Jefferson, T. (2000). *Doing qualitative research differently: free association, narrative and the interview method*. London: Sage.

Focus groups

Krueger, R.A. (1994). *Focus groups: a practical guide for applied research* (2nd edn). Newbury Park, CA: Sage.
Morgan, D.L. (1997). *Focus groups as qualitative research* (2nd edn). Newbury Park, CA: Sage.
Vaughn, S., Schumm, J.S. & Sinagub, J. (1996). *Focus group interviews in education and psychology*. Thousand Oaks, CA: Sage.

REVISION QUESTIONS

1 What are the advantages of semi-structured and depth interviews?
2 Describe some effective techniques for encouraging interviewees to talk freely.
3 How can you ensure that ethical standards are maintained when publishing quotations from research interviews?
4 What differences are there between focus groups and group interviews?
5 What is the role of the moderator in a focus group?

4 CONTENT AND THEMATIC ANALYSIS

Hélène Joffe and Lucy Yardley

AIMS OF THIS CHAPTER

(i) To introduce the basic principles of content and thematic analysis.
(ii) To explain in detail how to code qualitative data.
(iii) To consider the role of computer software in qualitative data analysis.
(iv) To discuss the advantages and limitations of content and thematic analysis.

Content analysis is the accepted method of investigating texts, particularly in mass communications research. Most content analysis results in a numerical description of features of a given text, or series of images. **Thematic analysis** is similar to content analysis, but pays greater attention to the qualitative aspects of the material analysed. This chapter considers the thinking that lies behind each of the two methods, as well as showing how content analysis and thematic analysis are conducted. The roles played by theory, coding and computer packages in such analyses are highlighted.

INTRODUCTION TO CONTENT ANALYSIS AND THEMATIC ANALYSIS

Content analysis involves establishing categories and then counting the number of instances in which they are used in a text or image. It is a partially quantitative method, which determines the frequencies of the occurrence of particular categories. However, while early proponents (for example, Berelson, 1952) conceptualised content analysis solely in terms of counting the attributes in data (for example, words), more recent writings on content analysis (for example, Krippendorf, 1980; Bauer, 2000) contain a broader vision. Krippendorf's point of departure is that social scientists tend to regard data as symbolic phenomena, and since symbolic data can always be looked at from different perspectives, the claim that one is analysing *the* content is untenable. In other words, talk about, for example, 'distress' cannot be taken as a straightforward observation of the phenomenon distress in the same way that a measurement of heart rate may be taken as a direct observation of one aspect of heart functioning. This is because talk *about* distress has a much more complex symbolic relationship to feelings of distress than heart rate does to cardiac functioning. Thus while 'content analysis is a research technique for making replicable and valid inferences from data to their context' (Krippendorf, 1980: 21), messages do not have a single meaning waiting to be unwrapped. The person analysing communications always has to make *inferences*, but these should be made by systematically and objectively identifying characteristics of the text.

The content analytic method is appealing because it offers a model for systematic qualitative analysis with clear procedures for checking the quality of the analysis conducted. However, the results that are generated have been judged as 'trite' (Silverman, 1993) when they rely exclusively on frequency outcomes. Researchers employing this method are also sometimes accused of removing meaning from its context. The problem is that a word or coding category such as 'pain' may occur more frequently in the talk of one person or group of people than another for many reasons; frequent occurrence could indicate greater pain, but might simply reflect greater willingness or ability to talk at length about the topic, or might even occur in repeated assertions that pain was *not* a concern. Thematic analysis comes into its own in terms of these two criticisms. Ideally, it is able to offer the systematic element characteristic of content analysis, but also permits the researcher to combine analysis of the frequency of codes with analysis of their meaning *in context*, thus adding the advantages of the subtlety and complexity of a truly qualitative analysis.

Thematic analysis shares many of the principles and procedures of content analysis; indeed, in Boyatzis' (1998) conceptualisation of thematic analysis the terms '**code**' and '**theme**' are used interchangeably. A theme refers to a specific pattern found in the data in which one is interested. In thematic and content analysis, a theme of a coding category can refer to the **manifest** content of the data, that is, something directly observable, such as mention of the term 'stigma' in a series of transcripts. Alternatively, it may refer to a more **latent** level, such as talk in which stigma is implicitly referred to (for example, by comments about not wanting other people to know about an attack of panic or epilepsy). Thematic analyses often draw on both types of theme, and even when the manifest theme is the focus, the aim is to understand the latent meaning of the manifest themes observable within the data, which requires interpretation.

A further distinction in terms of what constitutes a theme (or coding category) lies in whether it is drawn from existing theoretical ideas that the researcher brings to the data (**deductive coding**) or from the raw information itself (**inductive coding**). Theoretically derived themes allow the researcher to replicate, extend or refute prior discoveries (Boyatzis, 1998).

For example, the researcher might code patients' talk about a treatment programme that they were about to follow using coding categories based on the elements of the Health Belief Model or the Theory of Planned Behaviour, in order to determine to what extent each model seemed to capture their spontaneously expressed attitudes and beliefs. However, more inductive themes, drawn from the data, are often useful in new areas of research (although it should be noted that no theme can be entirely inductive or data driven, since the researcher's knowledge and preconceptions will inevitably influence the identification of themes). A key dilemma facing the analyst is whether to 'test' theory, or to explore new links. For example, if a theme corresponding to an expressed belief in an African geographic origin for an epidemic emerges prominently in two consecutive studies looking at western respondents' ideas about epidemics, is it an inductive theme in the first and deductive in the second, or inductive in both? In addition, such a theme refers to manifest content (the African origin of the disease), but also conveys strong latent meaning when it is westerners who consistently utter it (attribution of the origin of the disease to a distant place and alien culture).

In the type of thematic analysis proposed in this chapter, existing theories drive the questions one asks and one's understanding of the answers, so that one does not 'reinvent the wheel'. This is important since qualitative work, to a greater degree than quantitative research, has the potential to underplay evidence that contradicts the assumptions of the researcher. Therefore, it is advantageous to hold a model of 'testing' in mind, regarding taking counter-evidence seriously, even though it is only in quantitative work that the researcher tests theories in a statistical sense.

CONDUCTING CONTENT AND THEMATIC ANALYSES

What to code

In clinical and health psychology, transcripts of interviews often form the data upon which the content or thematic analysis is conducted, although open-ended answers to a questionnaire, essays, media and video-taped materials can also be used (Smith, 2000). While the steps involved in conducting a content analysis are well established (see Bauer (2000) for a review of the different types of content analytic design and how to sample material for a content analysis), there are surprisingly few published guides concerning how to carry out thematic analysis, and it is often used in published studies without clear report of the specific techniques that were employed. These techniques will therefore be detailed and evaluated below.

For both content and thematic analysis there is a need to create conceptual tools to classify and understand the phenomenon under study: 'This involves abstracting from the immense detail and complexity of our data those features which are most salient for our purpose' (Dey, 1993: 94). This is done by way of coding, which is the widely accepted term for categorising data: taking chunks of text and labelling them as falling into certain categories, in a way that allows for later retrieval and analysis of the data.

What one chooses to code depends upon the purpose of the study. Bauer (2000) warns against adopting a purely inductive approach where one codes whatever one observes in the text. Rather, codes need to flow from the principles that underpin the research, and the specific questions one seeks to answer. The total set of codes in a given piece of research comprises the **coding frame** (a term used interchangeably with 'coding manual' or 'coding book'). Such a frame is given coherence by being derived from higher-order ideas, and Bauer's argument is that codes should be derived from existing theory. However, there would be little point in doing research if one were not simultaneously open to the data and what they might offer anew in terms of the theory's development or refutation. The point of the coding frame is that it sets up the potential for a systematic comparison between the set of texts one is analysing (Bauer, 2000); it is by means of this frame that one is able to ask questions of the data (see below).

How to code

Coding in content and thematic analytic research is taxing and time-consuming because there are generally no standardised categories. The researcher codes in order to answer the research questions, and the coding frame is developed in a manner that allows for this. Coding involves noting patterns in the data and dividing up the data to give greater clarity regarding their detailed content. In order to do this, the patterns are labelled with codes. Distinctions are drawn between different aspects of the content by organising the data into a set of categories.

An early decision must be taken regarding what the unit of coding will be, that is, whether codes will be attached to each line of text, sentence, speaker turn, interview or media article. For example, one might simply want to know how many interviewees or newspaper articles mentioned 'stress', in which case the coding unit would be the entire interview or article. However, generally coding is much more fine-grained, using a coding unit such as the sentence or a phrase, which allows the researcher to count how often in a single interview or article the code occurs, and to analyse the relationship of this code to other codes, in terms of co-occurrence or sequencing. For example, one could then analyse whether mention of 'stress' was typically associated with mention of 'work', and whether talk about work was typically followed by talk about stress (which might be an indication that work was viewed as leading to stress) or whether talk about stress usually preceded talk about work (which might reflect talk about the impact of stress on work).

A related issue that the researcher must resolve is whether each coding unit must be coded exclusively into just one category, or can be coded into multiple categories. The larger the coding unit, the more likely it is that it will contain material that could be coded into more than one category. Note that for some quantitative analyses of codes the codes *must* be **exclusive**, since statistical analysis of the relationship between codes will assume this (for example, it is not possible to calculate the correlation between two codes if they are not independent – in other words, if a single text segment can be assigned both codes). Exclusive coding has the advantage that it forces the researcher to develop very clearly defined coding categories, and this can enhance the development of the theoretical basis for these coding decisions. For example, if one wishes to code exclusively using the concepts of 'coping strategies' and 'handicap' (changes in lifestyle due to illness), then the task of deciding which text segments should be assigned which code will oblige the researcher to think very carefully about the definition of and relationship between these concepts; if someone with dizziness says that they were so dizzy that they 'had' to hold on to a railing, should this be coded as an instance of coping (by holding on) or handicap (as they were unable to walk unaided) or both? In a more qualitative analysis the researcher may reject the necessity of making such a distinction, which may appear arbitrary and artificial, and will instead allow the codes to overlap on occasion. However, it is important that codes should not be too broad and overlapping, or they will not serve the intended purpose of making distinctions between different aspects of the content, and the researcher will find that he or she is categorising large chunks of the data using the same multiple set of codes.

A code should have a label, an operationalisation of what the theme concerns and an example of a chunk of text that should be coded as fitting into this category. For example, the range of codes that arose from asking a sample of Zambian adolescents to talk about the origin of AIDS is shown in Figure 4.1. This example shows how coding categories very often form a hierarchy, with a small number of higher level categories (such as 'origin' in this example) that can be progressively sub-divided into lower level sub-categories (in this example the first level of sub-category is 'geographical' vs 'God' or 'practice', and the lowest level of sub-category corresponds to the continents within the sub-category 'geographical' and the types of behaviour under the sub-category 'practice'). Sometimes this hierarchy is created by coding the text first at the highest level, and then developing finer coding discriminations that can be used to create sub-categories that fall lower down in the hierarchy. For example, if using predefined theoretical high level categories for deductive coding, such as the elements of the theory of planned behaviour, the researcher might first code the text into material relating to attitudes, subjective norms and perceived control, and then inductively construct coding categories which distinguish between different sub-categories of attitudes, norms and control. However, the researcher might decide that two or more sub-categories within a code are

Code Name	Description	Examples
Origin-geographical-Europe	AIDS came from Europe	'I only know it came from Europe and not from Africa'
Origin-geographical-US	AIDS came from the US	'Though people think that AIDS came from the black man, it actually came from the white men in USA, I think New York'
Origin-geographical-Australia	AIDS came from Australia	'It came from Australia'
Origin-geographical-Africa	AIDS came from Africa	'Monkey was a male and happened to rape a black African woman'
Origin-God/Immorality	AIDS is a punishment/result of the immorality of people. Includes sex before/outside of marriage	'It's God's disease', 'It is God-given, God is the one who has brought this disease as a punishment for those people who like moving up and down'
Origin-practice-bestiality	Includes sex with monkeys, chickens, dogs	'They went and slept with some monkeys and then those monkeys were said to have a certain disease . . . those diseases were passed on to those people'
Origin-practice-science	AIDS was manufactured in a laboratory by scientists	'AIDS was scientific, I hear some people were carrying out an experiment'
Origin-practice-anal sex	AIDS is a result of anal sex	'I think it came by having anal sex . . . I think it came from those people like homosexuals'
Origin-practice-mixing	AIDS is a result of inter-racial sex	'It came from the white people, it's like they were mixing with us Africans'

Figure 4.1 *Example from a coding frame relating to representations of origin of AIDS (reproduced from Joffe & Bettega, 2003, forthcoming)*

so distinct that two entirely new, separate codes need to be created by **splitting** the original coding category.

Alternatively, the researcher may begin by using very specific low-level codes when coding at the initial textual level (as in grounded theory analysis, see Chapter 5). For a coherent analysis, fewer, more powerful categories will usually be required and so the initial textual categories are integrated into conceptual categories by way of **splicing** and **linking**, according to Dey (1993). Splicing can be thought of as the opposite of dividing up material. It is the fusing together of a set of codes under an overarching category. It involves increasingly focusing the categorisation activities in the knowledge that it will be impossible to incorporate all codes into the final analysis. This process of fusion involves the researcher thinking through what codes can be grouped together into more powerful codes. For example, the codes European, US and Australian origin, in the coding frame above, could be fused into a 'western origin' code. An alternative to actually splicing codes is to create links between codes. Multiple themes can be clustered into groups – the particular cluster or link is a higher order theme allowing for higher order abstraction and interpretation. One might do such clustering to show a conceptual relatedness of themes, or to show the sequential relatedness of sets of themes across the data. Thus, if the codes European, US and Australian origin were clustered rather than spliced, it would be possible to analyse them jointly, to explore themes which were common to western origin countries, and also separately, to determine whether there were themes unique to particular countries. The splicing and linking processes can be driven by theoretical concerns, policy issues or purely grounded in the data itself.

Moving from coding to analysis

Once the codes have been developed, refined and clearly described in the coding manual, the researcher may determine the reliability with which the codes can be applied. An initial impression of reliability can be gained by applying the codes to the same piece of text on two occasions separated by a week or so (a kind of 'test-retest' reliability). Although the coding will be influenced by similar subjective processes on both occasions, consistent coding by the researcher at least indicates that the distinctions made between codes are clear in the researcher's mind – if *you* cannot apply the codes consistently, there is no possibility that anyone else will be able to! The stronger test of reliability is to calculate the correspondence between the way in which codes are assigned to the text by two independent coders (see Chapter 7 for details of methods of calculating **inter-rater reliability**). If you wish to claim that your codes are objective, reliable indicators of the content of the text then you must demonstrate that the inter-rater reliability of your coding frame is good. Reliability testing is commonly used in content analytic work, especially if quantitative analysis is to be employed.

Inter-rater reliability checks are not always used in thematic analytic research since there is scepticism regarding such tests: it can be argued that one researcher merely trains another to think as she or he does when looking at a fragment of text, and so the reliability check does not establish that the codes are objective but merely that two people can apply the same subjective perspective to the text. However, this criticism overlooks the value of having to make the interpretations of the data very explicit and specific in order to achieve reliable coding. The more clearly the rationale for coding decisions is explained in the coding manual, the higher the inter-rater reliability will be; for example, it may be helpful to detail the logic underlying subtle coding discriminations (which may have been debated when disagreements arose between two coders), or to provide 'negative' examples of text segments which might appear to belong to that coding category but actually do not. When carrying out a complex thematic analysis, inter-rater comparisons provide a valuable opportunity to open up the rationale for the coding frame to the scrutiny of others, to examine and discuss the reasons for any differences in coding decisions, and hence to fine-tune the theoretical bases and operational definitions for the coding categories. This process means not only that the second researcher will code most of the transcript in a similar way to the first researcher, but also that other researchers looking at the system of coding used will find one that is fairly transparent, coherent and understandable, as opposed to an idio-syncratic, opaque system of interpretation devised by a single researcher.

Box 4.1   *Key features of coding*

- Coding involves noting patterns in the data and labelling these patterns to allow distinctions to be drawn and research questions to be answered.
- The researcher must decide whether to code manifest or latent themes, using deductive or inductive coding categories.
- As coding progresses, categories are refined by splitting, splicing and linking codes.
- The codes are described in a coding frame, which should list their labels, detailed definitions, and one or two example text segments.
- Checking the inter-rater reliability of coding ensures that coding decisions are made explicit and consistent.

When all of the data have been categorised, the analysis can begin. A code can be used in a primarily quantitative manner, in which the numbers assigned to codes form the basis for a statistical analysis. Depending upon the way in which codes have been applied to the data (see Boyatzis, 1998: 141–2), statistically based analyses such as correlations, group comparisons (for example, using the chi-square test), cluster analysis or even multiple regression can be conducted. This would be the more usual route for a content, rather than a thematic, analysis. On the other hand, codes can be used for a purely qualitative analysis, where the focus tends to be on description of verbal patterns. Perhaps it is a point between these two positions that is most appropriate for a thematic analysis: the nuances of the high frequency themes are explored in depth. This approach is particularly fitting for research that is driven by social representations tenets; themes widely shared within particular groups are taken to illustrate the existence of social representations (see Joffe & Haarhoff, 2002).

Huberman and Miles (1994) spell out a useful sequence that summarises the method of generating meaning from a set of transcripts. Patterns and themes are noted; themes are counted to discern whether a theme is common or more rare; a plausible story is extracted from the data that can be related to the literature review; differences in terms of gender, class or other groupings are looked at; disconfirming as well as confirming evidence is examined. In line with a loose definition of 'testing' a research question, one looks at whether the original hunch can be sustained or not, and whether it needs modifying, as well as at the direction in which further research might go. New insights can often be provoked by attempting to understand what appear to be anomalies.

COMPUTER ASSISTED QUALITATIVE DATA ANALYSIS SYSTEMS (CAQDAS)

Over the past decades a series of computer packages (for example, Ethnograph, Atlas ti, NUDIST) which aid content and thematic analyses have been produced. Their role in the process of analysis, and their advantages and disadvantages require careful consideration.

The central analytic task of thematic analysis, in particular, is to understand the meaning of texts. This requires researchers' minds to interpret the material. The computer is a mechanical aid in this process. Computers cannot analyse textual data in the way that they can numerical data. Yet, as a mechanical aid, the computer is able to make possible higher quality research for the following reasons. CAQDAS allow researchers to deal with many more interviews than manual analyses can. Consequently, useful comparisons between groups can be made due to the inclusion of large enough numbers of participants in each group. The researcher is also assisted to look at patterns of codes, links between codes and co-occurrences in a highly systematic fashion, since retrieval of data grouped by codes is made far easier. CAQDAS permit retrieval of data combinations in a manner similar to literature search computer packages, typically using combination retrieval terms such as AND, OR and so on. The researcher can therefore instantly retrieve, for example, all text segments from older female interviewees which were categorised as relevant to 'perceived control', and compare these with similarly coded text segments in interviews with younger women, or with older men. If this process is carried out using, for example, cut-and-paste techniques (using either actual printed transcripts or a word-processing package), it is not only much more time-consuming, but literally cuts the text segment out of the (con)text, whereas the packages also allow the researcher to view easily the context of a particular coded text segment, so that the contextual meaning is not lost. Packages such as Atlas ti allow researchers to examine the patterning of themes across the range of interviews, and the common pathways or chains of association within interviews. More specifically, the filtering functions of packages such as Atlas ti allow the researchers to retrieve the patterns of codes prevalent in particular demographic groups, and such patterns can be retrieved as frequency charts, lists of textual excerpts, or visually, as visual networks.

Figure 4.2 provides an example of a visual hierarchy generated in Atlas ti, based upon the codes shown in Figure 4.1 (with the European, US and Australian geographical origin codes fused into a 'west' origin code), which

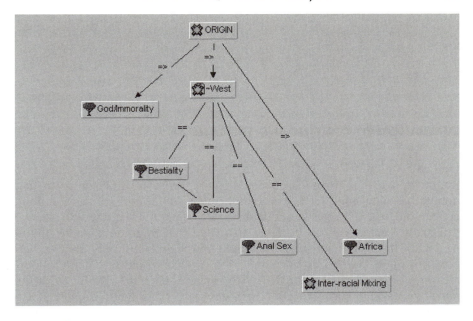

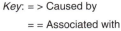

Key: = > Caused by

= = Associated with

Figure 4.2   *The origin of AIDS according to a sample of urban, Zambian adolescents (reproduced from Joffe & Bettega, 2003, forthcoming)*

shows how such a package can usefully illustrate the findings of a thematic analysis. The higher up the code is in the table, the greater the number of people who mentioned it spontaneously. This figure makes it possible to see at a glance, for example, that a western origin of AIDS is associated, in the minds of Zambian adolescents, chiefly with the practices of bestiality and science, which are viewed as linked, and to a lesser extent with anal sexual practices and inter-racial mixing. A diagram summarising the views of westerners would be visibly very different to this (see Joffe, 1999).

In summary, CAQDAS can provide an efficient means of retrieving text segments for systematic comparison, enumerating the degree of empirical support for different themes, and mapping the relationships between themes. It cannot fulfil the central task of textual analysis – to decode the meaning of the text – but as a mechanical aid to managing material it can facilitate it. Not only can it allow development of increased complexity of thought, since it can store and retrieve many more links than researchers can store in their minds, it also helps the researcher to assess how much counter-evidence exists for alternative interpretations. This is important, as qualitative work, in particular, has been accused of failing to take heed of trends that run counter to those that the research highlights. If the researcher is using qualitative and quantitative methods in tandem, the package can convert codes into frequencies and transfer them to the Statistical Package for Social Sciences (SPSS) for quantitative analysis, provided that the categorisation process meets the criteria for a more quantitative analysis (see above). When used in a thoughtful way, computer packages allow one to be highly systematic in a manner that is faithful to the data.

EVALUATION OF CONTENT AND THEMATIC ANALYSIS

Hollway and Jefferson (2000) challenge the practice of coding data into fragmented text segments in order to make sense of it. They claim that qualitative data analysis is one of the most subtle and intuitive human epistemological enterprises, and is therefore one of the last that will achieve satisfactory computerisation. They also state that fragmentation results in neglect of the whole, whereas the whole interview is not only greater than the sum of its parts, but by 'immersion' in the whole one gains understanding of the parts, rather than vice versa. Their work, in line with the narrative psychological tradition, consequently stays with people's storyline as a whole. Their critique is similar to the more general critique of thematic analysis, that it abstracts issues from the way that they appear in life, organising material according to the researcher's sense of how it connects, rather than the inter-relationship of themes in the participant's mind or lifeworld (see Boyatzis, 1998). However, it can be argued that the goals of thematic and content analysis are simply different from those of, for example, narrative analysis. The aim is to describe how thematic contents are elaborated by groups of participants, and to identify meanings that are valid across many participants, rather than to undertake an in-depth analysis of the inter-connections between meanings within one particular narrative.

Contemporary uses of content analysis reveal a rather rich interpretation of the method; systematic research need not be sacrificed in the name of a complex unravelling of data. This mixture of systematicity and complexity appears to be an aspiration of content and thematic analysis alike. However, there are cases in which one or other should be used. Clearly, content analysis should be used if the aim is to carry out quantitative analysis. However, on a small sample size only the descriptive use of thematic coding is advisable, since it is meaningless to assign numbers to a data set that is too small to meet the usual minimum requirements for statistical analysis. For instance, if the sample cannot be regarded as large enough to permit reliable statistical generalisation to the population from which it was derived then it may be misleading to report the frequencies of codes, as this would seem to imply that the frequency of occurrence in the sample was in some way representative of the likely frequency of occurrence in the wider population. Nonetheless, it can be helpful to give some indication of whether themes occurred rarely or commonly, although this can of course be conveyed using qualitative terms such as 'most', 'some' or 'a few'.

A good content or thematic analysis *must* describe the bulk of the data (Dey, 1993), and must not simply select examples of text segments that support the arguments one wants to make (see Silverman, 1993). Moreover, even if one quantifies the text for purposes of analysis, the analysis remains partially qualitative. In other words, it is vital to remember that numbers do not tell the whole story – that the number of times a category appears does not necessarily indicate the extent to which it is relevant to interviewees. A point that is only mentioned once, by one person, can still have great empirical relevance and conceptual importance. The aspiration of thematic analysis, in particular, is to stay true to the raw data, and its meaning within a particular context of thoughts, rather than attaching too much importance to the frequency of codes which have been abstracted from their context.

Box 4.2   *Key features of content analysis and thematic analysis*

- Content analysis is a method for counting particular features of a text or visual image. Statistical tests can be used to analyse the frequency of codes when content analysis has been carried out on a large, representative data set and the codes have been shown to have good inter-rater reliability.
- Thematic analysis is similar to content analysis, but also involves more explicit qualitative analysis of the meaning of the data in context. It is useful for systematically identifying and describing features of qualitative data, which recur across many participants.
- When using both methods it is important a) to examine *all* the data carefully to 'test' how much of it fits the description presented in the analysis, and b) to remember that coding is an interpretive process, and that the frequency of codes does not necessarily reflect their importance.
- Computer packages to assist qualitative data analysis help the researcher to retrieve relevant text segments for analysis, and to assess the frequency and co-occurrence of codes, but cannot fulfil the central task of qualitative analysis, that is, interpreting the textual or visual data.

SUMMARY

Content and thematic analysis share the potential to be systematic, to rely on naturally occurring raw data, and to deal with large quantities of data. Thematic analysis, conducted in the way laid out in this chapter, allows for systematic analysis of the meanings made of the phenomena under investigation. Moreover, it is a form of analysis that is acceptable and meaningful to both researchers who normally employ quantitative methods and those who prefer a qualitative approach (Boyatzis, 1998). However, 'The challenge to the qualitative researcher is to use thematic analysis to draw the richness of the themes from the raw information without reducing the insights to a trivial level for the sake of consistency of judgement' (Boyatzis, 1998: 14).

The chapter has demonstrated that computer packages, counting and the theory-driven nature of questions and means of answering them can contribute to the quality of work on naturally occurring texts (and indeed images). When used in a considered fashion, content and, particularly, thematic analysis allow the researcher to be faithful to the data while producing high quality social science.

RECOMMENDED READING

Books

Bauer, M.W. (2000). Classical content analysis: a review. In M.W. Bauer and G. Gaskell (eds) *Qualitative researching with text, image and sound*. London: Sage. pp. 131–51.
Boyatzis, R.E. (1998). *Transforming qualitative information*. London: Sage.

Websites

www.gsu.edu/~wwwcom/
www.qualitative-research.net/fqs/

REVISION QUESTIONS

1 Explain the difference between inductive and deductive coding.
2 What are the advantages and disadvantages of allowing each piece of text to be assigned exclusively to only one coding category?
3 Describe the steps in developing a reliable coding frame.
4 What are the arguments for and against carrying out inter-rater reliability checks?
5 What differences are there between content analysis and thematic analysis?

5 QUALITATIVE ANALYSIS OF EXPERIENCE: GROUNDED THEORY AND CASE STUDIES

Kerry Chamberlain, Paul Camic and Lucy Yardley

AIMS OF THIS CHAPTER

(i)   To consider how the analysis of experience can be undertaken.

(ii) To provide a brief overview of phenomenological analysis of subjective experience.

(iii) To outline and illustrate the steps involved in a grounded theory analysis.

(iv) To discuss the advantages and goals of qualitative case studies.

(v)   To describe the procedures involved in pragmatic qualitative case analysis.

INTRODUCTION

Health care psychology researchers are interested in many questions that centre on what it is like for people to experience physical and psychological health and illness-related episodes in their life, or to provide assistance to people in these situations. To answer these questions, a number of qualitative approaches have been developed for examining subjective experience, including **phenomenological methods**, **grounded theory**, **case study**, ethnography, biographical and life history analysis, and narrative inquiry (Creswell, 1998).

The attempt to study subjective experience raises some fundamental philosophical questions concerning the extent to which one person's private experience can be revealed to or understood by another person. If each person's private experience and perspective is different, then surely that of the researcher can never map on to that of the people who are studied? Early phenomenologists attempted to overcome this problem by seeking to 'bracket' their preconceptions – by trying to leave aside their existing understandings and assumptions in order to be open to new meanings, including those of others. However, setting aside one's own habitual way of thinking can prove a virtually impossible task. Most researchers now consider it preferable to accept that the meanings generated in an analysis of subjective experience will be a product of the perspectives of both the researchers and those of the people whose experiences are being studied. If this is the case, then an important part of the analysis is to acknowledge and, where appropriate, explicitly *reflect* on the influence of the researchers' own perspectives on their interpretation of the subjective experiences of others. This self-consciously interpretive approach differs from content analysis (see Chapter 4), which seeks to minimise (albeit not exclude) the influence of subjective interpretation of the text by using very explicit, objective coding procedures, and quantitative analysis of the patterns of codes in the data. It also differs from discourse analysis (see Chapter 6), which is concerned primarily with the processes by which meanings are constructed through language and social interaction, rather than with analysing the content and structure of the subjective meanings which result from this process. Nevertheless, an understanding of discourse analysis can contribute to interpretive analysis of subjective meaning, since an understanding of how language and talk can be used to construct meaning can assist the interpretation of subjective accounts.

This chapter provides a brief overview of phenomenological approaches to the study of subjective experience, and then focuses in detail on grounded theory and the case study, in order to illustrate the methods and analytic processes involved in examining experience (see Chapters 6 and 7 for analysis of experience using narrative analysis and ethnography, respectively). Grounded theory was selected because, while it shares many of the features of other approaches to the analysis of subjective experience (especially phenomenological analysis), it provides a more explicit, systematic set of procedures for interpretive analysis, can be adopted by analysts with very different epistemological approaches (for example, post-positivist or constructivist), and can be used to analyse virtually any kind or combination of qualitative data. The detailed procedures of grounded theory analysis can prove particularly useful for novice analysts, as they offer a step-by-step approach to ensuring that the analysis is grounded in the data, is thorough and comprehensive, and goes beyond description or superficial explanation to build a coherent and potentially generalisable theory.

The case study shares many of the advantages of grounded theory, including the capacity to encompass many different data sources and analytic perspectives, and also has a special relevance to health care research. Case-based learning has close parallels with real-world problem-solving (Fishman, 1999); consequently, the case study has been used since the earliest days of health care as a means of undertaking a holistic analysis of typical or special people, health care practices or settings, and communicating this interpretation in a manner that is meaningful to practitioners.

PHENOMENOLOGICAL ANALYSIS

The origins of phenomenological analysis can be traced back to the philosopher Kant, who advocated the systematic investigation of 'phenomena', by which he meant the content and organisation of conscious experience. Phenomenological analyses of subjective experience have subsequently been undertaken by a succession of philosophers, including in the twentieth century Heidegger, Husserl, Sartre, Merleau-Ponty and Ricoeur, and each of these writers has adopted a somewhat different approach. Consequently, while all phenomenological analyses attempt to analyse the essence of subjective experience(s), there is no single phenomenological perspective or prescriptive method. Nevertheless, many phenomenological researchers advocate broadly similar procedures (see, for example, Anderson, 1998; Creswell, 1998; Giorgi & Giorgi, 2003; Smith, 1999). These consist of: collecting in-depth descriptions from people who have experienced a particular phenomenon; abstracting and summarising key meanings in these subjective accounts; and using these as the basis for an interpretation of the essential features of the phenomenon.

A key advantage of phenomenological approaches is that phenomenology foregrounds the experience of the individual, and thus provides a 'space' or a 'voice' for the lived experiences of different people, which are not adequately represented or analysed by methods which aggregate statistics from large samples, such as randomised controlled trials or epidemiological surveys. Anderson (1998) argues that the clinician's understanding of patients' perspectives and decisions can be greatly enriched by entering into a dialogue with their accounts, which can reveal ethical and moral dimensions of their lives that cannot be captured or explained by scientific methods, and which may open up entirely new interpretations of their situation. For example, phenomenological analyses of accounts of chronic pain (Kugelmann, 1999; Osborn & Smith, 1998) have highlighted the sense of isolation or displacement that can result from pain – the feeling that one can no longer be a part of normal social life because pain traps the sufferer in a private world quite different from and incomprehensible to that of other people.

Whereas many approaches to research (both quantitative and qualitative) place great emphasis on showing that the conclusions have been derived by means of a series of approved procedures, in phenomenological analysis it is much more important to offer an interpretation that is imaginative, thought-provoking and compelling. Consequently, theory (often drawn from disciplines outside psychology, such as philosophy, sociology or anthropology) typically plays a much greater role in a phenomenological analysis than does methodological stringency, and a good analysis is able to go beyond existing and commonsense interpretations to suggest quite new insights or avenues for exploration. However, the freedom from methodological strictures also means that the inexperienced (or simply uninspired!) researcher lacks clear guidance as to how to achieve these insights, and may be unable to deliver more than a superficial description of the phenomenon, or an unoriginal interpretation formulated on the basis of pre-existing concepts or analytic frameworks. For researchers interested in subjective experience who lack the confidence to undertake an in-depth phenomenological analysis, the grounded theory method provides a very clearly defined set of procedures for moving from a rigorous analysis of the empirical data to abstract conceptualisation.

GROUNDED THEORY

Grounded theory was devised over 30 years ago (Glaser & Strauss, 1967) and has become very popular in recent years. It is now widely accepted and utilised in the field of health care, and has been employed to analyse experiences as diverse as: what it is like to experience breast cancer for older women (Crooks, 2001); how people adjust after surviving a serious traffic accident (Cagnetta & Cicognani, 1999); how general practitioners understand their role in implementing new genetic technology into their practices (Kumar & Gantley, 1999); or how the parents of children with autism make sense of this condition in email discussion groups (Huws, Jones & Ingledew, 2001).

Grounded theory is popular in part because it offers a detailed and systematic set of procedures for data collection, analysis and interpretation (see Strauss & Corbin, 1990). However, there is some debate about its use in practice. Some researchers argue that 'true' grounded theory must incorporate all the practices specified by the methodology, and critics of studies using grounded theory that have failed to do this have accused these researchers of eroding the methods (Stern, 1994), or of muddling methods (Wilson & Hutchinson, 1996). However, most writers, including the founders of this method, concede that grounded theory will evolve and develop over time (see, for example, Glaser, 1999; Strauss & Corbin, 1994). Others again argue that components of grounded theory methodology can be used selectively and usefully in general qualitative research practice (for example, Chamberlain, 1999). Bartlett and Payne (1997) suggest that research which uses only selected components may be better labelled 'grounded analyses' rather than grounded theory.

Grounded theory methodology provides a set of procedures which promote the development of a theory about the phenomenon under investigation. By following the procedures of grounded theory systematically and thoroughly, the researcher can devise an account of the phenomenon, such as experiencing surgery for colon cancer, which is grounded in the lived experience of the participants. Because it is grounded in the data, it will be relevant to the participants and those interested in their experience, and will fit the context in which it is researched. The procedures also promote a deep engagement with the meanings of the data, and operate to minimise researchers offering a purely descriptive account of experience.

It must be noted also that the processes of grounded theory analysis are interwoven, and are not carried out sequentially. This is most obvious where data collection and analysis are not conducted sequentially but are simultaneous and inter-related throughout the research process. This is in contrast to procedures such as content analysis, where it would be common to collect all the data before examining it for what it showed. The inter-relation of data collection and analysis is not unique to grounded theory, but the practices are certainly made explicit there. Although obtaining and analysing data are presented in separate sections below, this division, as you will see, is not applicable in the practice of grounded theory.

Obtaining the data

Psychology researchers, using grounded theory to investigate questions about experience, typically work with data collected in interviews, usually conducted one-to-one with the individual participant, but sometimes with data collected from couples, families or groups. Interviews are generally semi-structured or unstructured in nature, and the objective is to allow participants to talk freely about the topics of interest, and to give their own accounts (see Chapter 3). Interviews are typically tape-recorded and transcribed for subsequent analysis. However, there is no need to constrain data to come solely from interviews, and analysis could be undertaken of other texts, such as survivors' published accounts of their experience or internet discussions of illness experience or could include observational or ethnographic data (see Chapter 7). In fact, grounded theory encourages researchers to sample the field of the phenomenon under investigation as broadly as possible, and to draw on multiple sources of relevant data, although reliance on interview data alone continues to be very common in published studies using grounded theory procedures.

The data need to be transcribed in order to facilitate the analysis process, and this raises questions about the scope and detail of transcription required. In general, it is satisfactory to work from a complete account of what was said with some indications for pauses and breaks, and usually it is not necessary to record the timing of pauses and silences as suggested for some other forms of analysis. Because analysis commences as soon as data collection begins, it is important to transcribe the whole account, especially in the early stages of the research or if you are new to grounded theory analysis. Strauss and Corbin (1990) suggest that as the analysis, and consequently the theory, develops over the research, it may be possible to transcribe only selected sections of the interview, especially if you are an experienced researcher. However, because you will seek to confirm the developing theory in the data at all stages of the research, full transcriptions are usually best. It is also very useful to do your own transcribing, and to return and listen again to the tapes during the analysis. Both procedures assist in the interpretation of the transcripts.

The nature of the data and the role of the researcher also require some consideration. Under some assumptions, the data can be considered to be a factual account of experience, recounted to the researcher on request: a telling by the person as to what did happen to them and how they felt about it and reacted to it. However, most psychologists today, working with qualitative interview data, would consider the data to be a constructed account of experience, given for a specific purpose within a particular context: an account that may differ from occasion to occasion, and which is constructed to present this person in a particular light to this particular researcher. It may not be 'factual' in nature (see Nightingale & Cromby, 1999). We do not have space to discuss the assumptions underlying these perspectives, but only to note that it is possible to conduct grounded theory under either perspective (see Charmaz, 2001). Under the 'factual' or realist view, the researcher is considered to be a neutral observer, deriving theory from the data. Under the constructed view, the researcher is considered to be engaged in constructing the interpretation and the theory, and cannot be separated from either (see Hall & Callery, 2001).

Doing the analysis

The aim of the analysis is to develop a theoretical account of the phenomenon out of the data. Because interview data are rich and complex, analysis invariably means becoming immersed, and often initially overwhelmed, in the detail of the data, working through a series of possible interpretations and finally emerging or surfacing from the analysis as sense is made of the meanings in the data. This process is common to most qualitative research, but grounded theory is particularly helpful in achieving this through the procedures it utilises for making sense of data.

As noted earlier, analysis is not separate from data collection in grounded theory, and **theoretical sampling** connects these. What this means is that participants are included, or sampled, for specific reasons, which differ at each phase of the analysis according to theory development requirements. Early in the study, any suitable participants who have relevant experience related to the research aims may be included to provide data. Later on, as the theory starts to take shape, specific individuals are sampled who have particular experiences which could extend the theory by revealing new issues or relationships. This is a 'filling the gaps' phase. In the final phase, further specific individuals are sampled to 'verify' or test the theory, either to provide confirmation that the theory is complete, or sometimes to determine its limits, by selecting individuals to whom the theory should not apply. This sampling of data sources, usually individuals, proceeds in a systematic way, from convenience sampling to directed, systematic sampling, according to the needs of ongoing theory development.

This naturally raises the question of how much data you need. Grounded theory suggests that data collection can stop when **saturation** is reached. Saturation means that further data collection and analysis are contributing nothing new. It also has different senses of meaning at different times throughout the analysis, and is always a considered judgement on the part of the researcher. In early stages of analysis, it relates to concluding that new sources of data are not extending the specific codings but merely confirming them, and further input 'only adds bulk to the coded data and nothing to the theory' (Glaser & Strauss, 1967: 111). Further, because we want to develop a theoretical rather than a descriptive account, saturation (sometimes called theoretical saturation) is also considered in the later stages of analysis, when we attempt to judge whether the theory is saturated, full and complete. In this way, saturation is a criterion for establishing when both data collection and analysis have been taken far enough.

Phase 1: generating the initial codes   Analysis of data using grounded theory cycles through three phases, each interconnected with ongoing data collection and this with ongoing analysis. Each phase has a different function. In the first, data are collected and analysed to open up understandings. Grounded theory proceeds, for the most part, inductively: the researcher sets out to generate the theory from the data rather than verify hypotheses within it. Hence, grounded theory suggests that researchers approach the data collection and analysis, at least initially, without making a detailed reading of relevant literature. In this way, the researcher is open to ideas in the data and is free to find meanings in the data, rather than approaching the data with presuppositions about what it will contain. Therefore, the first phase of data collection is merely to obtain some data for analysis, and to allow analysis to commence. Data are obtained from any convenient sample of people who can provide information on the topic of interest, such as people who have gone through bowel cancer surgery, or caretakers of people with Alzheimer's disease, and so on – although even at this early stage it may be helpful to ensure that you sample from the range of people whose views you are interested in (for example, both men and women, old and young, newly diagnosed and experienced patients, etc.). As each interview is completed, the researcher begins analysis on the data obtained. Because this is to open up understandings, or 'break open' the data as grounded theory researchers describe it, in this first phase data collection procedures are termed 'open sampling' and data analysis procedures are termed 'open coding'.

Open coding involves going through the interview data systematically, listening to the recording, reading and rereading the transcript to become thoroughly familiar with it, and assigning labels, or codes, to sections of the text. In open coding you give labels (codes, or more commonly these are termed *categories* in grounded theory) to small segments of the text, indicating the idea or concept referred to. For example, you might note how the participant, in a particular segment of text, is talking about losing control, or being rejected, or feeling loss. In this phase, it is often recommended that you code the interview transcript line by line (see, for example, Charmaz, 1995) so that you focus on each small segment of the text in turn.

For the same reason, it is often recommended that you use 'in vivo' codes here: labelling the specific codes with words actually used by the participant. Although this is very useful, appropriate codes are not always available in this way, and some codings will be more abstract concepts than are conveyed by the participant's actual words. However, both of these recommendations are intended to compel you to stay close to the data, focusing on the detail of what participants said, and what it means. This works to prevent you assigning codes that are too broad or general at this stage, or codes which arise from your own presuppositions and that are not grounded in the data. Codes are created in analytic interaction with the data. This is quite different to content analysis, where codes are typically derived from a small initial sub-set of data and then applied to the whole data set subsequently.

As you collect more data, you will necessarily develop a more extensive list of codes. Inevitably, different participants will raise similar issues, giving rise to the same codings, but they will also raise different issues, and new codings. This leads you in two directions. Firstly, it will cause you to return to the earlier transcripts to determine if they contain any support for the new codes, and also to check that data given the same codes later on have the same meanings as the earlier codes. In grounded theory, this sort of comparison is a central feature of the analytic process, called the **constant comparative method**, and is used at all levels throughout the analysis. Secondly, the developing coding schemes can lead you to modify your data collection process, by extending the range of issues covered in future interviews and, once saturation is reached, by moving you into the second phase of analysis, selecting more participants who can confirm and elaborate the codings identified so far, and develop the emerging understandings to a more abstract level. The first phase of analysis will have produced a wide range of detailed codes (or categories) which have been established from the data. Some of these will be very specific; others may be more abstract. As the interpreter, you will have already begun to theorise connections and links between the codes or categories (using procedures we will discuss later). You will have established, by ongoing comparison, that nothing new is emerging from further open sampling, and that it is time to turn to the next phase of analysis.

Phase 2: elaborating more abstract codes   This second phase involves further data collection (through 'relational sampling') and further analysis (termed 'axial coding'). Whereas the first phase of analysis was to open up understandings and build a broad database for theory, this phase is to confirm what has been established and develop it to a more abstract level. It seeks to confirm and elaborate the scope of categories established earlier, to identify how they may be related, and to identify limits to their applicability. It is possible that new categories will be identified in this process, and this can require ongoing relational sampling and further axial coding analysis. As before, data collection and analysis proceed simultaneously, using saturation as a criterion for moving on. As analysis proceeds here, you will develop and establish a small set of general, more abstract categories, which will subsume the more specific and detailed codes established in open coding. During axial coding, you also specifically consider the properties of categories (how they are defined, when are they applicable, what is their function, and so on) and the relationships between them (which categories are superordinate, how are they linked to each other and to sub-categories). As with open coding, this stage of the analysis progresses using questioning and constant comparison. It results in the initial establishment of a theory of the phenomenon, built up and elaborated more fully as this phase proceeds. Although grounded theory is often categorised as inductive, you will now begin to work more deductively as theoretical ideas and understandings develop, and you go back to the data to consider their basis there. This requires theoretical sensitivity on the part of the researcher, an issue considered in more detail later. As the axial coding phase of analysis progresses, the researcher will progress to a more elaborated theoretical account, which is both simpler in structure than the diversity of codes established earlier, and more dense in the meaning of categories and their interconnected relationships. Once these are saturated, you move to the final phase – that of integrating and establishing the final theory to be presented.

Phase 3: verifying an integrated theory   The third phase also involves some further data collection and continuing analysis. Here, further participants are sampled, using 'discriminant sampling' to gather further data to confirm the overall theory, and to establish saturation of the theory as a whole. The analysis process here is termed 'selective coding', where you establish how the theory ties together as a whole, and establish the 'core category'. The core category is the over-arching category that encapsulates the theory and is related to, and superordinate to, all other categories. This is 'the one category which identifies what your research is about . . . the one which is abstract enough to encapsulate your storyline' (Bartlett & Payne, 1997: 193).

These three phases of grounded theory research have been presented sequentially here to enable them to be outlined clearly. However, it must be reasserted that these phases have fuzzy boundaries and are not clearly separable. Although progression is from raw data to final theory development, it is possible that you will cycle back through phases in order to extend, clarify and saturate categories. As the researcher, you need to use judgement as to when to move between one phase and the next.

Developing the theory

The aim of grounded theory is to develop a theory of the phenomenon. As will already be obvious, this is an ongoing process throughout the research, and cannot be separated from the data collection and analysis. The theory is built up systematically throughout the analysis, and developed into an abstract general account, grounded in the data, as the research proceeds. The theory is intended to emerge from the data, and is, like the codes and categories, created through the analytic interaction with the data. This interaction is enhanced by grounded theory procedures of questioning, **memo**-writing and diagramming, which are designed to ensure that the resulting theory is grounded in the data.

At all phases of analysis, you should be questioning the data and its interpretation. During open coding you will be asking questions such as: what is going on here? What is being said here? Who can say this, and who cannot? What led to this happening? What is being assumed? What is being left out? During axial coding, questions will be more general, such as: what are these codes an example of? Is this the same as this? How does this relate to this? What is the meaning of this? During selective coding, similar questions will be asked, along with questions about the structure of the theory, such as: does this category encompass this one? Are these categories at the same level? What is the most general category here? How do other categories relate to this general category? The application of questioning is made systematic through the use of the constant comparative method. This procedure involves comparing participants, codes and categories systematically for their similarities and differences. Such comparisons promote the need for further sampling (the codes for participants are still expanding and the data is not saturated), the development of new categories (these categories are not the same), and the synthesis of categories (these categories are the same), and so on. This process also facilitates an understanding of the properties of categories (when does this process apply or not apply) and the links between them (are these at the same level of abstraction). Constant comparison thus ensures that all data and its interpretations are considered systematically at all levels of analysis, drawing on questioning, but also interlinked with the processes of memoing and diagramming.

As the analysis proceeds, it is necessary to keep track of your ideas about the meaning and interpretation of codes and categories, and how they fit together. Grounded theory actively promotes memo-writing, or memoing, and diagramming as ways of doing this. Memos are merely notes to yourself, as the researcher. Memos are a record of developing thoughts, ideas and insights as the analysis progresses. These are an important component of many qualitative research methods (for example, field notes in ethnography, see Chapter 7) but grounded theory promotes their use at all stages of the analysis. Memos can be written about the context of an interview and reflect your understanding of it as similar or different to other interviews. Memos should be written about codes and categories (what do these cover? How are they defined? How are they limited?), as well as about more theoretical aspects (how do these categories fit together? What scope do they have for theory?). By incorporating memoing into the analysis, you are forced to reflect on the data and its meanings and interconnections. Comparing memos thus becomes an important part of the analysis, clarifying how different components inter-relate. Memoing throughout the analysis process forces your reflections to become both more abstract and more inter-related as you progress towards an overall theory. Diagramming – setting out inter-relationships in a visual memo – serves a similar function, organising your current understandings of how everything fits together. Diagramming is more relevant in later stages of the analysis, and assists in establishing the relationships between different categories in the theory – where and how they link, and where they do not (indicating more data collection and analysis may be called for). Frequently, grounded theory analyses are represented in publications in the form of the final diagram developed out of the analysis.

These processes, questioning, memoing and diagramming, in the context of data analysis using the constant comparative method, work to promote the development and elaboration of theory. Consistent use of these pro-cedures ensures that you will have to engage in abstract, analytical thinking about the data, its meanings, and how it all fits together. These procedures require you to make interpretations at a more abstract and theoretical level as the analysis progresses, and they promote more theoretical density and integration in your analysis. They work to promote and ensure the identi-fication of a grounded, saturated theoretical account of the phenomenon under study.

Box 5.1   *Key features of grounded theory*

- Data are 'theoretically sampled' from sources that allow the researcher to construct, elaborate and test emerging theory.
- 'Open coding' is used to inductively identify codes or categories that are grounded in the data. 'Axial coding' is then used to develop a smaller set of more general, abstract, theoretically based codes, which can encompass the initial grounded categories.
- The definitions of codes and the relations between them are elaborated and refined by 'constant comparison' between each coded data segment, in order to identify the similarities and differences between the charac-teristics and context of each instance of a particular code, relative to a) further instances of that code, and b) instances of different codes.
- Questioning, memos and diagrams are used to support and document the process of systematic theory construction.
- Finally, 'selective coding' is used to create a 'core category' that ties all the elements of the theory together, and 'discriminant sampling' is under-taken to verify that the theory has reached 'saturation', that is, provides an internally consistent and complete interpretation of the experience which closely fits data from a range of relevant sources.

A grounded theory example

To illustrate the processes involved in grounded theory analysis, we focus on a particular study of perceptions of non-pharmacological therapy (Yardley et al., 2001) and show how the analysis progressed through the phases outlined above. Phases 1 and 2 were undertaken by Karen Sharples, under the supervision of Lucy Yardley , and with assistance and input from an experienced complementary therapist (George Lewith). Phase 3 was undertaken by Lucy Yardley, using further data collected by a research nurse (Sandra Beech).

Phase 1   This project took as its starting point the question of how people evaluated chiropractic services, which was quickly reformulated in terms of the broader issue of what people wanted and expected from these services, and how they related their actual experience of treatment to these desires and expectations. A semi-structured interview schedule of five core questions was developed by the research team. The initial 'open' sample comprised eight consecutive people attending a chiropractic clinic for treatment of acute back pain. The interviews were tape-recorded and transcribed, and fieldnotes were kept recording the interviewer's reflections on each interview, with particular attention to interpersonal interactions (for example, interruptions by family members, apparent nervousness about who might hear the tape, or concern about whether what was said was similar to the accounts of other people), as well as documenting significant talk that was not tape-recorded, and noting the interviewer's immediate reactions (for example, that the interviewee seemed anxious to give socially desirable answers). Preliminary analysis was carried out in parallel with the interviews; the transcripts were read repeatedly so as to identify recurrent phrases and concepts, and possible themes, and memos were written regarding initial interpretations and questions. Open codes were then developed by continually comparing the emerging coding categories across different people, incidents and contexts, in order to develop and refine the codes (including their labels and definitions) to fit the data more closely and to address the questions 'when?', 'why?', 'how?', 'in what circumstances?'. A revised interview schedule was developed to seek clarification of emerging theoretical questions, and was administered to a further six consecutive patients with acute lower back pain. This resulted in saturation for this stage of the analysis – no significant new data seemed likely to be generated from this circumscribed population of patients who had a particular physical complaint and who were seeking therapy from a particular practitioner.

Phase 2   Open coding generated 78 coding categories, and these were tabulated in a form which allowed the researchers to identify which interviews contained an instance of each open code. For example, open codes relating to the theme of 'payment' included the concept that paying for treatment results in better service (voiced by seven participants), and the more specific concept (expressed by three patients) that payment entitled the patient to the exclusive attention of the therapist, an idea which was significantly expressed in the participants' words as a 'one-to-one' relationship. Using the method of constant comparison, the context in which these statements were made was established (for example, whether they were made by satisfied or unsatisfied patients), and these codes were linked and contrasted with other open codes; for example, a code which noted that payment could be a barrier to obtaining therapy, and a code relating to concern about whether payment would affect the chiropractor's treatment decisions. By this process the open codes could be integrated into a more abstract set of axial codes. At this point discussions between the researchers, reference to the literature, and the use of diagrams assisted with the development of an initial theory relating the ten axial codes that had emerged, which was written up as a coherent story mapping the trajectory of the participants over time from being passive NHS patients to becoming active consumers of chiropractic therapy.

Phase 3   The final phase of analysis sought to determine whether more general theoretical principles could be abstracted which would be applicable to people with different health complaints, receiving different forms of therapy from different therapists. A core category ('perception of treatment') was established which linked patients' abstract representations of therapy with their concrete experiences of the costs and benefits of treatment. Since changes in perceptions of treatment over time had emerged as a central concept, it was important to also seek longitudinal data to verify whether initial representations of therapy were influential in shaping subsequent treatment experiences, and whether they were modified as a result of treatment experiences. It was therefore necessary to employ 'discriminant sampling' to obtain longitudinal data from people with different symptoms, treatment and therapists to those in the initial sample. Fortuitously, the first author had already obtained a data set satisfying these criteria, consisting of transcribed interviews with 13 people seeking treatment for dizziness before and 6 months after treatment; these data were consequently employed to verify the emerging theory, rather than collecting further data for this purpose. Selective coding of these data could thus be used in order to test the theory that treatment perceptions and adherence to treatment would influence, and be influenced by, treatment experiences, such as perceived changes in symptoms and the relationship with the therapists. This systematic verification process provided partial support for the theory, but also permitted unexpected findings to emerge (for example, that treatment adherence could be maintained by positive treatment experiences even when not supported by the patient's abstract representations), suggesting that the cyclical process could usefully be continued by collecting and analysing further data.

CASE STUDIES

The case study (CS) is one of the most misunderstood research approaches in the social and behavioural sciences. Researchers do not even agree if the case study is a method, methodology, paradigm or approach (Hammersley, Gomm & Foster, 2000; Willig, 2001), let alone concur about its properties or methods of analysis. Added to this confusion – some would say chaos – are the multiple definitions of what constitutes a case study. In the practice of clinical and counselling psychology CS generally refers to a written narrative that describes a patient's course of treatment. Similarly, in law and business schools, the CS is presented as an example of a specific legal or corporate circumstance and utilised for educational and not research purposes. The case study, within psychological inquiry, is also confused with single-case experimental research (Aldridge, 1994), which employs an experimental or quasi-experimental design and measures observable behaviours that are manipulated by independent variables (Chapter 10; Barlow & Hersen, 1984). For the purposes of our discussion, the CS will be considered through the lens of a qualitative paradigm (Henwood & Pidgeon, 1994; Shweder, 1996), which may or may not incorporate quantitative data and statistical analysis (Patton, 2002), and will be looked at as a holistic methodology in which to approach research problems in health and clinical psychology.

The qualitative case study (QCS) makes use of data collection methods (interviews, observations, use of archival sources, visual data) and analytic methods (content analysis, pattern matching, coding and category development), which are shared with other qualitative methodologies (grounded theory, action research, ethnography) but maintains a distinct research design with different purposes and goals. In health care settings the 'case' may be considered a sole individual, a group of people experiencing the same condition or problem, a critical incident, an entire clinic or hospital, a specific intervention programme (for example, wellness for older adults) within a health care facility, or a treatment modality (for example, the use of biofeedback for stress in cardiac rehabilitation). The case is a 'specific, unique bounded system' (Stake, 2000: 436) that is clearly defined and can be examined through a variety of data sources.

The goals of the qualitative case study in psychological research in health care settings

An essential consideration when evaluating whether to use QCS methodology is the purpose of the research. Although most academic psychology research is oriented towards publishing findings that are statistically generalisable, not all research need have this as a goal. Research can serve the goals of a particular community or agency as well as have benefits for the wider health care profession. The issue of whether the QCS should be generalisable has brought forth considerable debate (Donmoyer, 1990;

Hammersley, Gomm & Foster, 2000; Guba, 1979; Schofield, 1990; Stake, 1995; Yin, 1994). Schofield writes:

> The goal is not to produce a standardized set of results that any other careful researcher in the same situation or studying the same issue would have produced. Rather it is to produce a coherent and illuminating description of and perspective on a situation that is based on and consistent with detailed study of that situation. (1990: 71)

The QCS allows the researcher the opportunity to delve deeply into a context-sensitive environment, to utilise data collection and analysis methods specific to the complexity of the situation or environment, and to produce a holistic understanding of the issue at hand (Patton, 2002). This method also allows the researcher to contextually examine issues related to *process* and *experience*, thus providing different information than pre-/post-treatment research designs.

In the last few years of research in clinical and health psychology in the United Kingdom and in North America, one finds relatively few studies that inquire about the experience of the patient, the process of treatment, or how a patient's perception of treatment may affect healing (Knight & Camic, 2003). Fewer studies explore the questions *how* or *why* some patients did not improve with treatment, or consider 'the patient' holistically within a biopsychosocial, cultural and socioe-conomic context. It is within these thornier, complex situations that the QCS can play a role.

Analytic strategies

The interpretive stance most often associated with a CS is that of social constructivism or critical theory (Denzin & Lincoln, 1998; see also Chapter 1), but it could also be used by a researcher using a post-positivist research design guided by a similar post-positivist epistemological position (Guba & Lincoln, 1998; Yin, 1994). The CS model we will describe is not limited to employing data from interviews, observations, case records and medical charts, but can also make use of data from medical and psychological tests, surveys and questionnaires.

There are two differing approaches weighing in on the issue of what constitutes a QCS and how data from these studies should be analysed. The 'naturalists' (Lincoln & Guba, 1985; Stake, 1998) contend that the QCS should be undertaken in naturalistic surroundings that are not created or manipulated by the researcher. Single rather than multiple cases are suggested as units of study and understanding the single case, *as a unit of analysis*, is considered a primary consideration. Analysis begins without a previously defined hypothesis as the researcher is urged to keep an open mind to what constitutes useful information and in essence is urged to pay attention to all raw data (Stake, 1995).

The second approach, which we are dubbing 'pragmatic' and describe in more detail below, was developed by Yin and Heald (1975) and further expanded by Yin (1994). Yin (1994) presents a well-developed discussion about the criticisms of the CS method and goes on to challenge his readers to design more rigorous and relevant case studies by offering a systematic outline of CS research strategy. Clinical and health psychology researchers are in a unique position to incorporate a range of data into CS research, making this method precise, thorough and relevant to contemporary issues in the field.

According to Yin, there are five steps in carrying out a QCS. A QCS must begin with well-defined research questions. For the intentions of a QCS, questions concerning 'how' and 'why' are most appropriate to the CS strategy. The questions that the researcher develops begin the analytic work, as they act to define the area of study, and also operate as a beginning guide that will determine what data sources the researcher will attend to throughout the study. For example, the question 'how does group psychotherapy improve the lives of women with breast cancer?' directs us towards the multifaceted lives of women who have breast cancer, and not only towards the variables of symptom reduction or improvement in mood. The question is a broad one and indicates that the researcher wants to know how participating in group psychotherapy improves the day-to-day life of women who have breast cancer. This question is also based upon the premise that the patient-subject possesses *a priori* knowledge that the researcher does not have, that is, context-dependent knowledge about a situation or problem – in this case group psychotherapy and breast cancer. The context in this situation would be defined as a specific group of clients undertaking psychotherapy with a particular therapist. The therapist and group of patients become a bounded case that is context sensitive and holistic (Patton, 2002: 447), and while not statistically generalisable to all other women with breast cancer undergoing group psychotherapy, nonetheless contains information that can be considered important, clinically valuable, useful and applicable to other women and psychotherapists in a similar context.

The second step in QCS research, and also a preliminary step in analysis, is the development of what Yin (1994) terms 'propositions'. Propositions serve a similar function to experimental hypotheses, but are more tentative and flexible, since in a QCS propositions may be revised during data analysis, whereas in experimental hypothesis testing the outcome of the analysis is simply that the hypothesis is either accepted or rejected. Propositions, by reflecting on important theoretical issues, help define key areas requiring attention in the study (Yin, 1994). This also helps the researcher identify relevant data and ignore other data which, while possibly interesting, may not be directly related to the work at hand. This is of particular relevance to the QCS, which may accumulate voluminous amounts of data during the course of any particular investigation. Yin also proposes that in order to improve the reliability and validity of a QCS the use of theory in helping to develop propositions is critical. A proposition, based on an existing theory, helps provide direction to the research while also supplying a benchmark from which to analyse information obtained from a case (internal validity) and from which to appraise the usefulness of the case findings to other settings (external validity).

In continuing with the example of women with breast cancer who are participating in group psychotherapy, three sample propositions and their supporting theories follow:

Proposition A: women participating in group psychotherapy receive benefits from both group participants and the therapist.
Supporting theory for proposition A: social support improves psychosocial functioning, lessens feeling of isolation and is a buffer against depression in people undergoing treatment for cancer.

Proposition B: group psychotherapy alters women's perception of self, including self-efficacy, self-concept, body image and self-statements.
Supporting theory for proposition B: for this proposition several theories are drawn from, including: an increase in self-efficacy improves emotional state; changes in self-concept and body image improve through continual and sustained emotional support; direct discussion of body image concerns, resulting from a diagnosis of breast cancer, improves body image through an increase in knowledge and understanding.

Proposition C: women engaged in this type of therapy increase their involvement with family, home life, employment, school and other activities and actions.
Supporting theory for proposition C: therapy provides a container for the worries and anxieties resulting from diagnosis and treatment of breast cancer through catharsis and empathy, which allows patients to more fully participate in life's activities.

The third step in a QCS is deciding upon the unit(s) of analysis. This decision is based upon both the initial research question(s) as well as the resulting proposition(s). Continuing with our example, the individual patient-participant would become our basic unit of analysis. Each member of the group would therefore be considered as an individual case. All of the preceding questions and propositions would be applied to each individual case and would guide the researcher in choosing the most appropriate data collection tools. Only when every basic unit of analysis (in this example, each group psychotherapy participant) is fully investigated should the researcher then proceed to the next unit of analysis, which in this instance could either be the psychotherapist-as-a-unit or the group-as-a-unit. The initial question, 'how does group psychotherapy improve the lives of women with breast cancer?' directs the researcher to consider the psychotherapist as the next unit of analysis. The reasoning behind this decision is quite straightforward: group psychotherapy cannot exist without a therapist; a therapist is a vital part of the group; a therapist possesses much information about the group from a different perspective than the group participants.

The fourth step in QCS research involves choosing the research tools and data sources which will yield most useful information about those units.

Based upon the research question and propositions in this study, an in-depth semi-structured interview (Kvale, 1996; Rubin & Rubin, 1995) with each group participant would be necessary. Additional sources of data might also include interviews with medical staff (physician and/or nurse practitioner), interviews with family members and a close friend, employer (often ethically difficult due to issues of confidentiality and privacy), and the group psychotherapist. Other data sources include things the patient may have produced during the course of therapy (for example, a personal journal which might include poetry, stories, drawings), photographs, observation of two or more group therapy sessions (or videotapes of these sessions), the therapist's clinical notes and any psychometric test summaries (for example, Beck Depression Inventory, State-Trait Anxiety Inventory, one of many quality of life inventories, etc.).

The sources of data listed above include interviews, written documents, physical artifacts, direct observation, participant observation and psychometric instruments. The fifth step involves both mechanical and intellectual operations on the part of the researcher that make use of all these data sources in relation to the study's guiding propositions (Patton, 2002). These three propositions were developed from the study's initial guiding question ('how does group psychotherapy improve the lives of women with breast cancer?') and based on information from existing literature. A **coding** scheme, based in part upon the propositions and the existing research literature, is now developed. We say 'in part' because information may be discovered during the initial coding procedure that is not related to a proposition but that the researcher decides is valuable. A good QCS will always allow some flexibility; the result of a QCS using this method of inquiry may be to modify a proposition, to propose a new proposition, or to develop a new theory about the case under investigation, in addition to addressing causal relations (Yin, 1994).

Deciding what to code is one of the most challenging tasks any qualitative researcher encounters. Propositions provide theoretical and practical direction concerning what to examine. For example, in proposition A (women participating in group psychotherapy receive benefits from both group participants and the therapist), the researcher has *a priori* identified two possible sources of benefit that a woman may find from this type of therapy. In developing codes and subsequent categories, the proposition is used as a guide to direct the attention of the researcher to these two potential sources of benefit.

Analysis continues with each proposition guiding the development of codes and subsequent category development. Depending on the purposes of the study, the researcher has three primary options for further analysis: explanation building, pattern-matching or time-series analysis (Yin, 1994). The goal of explanation building is to analyse the data by constructing an explanation about the case (Yin, 1982). Findings from an initial case are compared against a proposition. The proposition is revised until it matches the case. The case is then compared with the revised proposition. The proposition is further revised if needed. This second revision of the proposition is then compared to all remaining cases. The process, which can be a lengthy one, is repeated as needed to come up with a holistic and final explanation (revised proposition) that is based upon the data obtained in this CS. This allows the researcher to entertain 'other plausible or rival explanations' (Yin, 1994: 111) and to show how they are not supported by the data.

Pattern-matching is a type of QCS analysis derived from quasi-experimental design (Cook & Campbell, 1979). It compares an empirically based pattern with a predicted one, thus helping to increase internal validity and lend support to using a QCS in determining causal relations (Yin, 1994). This design requires the researcher to state predicted patterns for each case prior to analysis but, unlike experimental design, makes room for alternative patterns that may be discovered during the analysis. In our example of group psychotherapy, a stated pattern based on proposition B (group psychotherapy alters women's perception of self, including self-efficacy, self-concept, body image and self-statements) might be: increases in self-efficacy and self-concept will be noted in group participants by the end of therapy. Through examining multiple sources of data, such as interviews with the group participants, therapist and physician, examination of case records and observation of group sessions, empirical evidence is collected that supports the previously stated pattern, requires it to be modified in some way or rejects it as lacking support. If the pattern is rejected, however, it is necessary for the researcher to seek an explanation for what he/she has observed in the data. This may require developing an alternative proposition, seeking new coding strategies or, in extreme cases, revisiting the initial research question(s).

The third analytic strategy, time-series analysis, is not dissimilar to the time-series analysis design of quasi-experimental research (Cook & Campbell, 1979), and was first employed as a qualitative method by Louise Kidder (1981) in her analysis of participant observer studies. The time-series analytic strategy is appropriate for those studies where the time sequencing of events is important. A theoretically important proposition is specified before data collection begins, and must specify three circumstances: 1) points in time where events are anticipated to occur, 2) a rival or competing trend that is also supported by the literature and, 3) any trend that is based on artifact or other presently non-accountable factors (Yin, 1994: 114). For example, proposition C (women engaged in this type of therapy increase their involvement with family, home life, employment, school and other activities and actions), in order to be used in a time-series analysis, would need to be modified to specify points in time where increases in family involvement, home life, employment, etc. are anticipated. These points in time are not selected arbitrarily but are related to existing research findings in group psychotherapy for women with cancer. A subsequent proposition (C-2) is necessary to specify a possible rival trend or explanation, and a third proposition (C-3) to account for effects from artifacts, historical factors or other threats to internal validity.

This discussion of CS research has introduced the topic as a viable approach, but one in need of additional development. Just as grounded theory has evolved over the past decades, methods of CS should continue to develop and diverge as each investigator finds new ways of analysing different experiences and problems.

Box 5.2   *Key features of pragmatic qualitative case study.*

- The researcher develops a broad research question, and a set of related propositions derived from theory (which may include propositions about change over time).
- The question and propositions guide selection of relevant units of analysis (such as individual participants, groups or settings) and research tools and sources of data (such as interviews, observations, psychometric measures, physical data and written documents).
- A coding scheme is developed which allows the researcher to relate these data to the research question and propositions. Analysis may seek to modify the initial propositions to match the data or (if the existing propositions are not supported) to develop new propositions.

SUMMARY

This chapter has briefly introduced phenomenological methods and then illustrated how both grounded theory and case studies can be used to build and test theory. Both approaches retain a holistic appreciation of the topic which encourages analysis of the influence of contextual factors and unfolding processes. Both approaches are also able to convey the unique flavour of the particular situations studied – the rich, personal perspectives which qualitative research is best able to capture (see Chapter 1). But while every situation is unique, the theoretical principles abstracted by these methods are intended to have a wider relevance that can be appreciated by people engaged with similar situations. The concrete, contextualised accounts upon which interpretations are grounded in these types of analyses, and by which they are illustrated, can provide a means of vividly communicating these insights to others.

RECOMMENDED READING

Grounded theory

Chamberlain, K. (1999). Using grounded theory in health research: practices, premises and potential. In M. Murray & K. Chamberlain (eds) *Qualitative health psychology: theories and methods*. London: Sage, pp. 183–201.

Strauss, A. & Corbin, J. (1990). *Basics of qualitative research: grounded theory procedures and techniques*. Newbury Park, CA: Sage.

Case study

Yin, R.K. (1994). *Case study research: design and methods* (2nd edn). London & Thousand Oaks, CA: Sage.

REVISION QUESTIONS

1 What are the characteristics of phenomenological analysis?
2 What is 'theoretical sampling', and why is it used in qualitative research?
3 Explain the difference between open coding and axial coding in grounded theory analysis.
4 How does memo-writing contribute to a grounded theory analysis?
5 Describe the steps involved in a 'pragmatic' case study.

6 QUALITATIVE ANALYSIS OF TALK AND TEXT: DISCOURSE AND NARRATIVE ANALYSIS

Lucy Yardley and Michael Murray

AIMS OF THIS CHAPTER

(i) To describe how discourse analysis can be used to examine the ways in which social actions are accomplished through talk.

(ii) To describe the use of discourse analysis to examine the social context and functions of common linguistic terms and practices.

(iii) To consider how the narrative form is used to structure experience, and how this can be analysed.

INTRODUCTION

In traditional realist research it is generally assumed, firstly, that language takes its meaning from its correspondence with objective reality, and secondly, that what people say is a more or less accurate reflection of what they think. In contrast, constructivist research takes a radically different perspective on language and talk (Potter, 1996). Drawing on theory developed by philosophers such as Wittgenstein, Foucault and Derrida, constructivist researchers regard language as actively *constructing* meaning through social interaction, rather than deriving meaning from reference to reality (Yardley, 1997). Consequently, they view talk not as a simple exchange of information or thoughts, but as a complex socio-cultural process of negotiating the meaning of what is spoken about. For example, a realist interpretation of the statement 'I have back pain' would be that it conveys to the listener more or less accurate information about the internal psychophysiological state of the speaker. However, a constructivist would examine the statement in the context of the social interaction in which it was made, to discover its social meanings and functions. Viewed from this perspective, the statement might prove to be serving the purpose of a justification to a physiotherapist for failing to carry out prescribed exercises, an excuse to an employer for refusing to undertake physical tasks, or a plea for sympathy from family members.

Constructivism has given rise to a potentially bewildering diversity of new approaches to researching the socio-cultural dimension of human experience, as featured in talk and text. Typically (but not invariably) referred to as forms of **discourse analysis**, these include analysis of the *process* of how meaning is created in everyday interaction, and analysis of the socio-cultural context and effects of the *product* or elements of talk, that is, the concepts and categories used (Taylor, 2001). In addition, narrative analysis has focused on how people use the story form to make sense of their lives to themselves and others (Murray, 2003). It is beyond the scope of this book to describe all of the varieties of these methods in detail, but this chapter provides an introductory overview of each of these approaches.

ANALYSES OF THE PROCESS OF TALK

Analyses of discourse as a form of social interaction examine how people use language to accomplish social acts, such as constructing meanings, roles and identities (van Dijk, 1997). These ends are achieved not only through the content of what is said – what is selected, implied or omitted – but also through the structure and patterning of talk. For example, early discourse analytic work by Mishler (1994) showed that in interactions between doctors and patients the dominance of 'the voice of medicine' was maintained by a pattern of talk in which the doctor asked a series of closed questions to which the patient must make focused replies, and interrupted or ignored any talk which strayed from the biomedical agenda.

Potter and Wetherell (1987) were the first to outline a method of applying discourse analysis in psychology, which has been further developed as a particular approach known as 'discursive psychology' (Potter, 2003). Drawing on conversation analysis, Potter recommends that researchers should tape-record naturally occurring dialogue, in order to gain insight into how social actions are performed in real-life contexts. Coding in discursive psychology is simply a matter of identifying segments of talk that contain and illustrate the discursive actions of interest. For example, one might identify all talk segments in doctor–patient interactions in which the patient tries to introduce non-biomedical talk into the interaction, in order to determine how this action is successfully resisted by the doctor (the usual pattern of doctor–patient interaction) or, exceptionally, is successfully accomplished by the patient. Note that transcription is *extremely* time-consuming in discourse analysis (the transcription process taking up to 20 times as long as the duration of the talk transcribed), as it is necessary to convey as much detail of speech as possible, including the length of tiny pauses, the stresses laid on words, and overlap between different speakers (for basic transcription conventions, see Wood & Kroger, 2000; for a detailed discussion, see ten Have, 1999). Analysis involves trying to establish what are the usual patterns of discourse (or **discursive strategies**) whereby social actions are successfully accomplished; this can often best be clarified by comparison with 'deviant cases' in which the usual pattern is disrupted, leading to conversational awkwardness. A multitude of commonly used discursive strategies have already been identified (see Wood & Kroger, 2000), and it is necessary for the researcher to become familiar with these through immersion in the relevant literature in order to carry out a well-informed analysis that does not simply describe already known discursive patterns.

The 'discursive psychology' approach to discourse analysis outlined above sets out very clearly defined methodological criteria; for example, that the interactions studied should be naturally occurring, and analysis should be based solely on what is said and done in the interaction. However, there are a wide variety of different discourse analytic approaches, and proponents of some of these alternative approaches claim that analysis of the process of talk can be carried out very effectively using interviews and focus groups as sources of data (see Chapter 3, and Bevan & Bevan, 1999). Many analysts argue that it is important to take into account the context of the interaction beyond the transcription, such as the social relationship between the participants, their lives and roles, and the history and culture in which the excerpt of dialogue is embedded (Edley, 2000; Wetherell, 1998). In this way, researchers can combine analysis of the process of how actions are accomplished with an understanding of the influence on this process of the socio-cultural products and elements of discourse (see next section). An excellent example is provided by Wilkinson and Kitzinger (2000), who analysed interactions between women with cancer in focus groups, and showed that talk about 'thinking positive' does not necessarily constitute evidence for a particular coping style, but rather functions as a discursive device whereby the speaker can maintain a normative, acceptable 'positive' social identity and conversational tone when disclosing extremely distressing events.

ANALYSES OF THE PRODUCT AND ELEMENTS OF TALK

Some forms of discourse analysis focus primarily on the influence on meaning of wider social and linguistic structures and practices. This type of discourse analysis has its origins in the post-structuralist philosophy of Foucault and Derrida, and neo-Marxist critical theory; in clinical and health psychology it is therefore often linked to critical approaches (for example, Crossley, 2000; Stainton-Rogers, 1996; Stoppard, 1998; Willig, 1999; Yardley, 1997). Derrida argued that meaning in language is not the result of linking words with pre-existing categories in the world, but is actively constructed through the creation of value-laden dichotomous distinctions, such as well/normal/good versus ill/abnormal/bad. By **deconstructing** linguistic terms it is possible to understand how they engender certain ways of viewing things and suppress others (Feldman, 1995). Foucault conducted historical analyses of how social practices, institutions, concepts and technologies 'construct' and 'regulate' the categories and meanings that we take for granted. For example, he showed that the contemporary concept and role of the patient in western medicine was created by a radical change in thinking, which entailed abandoning the pre-scientific concept of each person as a unique, sacred holistic entity in order to analyse them as comparable physiological 'cases' of a disease; moreover, this change in thinking was only possible because of changes in social practices such as permission for dissection of bodies, and the establishment of clinics in which many people with similar symptoms were treated (Foucault, 1989).

Although there are few methodological restrictions associated with this kind of analysis, in order to develop a sophisticated understanding of the socio-cultural origins and implications of discourses it is necessary to be familiar with relevant socio-cultural theory and research (which is typically cross-disciplinary, and may be located in the sociological, anthropological, feminist or other literature). Suitable sources of data can include conversations recorded in everyday settings, interviews and focus groups, observation (for an example, see Chapter 7), written texts (such as health promotion messages, medical records or textbooks), and even questionnaires. For example, Moulding and Hepworth (2001) interviewed health professionals responsible for managing a programme to reduce body image dissatisfaction and unhealthy eating behaviour, in order to identify the discursive themes that recurred in the talk of those involved in this intervention. They then analysed how the dissociation of individual and social causes of body image dissatisfaction in the dominant discourses of the health promotion workers might link with their reliance on professional rather than community interventions, since individual change is constructed as independent of social change. Brown (1999) analysed a sample of published self-help texts to identify some of the rhetorical devices used to construct stress as ultimately a form of subjective malfunction that should be corrected by the individual. Ville, Ravaud, Diard and Paicheler (1994) used responses to a questionnaire as the springboard for their social constructionist analysis of the way in which terms such as 'adjustment' and 'coping' have historically had the effect of oppressing people with disabilities, assigning to them the responsibility to conform to the requirements and constraints of able-bodied society. Some analyses simply draw on concepts or terminology in the public domain, rather than a discrete body of empirical data. For instance, Lupton (1993) has shown how the discourse of 'health risk' can be used as a justification for exerting control over the private behaviour of individuals, and a means of diverting blame for poor health from structural factors which are the responsibility of society (for example, relative poverty) to factors which are deemed the responsibility of individuals (for example, risky behaviour).

An illustration of an analysis of the product and elements of talk

This example is based on a study of accounts of coping with dizziness generated in interviews with 37 sufferers (Yardley & Beech, 1998). It is beyond the scope of this example to summarise the full analysis, and so the focus below is on the part of the analysis that considered the socio-cultural meaning and function of talk about 'coping'.

The analysis was undertaken from a perspective which views coping behaviour as a mode of interaction between the individual and society, rather than as simply a matter of individual self-regulation. The assumption was that the socio-cultural, and indeed material, context of such talk was highly relevant, since the roles and meanings constructed in talk are grounded in, and impact upon, the activities and relationships of daily life (Yardley, 1997). The analysis sought to 'deconstruct' talk about coping by revealing the ideological constraints on what can and cannot be said, and the dichotomies that connect dominant discourses to those that are hidden or stifled. This kind of analysis can be undertaken without reference to any specific text, by simply considering the contemporary socio-cultural functions of the concept of 'coping' (see Pollock, 1993). However, in this study we chose to ground the analysis more specifically in the talk of people with chronic dizziness, by determining the dominant discourses on which these participants were drawing and then exploring their functions and implications.

For this study we chose to employ content analysis to identify the most common or dominant elements of talk. Discourse analysts would usually avoid employing research methods, such as content analysis, which might be taken to imply that the coding categories constructed for the purpose of analysis correspond to objective, unchanging, context-free psychological phenomena. Nevertheless, we felt that this method would serve a useful rhetorical purpose in our study, since we wished the analysis to be meaningful and persuasive to quantitative researchers, who would normally expect some kind of 'evidence' to warrant claims that particular elements of discourse are 'typical'. From the content analysis, we drew up tables of the most common elements of the talk, and constructed a chart to show which interviewees had made statements classified in each coding category, in order to reveal the pattern of statements of each interviewee. The implications and functions of the dominant discourses were then analysed by searching the relevant text segments for characteristic phrases or contexts, by examining the inconsistencies, omissions and moments of conversational awkwardness within accounts, by comparing the transcripts of prototypical accounts with those which departed from the dominant pattern of discourse, and by reference to the relevant literature. Since a disadvantage of content analysis is that it strips away the precise linguistic content and context of the coded elements of talk, brief excerpts from the transcripts were also included in the report to demonstrate how these elements functioned in the interview dialogue.

The content analysis identified several elements of talk about coping behaviour that were present in the accounts of at least two-thirds of interviewees. These included talk about coping by consulting a doctor, coping by restricting activity so as to minimise the provocation or effects of dizziness, the impossibility of coping with or controlling the dizziness, and assertions that the sufferer was able to cope and carry on as normal. The normative constraints on how people with chronic illness must present themselves can be easily identified by considering the opposing meanings which these four dominant discourses suppress: that the interviewee does not consult a doctor, can act as normal, is actually able to control their illness, but makes no effort to cope – in other words, fits the social definition of a malingerer rather than a patient.

The first two themes raise some interesting questions about whether adopting the traditional passive role of the handicapped patient can or should be classified as a coping strategy. Clearly depending on medicine is a way of actively solving some of the social and physical problems posed by illness, since it can provide a reassuring explanation for the illness, a medical regimen for managing the illness, and a social justification for failing to behave normally. However, in the case of chronic illness it can result in an extremely disempowered and stigmatised position as a chronic invalid, unable to take up an active and competent role in society or in the management of the illness. This tension is also evident in the contradictions between the latter two themes (being unable to cope vs carrying on as normal), which point to a dilemma between the need of interviewees to warrant their claim to the social role of a patient by describing themselves as a helpless victim of illness, while simultaneously demonstrating their social worth by depicting themselves as successfully making the commendable effort to overcome their disability. The co-occurrence of these apparently inconsistent elements of talk can be seen in the following excerpt. The interviewee first describes her partial disability in such a way as to elicit sympathy for her predicament as a sufferer. However, when confronted with a request to explicitly state in what ways she is disabled, she evades admitting to any specific incapacity and instead asserts an identity as a successful coper, marking the awkwardness of negotiating the tension between these apparently inconsistent discourses and positions with laughter:

> MA: It's very frustrating you know, 'cause, er, I like to do things, get up and get out and all that, and you're restricted really.
> SB: Is there anything in particular you have stopped doing because of this?
> MA: Not really, no . . . you got to be a bit more careful, got to watch it. [Laughs] You got to live with it, you just got to get on with it sort of thing. But it's a thing I could do without. [Laughs]

We linked this dilemma to a modern western cultural context in which the threat to the dominance of the rational mind posed by a 'misbehaving' body should ideally be contained by the rational power of medicine. Medicine should firstly supply an explanation for illness-related deviance that does not disturb the social order, and secondly provide a reassuring demonstration of scientific control over the body's functioning, by curing the illness. Unfortunately, when this proves impossible (as in the case of dizziness) responsibility falls on the sufferers to try to master their deviant bodies by deploying 'mind over matter' (Pollock, 1993) – or at least to depict themselves as successfully doing so. Moreover, when diagnosis and treatment are problematic, there is a tendency for the authority of medicine to be upheld by querying the authenticity of the patient's claim to a physical problem (Fabrega, 1990). Those with ill-defined, chronic complaints are therefore constantly obliged to justify themselves in anticipation of the unspoken but implicit question which lurks beneath discussions with doctors, family, colleagues and research interviewers: are they 'real' victims or poor copers? This harsh dichotomy provides the context within which the tensions and contradictions in accounts of coping with dizziness can be understood, while the passive behaviour of sufferers is consistent with modern western discourses and practices that construe illness as a purely medical problem, and offer patients no clear role in either defining or controlling it.

Deconstructing participants' talk in this way poses a difficult ethical issue: is it ethical to offer interpretations of the talk of participants which they might resist, since such deconstruction has the potential to reveal and therefore undermine the social objectives of the talk? For example, is it ethical to depict accounts of disability as justifications for adopting the patient role, rather than as simple descriptions of a physical reality? Since very few participants would be able to offer informed feedback on such an esoteric analysis, before commencing the study we took as our guiding principle that our interpretation must remain sympathetic to the position of our participants. Happily, we later received feedback that we had achieved this objective from a constructivist researcher with dizziness at a conference where we presented this analysis.

NARRATIVE ANALYSIS

Narrative research begins with the premise that we organise the accounts we exchange about our life experiences in the form of **narratives**, in other words we tell stories about our lives. From this seemingly simple premise a number of philosophers and social scientists have developed a complex theory of the self and of social interaction. The philosopher Paul Ricoeur (1984) has argued that since we live in a temporal world it is necessary to represent it in a narrative form in order to make sense of it to ourselves and to others. If we did not, the world would seem like a constantly changing meaningless ferment over which we could not exercise any control. Imposing a narrative structure on this ferment gives it a sense of order and a meaning. From the narrative perspective, the layperson does not speak or indeed think in abstract terms but more in narrative form. Jerome Bruner (1990) has distinguished between paradigmatic and narrative thought. He has argued that while the scientist prefers the former, the latter is the everyday thought of the layperson. Yet scientists are also laypersons and so bring narrative ideas into their scientific thinking. In contemporary society there is sustained movement between narrative and scientific domains.

It can also be argued not only that we represent the world in narrative form but also that we live through the narratives that we create and those that surround us (Maines, 1993). According to this argument extensive social narratives shape the world into which we are born and our very own life histories. We are born into societies, communities and families each of which has particular stories about our ancestors. From these stories we develop a particular narrative sense of our history and of whom we are. It is through these narratives that we locate ourselves in the cosmos and orient ourselves for future actions.

Western society promotes the idea that our lives have a sense of orderliness (see Becker, 1997). Events do not happen by chance but rather because someone or some group of people exerted some force for change. Thus when we observe a change we attempt to identify the narrative structure behind that event. For example, when someone asks us to explain what seems to be an inconsistent or deviant act we attempt to locate it within some narrative structure. Sometimes it is difficult to provide a sense of order. Instead the participant is left with a sense of unease and perhaps of frustration. It is through narrative that we can assert a sense of continuity and coherence in our own lives. When our ability to make these connections is frustrated then we feel uncomfortable. Some clinical practitioners have used narrative theory as a framework for developing a particularly dynamic form of psychotherapy that combines reassessing the past story of our lives with deliberation on the shape of potential future stories (White & Epston, 1990). The aim of this narrative therapy is to provide a new sense of coherence to a life that previously was perceived as disordered.

On a societal level, a coherent narrative gives a sense of meaning and orderliness to changes in society. However, major threats to a society can sometimes be difficult to integrate into a society's sense of narrative coherence. For example, one of the challenges faced by historians of the horrors of the Holocaust is that it occurred in a very sophisticated and modern society where irrational racial prejudices were supposed to have been overcome. Instead there occurred one of the major horrors of the modern era. This search for narrative coherence clashes with the need to bear continued testimony to the victims. Langer (1991) has argued that if society finds a comforting narrative coherence for this tragedy, the tendency would be to allow the memory to drift out of our consciousness. Conversely this inability to provide narrative coherence preserves the memory of the horror.

Adopting the narrative approach to research leads us to look for the narrative structure underlying everyday accounts. Frequently qualitative researchers have ignored this narrative structure both in the collection and in the analysis of interviews, which have instead been designed to elicit and extract themes common to multiple interviewees (see Mishler, 1986). From the outset the narrative researcher is keen to collect narrative accounts from the study participants and will facilitate this in the interview by encouraging extended accounts and by encouraging the participant to reflect upon the temporal sequence of events. Often in the interview the participant will provide a series of brief narrative accounts to illustrate what is meant. For example, they will say things like 'I'll give you an example of what I mean'. Further, when they are given the opportunity participants will often provide extended narrative accounts of particular experiences they have had. In a life history interview the deliberate aim is to encourage the participants to reflect on their lives or a particular component of their lives, for example, their school life. The researcher can help contextualise these narrative accounts by collecting information from other sources about particular events.

Although narrative accounts are often collected from individual participants we can also explore shared social narratives through group interviews or focus groups (see Chapter 3). In these the aim is to encourage the participants to reflect upon common experiences, for example, growing up in a particular neighbourhood. These group interviews can help clarify the extent of commonality and conflict in a community's narratives. They also identify the extent to which particular individuals identify themselves as part of that community.

In the data analysis the narrative researcher deliberately looks for the underlying **narrative structure** in accounts obtained. As mentioned, there may be a series of mini-narratives that convey the participant's interpretation of certain experiences. Each of these narratives can be considered independently with reference to the particular phenomena under investigation. They can also be considered together to unravel the participant's broader approach to life. Thus the participant might recount a series of incidents that convey a sense of frustration or anger. The researcher attempts to reveal not only the content of the narrative accounts but also their structure and their trajectory.

In analysing the narrative accounts the researcher can begin by preparing a summary of the account that includes some detail of both narrative structure and **narrative content** – what the narrator is talking about (for example, a car accident) and how the account is structured (for example, what was going on before the accident occurred? what exactly happened during the accident? and what happened afterwards?). The researcher can detail the overall emotional tone of the narrative (for example, anger, sadness) and its connection with the person's identity (for example, sense of responsibility). The researcher can also consider how the narrative is structured within the particular interview setting, how the narrative is shaped to convey a particular argument, for example, the extent to which the participant accepts responsibility for the car accident.

In developing a more sophisticated narrative analysis the researcher connects the narrative account and summary with a broader interpretive framework. There is no set form of narrative analysis, rather the form depends upon the researcher. For example, the researcher might be particularly interested in the narrative identity of the participant and how this changes depending upon the interview setting. Alternatively, the researcher might be interested in the unconscious processes underlying the narrative (for example, fear and anxiety) that connect the immediate narrative account with previous experiences of the narrator (see Hollway & Jefferson, 2000). Thus the researcher must enter into a form of dialogue with the narrative.

An excellent example of narrative analysis is provided by the study of agoraphobia carried out by Capps and Ochs, who were interested in 'how agoraphobia is realized through the activity of storytelling' (1995: 407). They carried out an in-depth ethnographic study including 26 months of participant observation of family life, with video- and audio-recording, and in-depth interviews. For this analysis they selected 3 interviews and 3 recorded dinner-table conversations and identified all narratives in which the person with agoraphobia ('Meg') was the principal storyteller and was talking about panic. Capps and Ochs then analysed the 14 narratives that met these criteria in two ways. Firstly, they examined the organisation of the narrative, including the sequencing, setting, problematic event, psychological response, attempts to resolve the problematic event, and the consequences. Secondly, they focused on the lexical and grammatical features that indexed the onset, experience and outcome of panic episodes. Their analysis showed that panic episodes were constructed as a temporal sequence in which a problematic event precedes and triggers a panic response of feeling overwhelmed, helpless and trapped, leading to a series of attempts to escape that were themselves typically described as problematic and therefore feeding into a spiral of further panic. A variety of grammatical strategies were used to convey the helplessness of the teller. The teller was cast in non-agentic semantic roles as the object of events: for example, 'the anxiety rea::ly got to me' or 'all of this came <u>down</u> on me', rather than the agentic form 'I was anxious'. Intensifiers were used to amplify the sense of vulnerability, such as increased volume and duration of words for emphasis: 'It was <u>SO::</u> awful'. Whenever positive agentic activity was described it was weakened by deintensifiers such as 'just' and 'sort of': 'just thinking if I (.3) do <u>any</u>thing to just sort of burn off some of this nervous energy'.

The authors suggest that these **narrative strategies** function to present the teller's explanation or theory of panic, which is that it is a state that renders them powerless. However, they point out that paradoxically the state of panic actually seems to empower the teller to exert considerable control over the activities of themselves and others, while allowing the teller to continue to portray themselves as powerless. Capps and Ochs therefore offer a radical interpretation of agoraphobia as a communicative disorder whereby the sufferer is unable to explicitly communicate reservations about undertaking an activity they wish to avoid, and to openly negotiate a solution to the conflict between their wishes and those of others. They are only able to assert their needs belatedly and obliquely through the extreme emotional state of panic.

Box 6.1   *Key features of constructivist approaches to analysis*

- Analysis of how social actions are accomplished in talk involves: tape-recording naturalistic dialogue; transcribing this in minute detail; identifying text segments in which the action(s) of interest are accomplished; identifying the discursive strategies by which the action(s) are accomplished (referring to the body of literature describing previously identified discursive strategies); optionally, drawing a comparison with text segments in which the same social action(s) are not successfully accomplished.
- Examination of the socio-political context and functions of common socio-linguistic practices involves applying socio-cultural theory to the analysis of common discourses (for example, commonly used categories, phrases or concepts, published texts, or discourse generated in interviews or conversation) to show how discursive elements and practices construct value-laden meanings that serve socio-political functions.
- Narrative analysis involves eliciting extended narrative accounts of events, examining the content, structure and trajectory of these narratives, and interpreting these features of the narrative in relation to a broader theoretical framework.

SUMMARY

This chapter has provided an introduction to some constructivist approaches to analysing talk and text, outlining their purpose, and briefly describing a variety of different types of analysis, including analysis of the process and elements of talk, and narrative analysis. An illustration of how discourse can be analysed was given, and in conclusion we consider below how constructivist research can relate to more traditional approaches.

Undertaking discourse and narrative analysis requires adoption of a non-realist approach to research, and specialist knowledge – for example, of critical theory or of discursive strategies. For these reasons, these methodological tools are less easily embraced and combined with a more traditional programme of research than some other qualitative methods. However, the appreciation fostered by constructivist approaches of the way in which social and linguistic practices shape and constrain our understanding of such basic notions as 'health' and 'illness', 'normality' and 'disorder', has far-reaching implications for *all* forms of clinical and health psychology research. Such approaches provide thought-provoking challenges to the conventional view and usage of some of the most basic concepts and categories employed in the theories and questionnaires of mainstream health psychology, such as old age (for example, Conway & Hockey, 1998), risk (Lupton, 1993) or coping (Ville et al., 1994; Yardley & Beech, 1998). Perhaps more importantly, they also compel us to examine closely fundamental questions concerning the nature of meaning, knowledge and reality, and the role of the researcher (Wetherell, Taylor & Yates, 2001; see also Chapter 7).

RECOMMENDED READING

Murray, M. (2003). Narrative psychology and narrative research. In P. Camic, J.E. Rhodes & L. Yardley (eds) *Qualitative research in psychology: expanding perspectives in methodology and design*. Washington DC: American Psychological Association.

Wetherell, M., Taylor, S. & Yates, S. (eds) (2001). *Discourse theory and practice: a reader*. London: Sage.

Wood, L.A. & Kroger, R.O. (2000). *Doing discourse analysis*. London: Sage.

REVISION QUESTIONS

1　What are the aims and methods of discursive psychology?
2　What is meant by 'deconstruction' of linguistic terms?
3　Why is narrative structure important?
4　What is the value of discourse analysis to clinical and health psychology?

7 OBSERVATION AND ACTION RESEARCH

Claire Ballinger, Lucy Yardley and Sheila Payne

AIMS OF THIS CHAPTER

(i) To briefly describe the method of structured observation.
(ii) To outline and discuss different approaches to participant observation.
(iii) To consider varieties of action research.

INTRODUCTION

Most fieldwork in health and clinical psychology is carried out using questionnaires or interviews (see Chapters 3 and 8). Both methods rely on people *reporting* their behaviour, and the reasons for it. An obvious disadvantage of using these methods exclusively is that people do not always describe their behaviour or its causes with accuracy. Firstly, they may be unaware of certain aspects of their behaviour and factors that influence it. For example, their actions may be automatic, or prompted by environmental cues of which they are unaware, they may lack insight into their personal motivations, or they may be acting on the basis of taken-for-granted cultural assumptions or customs which seem so obvious to the participants that they are not mentioned. A significant component of social interaction consists of non-verbal communication of feelings (for example, sulking, boredom, disapproval, etc.) that is easily observable, but is not readily reported by the person concerned. Secondly, they may be unable to describe their behaviour accurately, perhaps because they lack the capability or the opportunity to do so. For this reason, observation has been used in health settings for research populations considered too young, too cognitively impaired or too ill to provide a self-report. However, even those with no reporting difficulties may be unable to report their behaviour accurately. An example is people who do not adhere fully to a recom-

mended course of treatment because they are forgetful or do not understand the instructions they have been given; such people are unlikely to
report non-adherence as they are unaware that they are not following the
recommendations. Finally, they may be unwilling to accurately report their
behaviour or its causes if they feel that these are sensitive topics, or are
concerned that they might be viewed as behaving in a socially undesirable
manner (a common cause of under-reporting non-adherence to recommended treatment). Indeed, discourse analysis suggests that nothing that
people say can be viewed simply as a straightforward description of their
experiences, since all talk serves the purpose of portraying oneself and
one's actions as socially valid (see Chapter 6).

This chapter reviews methods of research that do not rely on participants' accounts, but instead directly examine their behaviour, thus overcoming the limitations of research that is based entirely on the analysis of
self-report. Three very different research methods will be outlined, which
all share an observational rather than report-based method of data collection, but which are based on entirely different assumptions about how
research can and should be carried out, and the role that the researcher
must therefore adopt.

The first section of this chapter briefly outlines the techniques of **structured observation**, which is typically employed as a traditional, realist form
of observation, in which the researcher seeks to produce a precise, objective
description of what is observed. In order to do this, the researcher adopts
the role of a completely detached and neutral observer, and engages in
quantitative assessment of the behaviour of those who are observed.

The second section of the chapter describes the key features of **participant observation**, which is an interpretive method which assumes that
the researcher's understanding of what is observed is inevitably influenced
by his or her own perspective and activities. The aim of this approach is to
try to gain an understanding of the cultural perspective of those who are
observed. Consequently, the researcher must achieve a delicate balance
between becoming sufficiently immersed in the culture and activities of
those who are observed to understand the 'insider' perspective, and yet
maintaining enough distance to be able to record and critically analyse
what is observed, and to avoid exerting undue influence on the culture and
activities in which the researcher is participating.

The final section of the chapter is devoted to **action research**, an investi-
gative approach in which the roles of the 'observer' and the 'observed' are
combined, since *all* the participants are actively involved in the research.
This approach to research does not attempt to produce a form of knowledge
which can be detached from the interests, context and activities of the
researcher-participants. Instead, the aim is to collaboratively harness the
insights of participants, employing practical joint action as a means of
testing and developing the utility of this knowledge, with the ultimate
objective of empowering all those involved to better understand their
situation and how they can achieve their objectives.

STRUCTURED OBSERVATION

In structured observation, the observer attempts to remain neutral and uninvolved, and to collect observations as objectively as possible, usually for quantitative analysis. The way in which this method is implemented depends upon a number of important decisions which the researcher must take regarding the design, setting and focus of the research, and the sampling method and data-gathering medium to be employed.

Research design and setting

Depending on the objectives of the research, structured observation can be carried out either in a naturalistic or a structured setting. For example, videotapes of naturally occurring consultations provide the most eco-logically valid means of observing the degree of patient-centredness of doctors' normal consulting style (see, for example, Mead & Bower, 2000), since this style might alter in an artificial situation. However, in order to produce observation-based ratings of disability for comparison with self-report, it is necessary to ask participants to perform a structured set of tasks which allow comparability between respondents, and between the activities performed and those described in the self-report questionnaire (see, for example, Wijlhuizen & Ooijendijk, 1999). Similarly, the design of the research can involve observation of naturally occurring differences, or experimentally induced differences. For example, insight into abnormal infant feeding behaviour can be obtained by observing naturally occurring differences in the feeding behaviour of infants with feeding disorders and healthy infants (Chatoor et al., 2001). However, when circumstances permit an intervention in behaviour, a stronger test of causation for behaviour can be provided by an experimental design, as in the demonstration that observed use of the stairs increases when large posters are put up to encourage people to use the stairs instead of the escalator (Kerr, Eves & Carroll, 2001).

Research focus and sampling

The data available for observation are potentially limitless, and so a vital first step is to decide on the focus of the observation (Robson, 1993; Simpson & Tuson, 1995). The research may focus on the discrete actions by a single person or class of people or on patterns of interactions between two or more people, and on verbal or nonverbal behaviours. The researcher may be interested in the frequency, sequence, timing or quality of these events. For example, in their study of patient-centredness in video-taped consultations, Mead and Bower (2000) **coded** the observed talk of doctors and patients according to defined categories, and then compared the frequency of occurrence of each category of talk with the observers' subjective ratings of this quality on a five-point scale. They found better agreement between different observers for the more objective categorisations of talk than for the more subjective ratings of patient-centredness, but there was little correlation between the different methods of observation, perhaps because they were measuring rather different things.

If the frequency of events is of interest, this can be sampled by observing the total frequency within continuous periods of time; these must be chosen carefully to represent all the time periods of interest (for example, day and night). Alternatively, **time sampling** can be employed, whereby the observer records what is happening at instants sampled at random or fixed time intervals. The researcher may choose to code the directly observable **manifest** dimensions of behaviour, such as how often a patient groans, or the inferred (and hence more interpretive) **functional** dimensions of their behaviour, such as how often a patient expresses distress (which could be inferred from groaning, but also from wincing, complaining, crying, etc.). Considerable pilot work may be necessary in order to develop a set of clearly specified codes that is exhaustive (there is a code for every type of event of interest likely to occur) but not too complex (as this can make the observer's coding task impossible to perform reliably).

Data-gathering medium

Observation can be carried out by lay observers, such as nurses working with the patients who are to be observed, by trained researchers, or using video-recording (Ratcliff, 2003). It is vital to consider how the method of data collection might influence the observations gathered. A familiar person, or a discreetly placed camera to which those observed have become accustomed, may influence behaviour less than the presence of a stranger. However, trained observers using formal sampling and coding procedures have been shown to be more accurate than lay observers (see, for example, McCann et al., 1997; Simmons & Reuben, 2000), while a camera is unable to actively follow the focus of research as an observer can, and so is only suitable for observing events tied to a single location.

Data analysis

The frequency of, or covariance between, coded events or qualities can be examined using any of the standard methods of statistical analysis used for other types of quantitative data (see Chapters 9 and 10). However, it is first necessary to establish the reliability of the coded data, by calculating the correspondence between the codes assigned by two independent observers. A simple guide to **inter-rater reliability** is the proportion of agreement, which can be calculated by:

$$\frac{\text{(number of agreements)}}{\text{(number of agreements)} + \text{(number of disagreements)}}$$

A preferable method of calculating inter-rater reliability is to calculate 'Cohen's Kappa', as this corrects for the number of agreements that would occur by chance (this statistic can be generated using SPSS under **cross tabulations**). The coefficient calculated in this way inevitably tends to be noticeably lower than the proportion of agreement or simple correlation between the observers; consequently, a Kappa of only 0.40 to 0.60 is regarded as fair, 0.60 to 0.75 is good, and a Kappa above 0.75 is considered excellent (Robson, 1993).

Box 7.1   *Key features of structured observation*

- The aim is for a detached observer to produce objective, quantitative descriptions of what is observed.
- The focus of observation may be of naturally occurring events, structured tasks or the effects of interventions.
- The data of interest may consist of the frequency, sequence, timing or quality of events, and can be collected by a researcher, lay observer or video camera.
- It is essential to develop a set of clearly defined rules for comprehensively coding what is observed, and to establish the reliability of the codes by calculating the correspondence between codes assigned by two independent observers.
- The data can be analysed using conventional statistical techniques.

PARTICIPANT OBSERVATION

A long-standing qualitative tradition of observation is known as 'participant observation'. The use of participant observation is closely associated with **ethnography**, described by Fetterman as 'the art and science of describing a group or culture' (1998: 1). Ethnography has principally been used within anthropology and sociology, for example, to explore and describe ethnic groups about which little had been previously known (see, for example, Evans-Pritchard, 1940), or provide vivid accounts of the rules, habits and mores which characterise social behaviour among better known groups, such as Whyte's classic study of street gangs in Chicago (Whyte, 1955).

Ethnography has traditionally required the researcher to immerse him or herself within the culture of interest, for a period of between six months and two years or more. This period is known as 'fieldwork'. During this time, the researcher attempts to record the 'rich detail and flavour of the ethnographic experience' (Fetterman, 1998: 63), using a variety of tools such as notepad and pen, camera, and audio or videotape recorder.

With a greater appreciation of the potential contribution of qualitative methods within health care research (Chamberlain et al., 1997), there has also been a concurrent growth of interest in and use of participant observation within health care settings. It is seen as particularly useful because, as Mays and Pope (1995) note, observation can help highlight differences between what people say (for example, within the context of semi-structured interviews), and what they do. Hodgson (2000) identifies two functions for participant observation in health research: the exploration of cultural representations of illness, and investigation into the various cultures of health care workers as a means of explaining health care provision. Many of the examples used subsequently fall into one or other of these categories.

Within qualitative research more generally, there has been much debate about the implications of critical or relativist schools of thought for research methods and researcher positions (see, for example, Denzin & Lincoln, 1998). As Atkinson and Hammersley (1998) have recently observed in relation to participant observational studies, the means used and claims made for observational research are open to debate and critical scrutiny as never before. However, while Hammersley and Atkinson (1995) state that there are no right or wrong ways of doing ethnography, it is important that the researcher using any type of participant observation is able to justify decisions made about setting, personal involvement and modes of recording and analysis.

Gold (1958) described four different levels of interaction between the researcher/observer and the observed; 'complete participant', 'participant-as-observer', 'observer-as-participant' and 'complete observer'. This typology has been widely cited within participant observation research, and will be used in the following sections to explore aspects of participant observation about which the researcher is required to make an informed decision. The use of Gold's typology will permit clear illustrations of the differences between adopting a realist/positivist perspective as a neutral, uninvolved 'complete observer', and a critical or relativist perspective which reflexively considers the way in which the 'participant-as-observer' influences both the participants' behaviour and the analysis.

Features of participant observation

Selection of setting   Within participant observation generally, the primary requirement for site of the research is that it is 'naturalistic' – that it is a naturally occurring setting. In early ethnographic work, and in some more recent realist observational research, the choice of site is represented as relatively straightforward in that a specific research question is being asked, and the primary requirement of the research site is that it must permit the question to be answered. Pope (1991) for example wanted to investigate waiting lists within the National Health Service (NHS), and carried out her observational research within the admissions office of a hospital. This unproblematic selection of site and location of researcher concurs with the 'observer-as-participant'/'complete observer' end of Gold's (1958) continuum.

However, while theoretical choice of research site within observational research might be relatively easy, the negotiation and arrangement of access to such sites may be more difficult. This might be particularly so in the case of observational work, as opposed to other qualitative research methods, as the constant presence of the researcher within a health care setting may be physically difficult to accommodate, be viewed as compromising confidentiality within health care practice, and be viewed as a form of surveillance by health care staff. It is often the case, therefore, that the observer/ researcher has some *a priori* connection with the observed site, which facilitates access. Holland (1999), for example, was employed as a nurse teacher for the group of student nurses with whom she carried out her ethnographic study focusing on the transition from student to qualified nurse. Holland comments on the benefits of 'shared understanding [with students] of the cultural world . . . within practice areas' (1999: 231) in enabling joint construction of meaning with research participants. She also highlights dangers in being too close to data, and used the strategy of distancing to aid analysis. This approach corresponds to Gold's 'participant-as-observer'/'complete participant' positions. The researcher's personal association with the research site has obvious implications for the involvement of the researcher within the setting, explored in the following section. Such relationships also draw attention to ethical considerations within this type of research, for example the ease with which individuals can refuse to participate in the research, which are also considered in a later section.

Involvement of the researcher in the setting   Different levels of interaction between the observer and the observed are clearly described within Gold's typology. The 'complete observer' within naturalistic forms of observation aims to view the research participants acting as naturally as possible, with the observer having minimal influence, and to produce an accurate or true representation of social action within which the environment under investigation can be apprehended. The impact of the researcher on the environment and those being observed is considered to be less obtrusive once those being observed have begun to habituate to the researcher's presence, hence the necessity for 'prolonged engagement'.

In contrast, the term 'participant observer' implies that either by design or simply because of the nature of observation, as a researcher one will inevitably be interacting with people within the research site. Even within the broad church of participant observation, there are a variety of different views about the meaning of the term 'participation'. Merrill (2000) initially worked as a volunteer, and then subsequently as a clerk, in the community Well Women clinics where she based her ethnographic study of the role of volunteers within such settings, and as a participant therefore had a clearly defined and recognised role. Tsey (1997) grew up in the community of Botoku, Ghana, in which he carried out his participant observation into the practice of traditional medicine, and claimed the status of 'participant' as a member of that community. For others, the term 'participant observer' is used to acknowledge that the introduction of the researcher to the setting will mean that they inevitably participate in some way in the social action, and that a position of 'non-participant observer' is not viable (see, for example, Ballinger & Payne, 2002).

Within realist research traditions, the potential influence of the researcher on those observed is viewed as an undesirable feature of participant observation, although difficult to control. However, from a critical perspective, the participation of the researcher can be viewed reflexively as contributing to the developing analysis of data gathered from the research site. Defined as 'critical self-scrutiny' (Mason, 1996: 5), **reflexivity** makes explicit the assumptions and perspectives which the researcher brings to the research field, and can also highlight the skills and expertise which the researcher is able to bring to the analysis. Opportunity to reflect on how one is starting to understand and make sense of what one is observing, for example, might have broader implications for how others, of whom the researcher might in a general sense be representative, do the same. Within the context of research based around interviews, for example, Ballinger described how reflexive strategies enabled her to move beyond the initial assumptions she brought to bear in interpreting older people's accounts about falls (Ballinger & Payne, 2000), which she attributed to her experience and training as a health professional.

Strategies for recording From the position of observer, one's role as a researcher is to create as full and accurate an account of the setting under question as one is able, through the completion of carefully documented **field notes**. The challenges of maintaining as full a record as possible, without drawing attention to the recording process, or making those being observed self-conscious, are widely recognised. General advice is to write up field notes as close as possible to the actual timing of events. If the writing of notes at the site of the observation would impact on behaviour or interaction, it is suggested that the researcher record as soon as possible after the observed event (Mays & Pope, 1995).

Of questionable significance within realist observation traditions, the necessity of recording personal impressions is often highlighted as important in participant observation; for example, Banister et al. encourage the recording of 'reflections, personal feelings, hunches, guesses and speculations' (1994: 23). However, although acknowledged as important, for example through encouragement to the researcher to maintain a personal research diary, the status of these additional materials in relation to raw data or field notes is sometimes unclear, as is the way in which they are expected to contribute to the interpretation. In the example provided later, a conscious decision was made to include and code personal **memos** alongside field notes, and the same coding scheme was used for both types of data.

Time spent in the field Another issue, which more critical approaches to participant observation throw into sharp focus, is the optimum amount of time that researchers should spend in any particular setting. As previously described, prolonged engagement has been advocated in realist observation methods as a means of overcoming initial disjunctures to usual patterns of behaviour, otherwise known as the 'Hawthorne effect' (Roethlisberger & Dickson, 1939). As an observer (either 'complete observer' or 'observer-as-participant'), one needs to allow time for the actors to become comfortable and familiar with the presence of the 'alien' researcher. Once this has happened, social behaviour can resume its normal routines and interactions.

However, with the rejection of the availability of a more accurate reflection of culture from a critical perspective, the case for prolonged fieldwork has become less sustainable. It is also possible that it is precisely this strangeness and novelty at the beginning of a period of study that enables the researcher to make the most acute and sharply focused observations. As time passes, the routines, habits and customs which one is observing become more familiar, thus increasing the likelihood of the researcher themself becoming encultured within the environment in which they are carrying out their observational work. Several prominent academics who employ ethnographic methods have made the case for shorter or non-continuous periods in the field (for example, Fetterman, 1998). Aside from the methodological issues, this has obvious benefits in terms of time and resources.

Analysis   As an observer within a realist tradition, one's aim is simply to provide as accurate a representation of the setting which one is observing as possible. Mays and Pope, for example, describe the process of analysis of field notes in observational research as 'variants of content analysis' (1995: 184), and illustrate how the analysis of field notes from the study by Pope (1991) was conducted in this way.

Critical researchers are more concerned with how the analysis is influenced by the epistemological assumptions underpinning the research, and the strategies of analysis employed. By way of example, Hodgson (2000) highlights the different implications of using either of two distinct underpinning methodologies within observational work: interpretivism and symbolic interactionism. A wide variety of analytical methods can be adopted. The extended example of participant observation described later in this section makes use of discourse analysis as a methodological framework for participant observation. Using a different approach, Rapport and Maggs (1997) describe interpretive phenomenology as informing their participant observation study of district nursing, and use a process known as 'cognitive reasoning' to assist their analysis within a phenomenological tradition.

Ethical considerations   The use of observational methods, particularly within health care settings, poses difficult ethical challenges. There is now general agreement that covert observation, in which those being observed are totally unaware of this, is unacceptable. However, the extent to which informed consent is gained and documented, and the degree to which actors in the research setting remain aware of being observed, remain matters of debate. In theory, informed and documented consent to participate in observational research would require the researcher to speak with each individual who potentially might feature in an account of the setting, provide written information about the purpose of the research, and obtain a signature indicating agreement. In addition to logistical difficulties raised by the constant throughput of new actors in a busy research site, for example an outpatient clinic or an accident and emergency waiting room, this raises the question about what should be done if an individual does not choose to participate. All actors have the right to veto observation of themselves, but it is clearly problematic to provide an account of a research site in which non-consenting actors are written out, and do not appear. These same people might, for example, play key roles in particular events which take place, and their absence from the account might render it incomprehensible.

A frequent solution is to gain prior approval for the study from bodies such as Local Research Ethics Committees whose remit includes the protection of potential participants in medical research from exploitation or harm. Similarly, in the USA, Happ (2000) obtained permission from her University and Hospital Review Committees for her participant observation of critically ill older adults. Another solution is to gain prior informed consent from people who might be viewed as key or representative in some way of those participating in the setting. Within health settings this is sometimes restricted to staff groups, but could also include service user representatives. Another method of approaching this difficult issue is to encourage general discussion among those who would be affected, in order that the group can reach a consensus about whether or not to participate. The provision of written information about the research study in response to questions about one's apparently aimless purpose in the process of observing can help to fulfil the ethical obligations of the researcher and the curiosity of people who are the focus of the observation.

An example of participant observation

In order to better reflect the personal choices made regarding the focus and conduct of research described subsequently, this section is written in the first person, describing the experiences of Claire Ballinger, the first author. In addition to being an academic lecturer and researcher, I am an occupational therapist, and the work described here was undertaken as part of my doctoral research project.

Health promotion and rehabilitation for older people who fall are increasingly based on evidence derived from large epidemiological studies and intervention trials which employ statistical notions of risk (for example, Lord et al., 2001; Nuffield Institute for Health and NHS Centre for Reviews and Dissemination, 1996). However, the accounts of the patient participants in a preliminary study (Ballinger and Payne, 2000) seemed to allude to risks of a different kind, involving threats to choice and autonomy. I wanted to use discourse analysis to explore how different views of risk impacted on, and were enacted within, a day hospital that provided rehabilitation for older people.

Decisions regarding data generation method   In electing to use observation as my research method, I wanted to note the routines, customs and practices of the day hospital, which I believed would illustrate how risk was constructed and negotiated between the day hospital staff and the older people who attended. I described my method as 'participant observation', as I subscribed to the view that, as a researcher, I was intimately involved in what happened around me, and implicated in what I chose to describe, and how I interpreted it. Observation was to be supplemented by some analysis of documentary sources (such as information leaflets and the Operational Policy of the day hospital), and the design and timeframe of the study were deliberately flexible to allow for use of other methods if appropriate. In the event, semi-structured interviews with some older people attending the day hospital were also carried out towards the end of the project.

As a novice participant observer, I practiced observing and writing up different scenarios in which I found myself prior to the start of the study. I quickly became aware of the selective nature of what one as researcher chooses to record, and the necessity of reliable strategies for catching key moments and events. In general, the periods of observation in the day hospital were limited to around two hours maximum, and sometimes shorter, unless observing a specific clinic or meeting. This time period seemed to be optimum in terms of noting detail while maintaining focus and concentration. In a busier environment, this would have been more difficult to sustain. The data collection period extended over 11 weeks, with a two week break. Semi-structured interviews and analysis of documentary sources were also employed to supplement the participant observation.

Persona and positioning of researcher   As a participant observer, I was conscious that I had a number of choices with regard to how I presented myself to research participants, and who I claimed to be. I was particularly anxious to make conscious decisions with respect to these choices, as I had given the question of my 'persona as researcher' little consideration in a preliminary study immediately prior to this observational work. However, reflexive strategies such as a research diary and discussion with my supervisor had highlighted how my appearance and demeanour as a researcher had possibly reinforced patient misapprehensions about my involvement with them in a previous project. On visiting the ward, I had dressed smartly, carried information sheets and consent forms on a clip board, wore an identity badge and assessed patients' suitability for inclusion through accessing medical records and talking to nursing staff. Unreflexively I had behaved as a health professional would have done, and in turn, the accounts which patient participants provided me with corresponded to the type of accounts which would have been given to health professionals involved in their rehabilitation.

Within this second study, therefore, I consciously considered my identity within the research environment, and elected to describe myself as a student. I felt that this would be less intimidating than my 'professional' appearance and demeanour in the initial study. This identity also accorded with my purpose as a postgraduate, and was a role in which I felt comfortable. I therefore consistently introduced myself both verbally and in written material such as information sheets as a student, and dressed fairly informally, usually in trousers and jumper or shirt. I chose not to wear makeup and avoided carrying a briefcase, folder or other academic accessories.

Strategies to promote reflexivity   In addition to considering my research persona prior to the study, I used a number of strategies throughout the project to encourage reflexive thinking. In addition to field notes, I regularly wrote personal memos which reflected my own thoughts, feelings and perspectives about the experience of carrying out this research project. These were formally included as raw data, and were word processed, coded and included in the analysis. During regular meetings with my supervisor (the third author of this chapter), who was experienced in the use of qualitative research methods, I was encouraged to question and justify my developing interpretations. The drafting of an account of the research started before analysis was complete, and repeated re-drafting proved a useful means of testing new ideas and developing the interpretation. Concurrent reading of the newly emerging 'risk literature' in medical sociology, health psychology and other social science disciplines helped to inform my ideas. I found the regular presentation of ongoing work to a variety of audiences, together with noting of responses and questions, a useful practice. This enabled me to consider the relative contributions of contrasting perspectives (for example, academic and clinical occupational therapy), and think about the expectations and requirements of my work for different audiences.

Analysis   My analysis of the texts generated through the use of participant observation and personal memos was carried out according to discourse analytic principles (Parker, 1992). Raw data were read repeatedly, and comments and ideas noted. Preliminary codes were next identified, particular attention being paid to object and subject positions manifest in policies, routines and practices within the day hospital (Parker, 1992). The strategies I used to promote reflexivity ensured that my role as researcher was addressed within the analysis. The initial codes were refined, the raw data entered and recoded within the computer package 'Ethnograph', and finally a theoretical framework to explain the data was developed.

The use of participant observation as a method of generating texts for a discourse analysis is unusual and raises particular issues in that the raw data one is analysing have been initially recorded by oneself. Again, however, reflexive strategies can enable the researcher to access alternative perspectives or explanations about events observed, and highlight the authoritative position of the researcher in interpreting data generated within any qualitative methodology. The use of different data generation methods within discursive analysis has been explored by Parker et al. (1999).

My analysis suggested that the rehabilitation service was orientated towards the management of 'medical' risk, or risk of physical or bodily damage to older users of the service. This was manifest in such practices as storage of walking aids together at the side of a corridor, thus ensuring that the busy day room remained free of obstacles, although limiting unassisted mobility of frailer services users. Attenders at the day hospital were served hot drinks and lunch, rather than given the opportunity to make their own, and were encouraged to use the toilet at prescribed times, when more help was available.

In contrast, service users themselves seemed to orientate to the social environment of the day hospital, for example, expressing concerns about 'fitting in', or anger about being treated 'as a child' as a result of some of the routines (for example, some service users commented negatively about the nurses assuming responsibility for the dispensing of medication when they themselves were responsible for their own medication at home). Thus for service users, particularly as new attenders, social risks seemed to predominate, whereas the health care providers were preoccupied with physical threats or challenges.

Box 7.2   *Key features of participant observation*

- The aim is to gain an in-depth understanding of a set of cultural practices.
- An informed and reflexive choice must be made concerning the extent to which the observer participates in the cultural practices of interest.
- Prior to engaging in the culture the researcher must anticipate and resolve potential problems relating to: unobtrusively recording observations; obtaining informed consent; minimising the influence of the researcher on the practices observed; assuring the confidentiality of participants; maintaining analytical detachment.
- One or more of a wide variety of qualitative methods of analysis can be employed, ranging from realist content analysis to interpretive and constructivist analyses.

ACTION RESEARCH

Action research is less a method than an *approach* to research – one which can differ radically from conventional approaches. While there are many varieties, distinguished by different designations such as 'participatory research' or 'co-operative inquiry', a core element of all action research is the active involvement of the users or **stakeholders** in the research. Their involvement is regarded as essential for two reasons. Firstly, action researchers believe that the people who are actually living in the situation that is being researched have invaluable insider knowledge of it, which makes them uniquely well qualified to research it. Secondly, action researchers believe that the process of research (and not simply the products of research) should directly benefit the participants, in particular by empowering them to understand and make changes in their own lives. If stakeholders identify the questions, problems and solutions that will be researched then they can ensure that these address their specific objectives, and if they are actively involved in the research process then they will have direct access to and control over the knowledge produced.

Another defining feature of action research, as its name suggests, is that active intervention or change in the form of action is central to it. In this sense action research resembles a naturalistic experiment or clinical trial; rather than simply describing and analysing a situation (as in interview- or observation-based studies) action research actually tests the validity of the analysis by implementing the changes suggested by the analysis and then evaluating their effects. Because action research involves implementing and evaluating solutions to specific local problems, it bridges the gap between research and practice. This makes it a potentially useful research method for practitioners such as health professionals (Meyer, 2000). Similarly, the emphasis on active stakeholder involvement makes action research a potentially useful method for users of health care services (Consumers in NHS Research Support Unit, 2000; Kovacs, 2000).

Varieties of action research

The term 'action research' was coined by Kurt Lewin in the 1940s to refer to the novel style of democratic, naturalistic experimentation which he pioneered (Greenwood & Levin, 1998; Hart & Bond, 1995). Lewin worked chiefly in an industrial context, where the democratic aspect of action research involved including workers as equal contributors to the discussions, while the action component involved solving concrete industrial problems. The research process he proposed has three key iterative stages . Firstly, it is necessary for all the participants to collaboratively evaluate and analyse the current situation, in order to identify and describe problems and their possible causes and solutions. This analysis should produce one or more recommended courses of action, and so the second step is a **change experiment** which involves acting to implement these proposed solutions. Thirdly, the participants again observe, evaluate and reflect on the changed situation in order to determine the extent, benefits and drawbacks of the changes made, and the reasons for these. This process of reflection may suggest further changes, and so the iterative cycle can continue with further action and reflection.

Later developments of action research have tended to place greater emphasis on maximising its potential to empower and emancipate participant researchers. The Tavistock Institute in London adopted a more psychoanalytical approach, involving long-term therapeutic relationships which addressed clients' problems, rather than short-term change experiments. Another variant is 'co-operative inquiry' (Heron, 1996), which also emphasises the transformation of personal being through the inquiry process, as well as the development of practical skills through the experience of transformative action and collaboration. Heron suggests that co-operative inquiry is preferable to controlled trials as a means of studying treatment effects because it draws on experiential insider knowledge of combined physical and mental processes, and is also preferable to traditional qualitative research because it allows the participant researchers to develop their own interpretations and then to test their emerging theories in the crucible of action.

'Participatory research' in deprived communities and 'feminist participatory action research' seek to enhance socio-political awareness in participants, as a prelude to undertaking socio-political action to challenge oppression and change the social agenda (Balcazar et al., 1998). An example of participatory research in the field of health is the Merton Project (Taylor, 1999), which was commissioned by the housing and services department in Merton to determine how services could be developed to meet the needs of deaf people in ethnic communities. The project was publicised to the community through community leaders of ethnic groups, and proceeded through a series of consultations (including interviews and public forums) with these groups, users, public service providers, voluntary agencies and health professionals, concluding with an open workshop to ensure that participants' views were accurately represented.

As the previous examples illustrate, a wide range of methods can be employed in action research; essentially, *any* method can be used which the participants feel will help them to analyse the questions or problems they wish to address, and instigate the changes they wish to make. Methods of evaluation can include personal interviews or questionnaire-based surveys, small group discussions or large open meetings. Interventions could range from changes in inter-personal relationships or ways of working to joint political action, or randomised controlled trials of interventions in experimental as compared with 'control' communities. The form in which evaluations are reported also varies more widely than is customary in academic research; instead of a publication in a journal article, the participants might feel it is more relevant to disseminate the knowledge they have gained through a play performed to the target community, or an internet website that others in a similar situation might access.

The number of participants and nature of the participation can also vary greatly. Some action research projects are initiated by an outside body but

seek to reach a whole community; for example, initiatives to reduce problems associated with alcohol use have included working with government
agencies and the public sector to change drinking-related policies and
practices, and working with schools to develop educational poster cam-
paigns (Giesbrecht & Rankin, 2000). Alternatively, some projects are carried
out entirely within a small, committed group of people with a common
interest.

An excellent example of such small-scale participatory research is
described by Stewart and Bhagwanjee (1999). A therapist set up weekly
meetings for people with spinal cord injury, in response to a need for more
input and support after discharge expressed by six patients. The meetings
were open, and so group size and composition changed during the project.
The purpose of the group was to provide peer support and promote quality
of life through the sharing and learning of skills and coping strategies.
Group activities were chosen to reflect members' needs and interests, and
included educational, personal development and recreational sessions.
Initially the therapist acted as group leader, and assisted with the colla-
borative planning and implementation of group activities and the development of the participants' technical skills. As mutual trust and personal
confidence grew the leadership role began to be rotated.

After 18 months the group decided that the time had come to hold a focus
group meeting to determine how to evaluate their activities. They decided
to ask the therapist to develop a questionnaire, with feedback from members, which would inform group management and planning by gathering
information about members' views on the group's goals, programme,
structure and leadership. The therapist was asked to administer the questionnaire and to report the findings at a second focus group, which would
then engage in further in-depth discussion and analysis in order to decide
on future activities. The outcome of this evaluation process was that the
group decided to move on from their previous focus on peer support to
actively try to change attitudes to disability (for example, through media
work, a brochure, school presentations), to reach out to new members, and
to raise funds to achieve these goals. At this point they developed a new
group structure, in which the role of the therapist was restricted to occasional invited consultant.

Issues to consider when carrying out action research

Many of the issues and problems posed by action research are quite different from those encountered in other kinds of research, and require
thoughtful consideration, as outlined below (see also Graham & Chandler-
Coutts, 2000).

Initiating the project   Action research should ideally be initiated by the principal actors themselves. If the action research project has not been initiated
at a grass-roots level, gaining the trust and commitment of the participants

can present a challenge. In the first place, target groups for research (for example, adolescent drinkers or people with disabilities) may not welcome being targeted and hence implicitly labelled as a 'problem', and may not wish to instigate any change. Researchers will be more easily accepted if they have a long-standing link with the other participants, or a similar identity (for example, similar age group, or with a disability), and it is helpful to be able to offer an attractive benefit, such as funding for group activities, or a potential solution to a problem which the participants really care about. It is important to involve key informants with the social influence and skills to convince and motivate others – for example, in a medical setting the involvement of the consultant will facilitate involving more junior staff. However, as in observation research, forming close alliances with powerful figures may make it more difficult to gain the trust of other participants and, ideally, alliances must be carefully balanced between more powerful and less powerful participants, all of whom have an interest in the outcomes of the project.

Establishing roles and boundaries   It is important to establish as early as possible what involvement is expected and permitted with respect to each potential participant. It may be difficult to define the boundaries of who is involved; for example, in a hospital setting are the stakeholders in a particular project to be only health professionals, or all staff, or also the patients, or additionally their families? Owing to resource constraints and the difficulty of working collaboratively with a large group, it may not be feasible to include all who might affect or be affected by the research. Decisions also need to be taken about whether all participants will have access to all data (which might pose serious confidentiality problems, for example if clinicians have access to interviews with patients they are treating), and whether and how they will contribute to the design and analysis of evaluative measures, which may require particular skills.

A key question concerns the role of the professional researcher, which is much less dominant in action research than in traditional research, and is more one of a partner than a consultant. Action researchers assume that people have the capacity to solve their own problems if given the opportunity, and that the role of the 'expert' is therefore not to disempower them by analysing the problems and solutions on their behalf, but instead to facilitate the participants' capacity for informed, shared decision-making. In the context of participatory action research with people with disabilities, Balcazar et al. (1998) neatly encapsulate this role by inverting the question 'what role can consumers play in rehabilitation research?' to instead ask 'what of value can university researchers offer to people with disabilities trying to lead independent healthy lives?' Subject to instructions, monitoring and input from other participants, professional researchers can: provide an analytic framework and information from the literature, allowing wider comparisons to similar situations; articulate the tacit local knowledge of insiders (for example, by analysing interviews or writing reports of group conclusions); use their research training to question assumptions and systematically seek and test explanations; design evaluation instruments and collect and analyse data; provide training and support to allow other participants to carry out any of these roles. Another useful role is that, as an outsider, the professional researcher can (tactfully) flout local conventions; for example, suggest things that insiders cannot recognise or articulate because of long-standing conventions or relationships.

Agreeing on research questions, process and outcomes   Some of the most difficult compromises that must be reached will concern which questions to research, in what ways, and what outcomes to aim for and evaluate. The various participants will have different, and sometimes conflicting, priorities. A possible problem for professional researchers is that most participants are likely to prioritise local objectives, such as finding workable solutions to practical problems, ensuring harmonious and inclusive community collaboration in the process, and promoting a sense of personal growth and empowerment among participants. Collecting and disseminating conventional evidence regarding the outcomes of the project to the wider academic or professional community may be dismissed altogether as inappropriate to these goals. Moreover, the concrete, observable outcomes from a successful action project may occur *after* the professional researcher has ceased to be involved, since a successful action research project will have changed and empowered the participants to continue to address the problem themselves. For example, due to limited resources an initial intervention may not have had sufficient scope to achieve an effective solution to a problem, but might nevertheless raise awareness and change

---

Box 7.3   *Key features of action research*

- Action research is based on the assumption that those living in a situation have unique and invaluable insider knowledge of it and should therefore be actively involved in the research process.
- The aim of action research is to directly benefit participants by empowering them to define their own problems and develop their own solutions.
- Action research was originally based on an iterative cycle of: a) reflecting on the current situation; b) carrying out a change experiment; c) reflecting on the changed situation.
- Action research can draw on a very wide variety of methods, including long-term therapeutic relationships, socio-political action, surveys, meetings and experiments.
- It is important to establish at an early stage what involvement is expected from each participant and what the aims of the research are; note that academic and professional input and outcomes may not be a high priority.

attitudes, which after years of lobbying could lead to better-resourced interventions which *are* effective.

For these reasons, a conventional assessment of the success of an action research project may not be possible or meaningful, because the kind of local, subjective, embodied and practical knowledge and outcomes it seeks to generate cannot be adequately captured and conveyed in an abstract, generalisable form. Lewin is said to have expressed this intimate connection between theory, research and practice in the aphorisms 'nothing is as practical as a good theory' and 'the best way to understand something is to try to change it' (Greenwood & Levin, 1998) – or, to put it another way, 'the proof of the pudding is in the eating'! But while the outcomes achieved through an action research project may not be directly transmissible, the principles and process by which they were achieved can, like a recipe for a good pudding, be disseminated by descriptive case studies, or may be practically demonstrated by the example of 'good practice'.

SUMMARY

This chapter has outlined three extremely different approaches to under-taking research that is based on data which are directly observed rather than reported. These methods of data collection are not widely used in the fields of health and clinical psychology, perhaps because of the substantial resources required to record and analyse events on-the-spot, and the com-plexities and dilemmas associated with the more participatory forms of research. However, these research methods provide fresh avenues of inquiry and sources of insight that may complement, enrich or challenge the under-standings gained from the more common self-report research methods, and therefore provide an important alternative or addition to them.

RECOMMENDED READING

Structured observation

Simpson, M. & Tuson, J. (1995). *Using observations in small-scale research: a beginner's guide*. Scottish Council for Research in Education.

Participant observation

Fetterman, D. (1998). *Ethnography step by step* (2nd edn). London: Sage.

Action research

Greenwood, D.J. & Levin, M. (1998). *Introduction to action research: social research for social change*. London: Sage.

REVISION QUESTIONS

1 When may it be useful to use observation methods for clinical or health psychology research?
2 How can the researcher define what should be coded when carrying out structured observation?
3 Explain the goals of ethnography.
4 What are the ethical, practical, theoretical and analytical implications of an observer becoming involved as a participant in the setting that he or she observes?
5 What difficulties may researchers encounter when becoming involved in action research, and how can these difficulties be avoided or resolved?

8 QUESTIONNAIRES AND SURVEYS

David F. Marks

AIMS OF THIS CHAPTER

(i)   To describe the essential characteristics of the questionnaire.
(ii) To discuss the assessment of the reliability, validity and sensitivity of a questionnaire.
(iii) To describe the essentials of the survey method.
(iv) To illustrate the use of questionnaires and interviews with an account of a health and lifestyle survey.

INTRODUCTION

This chapter provides an introduction to the questionnaire and the survey, among the most useful and popular quantitative methods in clinical and health psychology research. The questionnaire is a basic tool not only for measuring individual psychological states, traits and processes, but for assessing health status and quality of life in healthy people and those suffering from illness. In the past, those carrying out research using questionnaires and surveys have followed the traditions of positivism and realism in making the assumption that human beliefs, experiences and behaviours are processes which have the status of entities that are sufficiently stable that they can be accurately reported and measured. Of course, these assumptions can be challenged, and the data collected by these methods can be contested on the grounds that the responses are contextually determined and socially negotiated. However, the bedrock of much of the social and health sciences would need to be replaced if we did not assume that at least some of the information obtained from these sources is related in a systematically meaningful way to people's subjective experience. For present purposes, it is necessary to assume – or we simply would be unable to continue – that information from questionnaires, interviews and surveys has a similar epistemological status to readings from an error-prone, semi-opaque thermometer, which, unless specifically evidenced, is without interval scale properties. Alternatively, questionnaires can be viewed as a particular form of communication between the researcher and the respondent. Responses to items can be used to convey a range of social positions and identities (for example, dissatisfaction, handicap) and, like any other form of discourse, these discursive moves are not arbitrary but are grounded in respondents' ways of living (see Chapters 1 and 6).

Surveys are generally conducted using structured interviews and/or questionnaires. Interviews have the advantage that they can take longer and include more complex and difficult questions. They are normally carried out in private, one-to-one. On the other hand, the self-completion questionnaire ensures greater anonymity and is economic to use. It is often less invasive and quicker to complete for the respondent, and may be presented in computerised format to large groups at the same time, sent through the post, or given to people for completion at home and postal return or published for completion using the Internet.

The analysis of questionnaire data can be efficient using **coding sheets** of responses and/or computerised scoring, or at the very least, with manual scoring templates to speed up the process. For complex applications such as psychiatric diagnosis, procedures have been developed which combine the interview method with standardised questionnaires and test batteries. A huge number of instruments are available for assessing everything from mental and physical health status to specific symptom questionnaires. New measures are being developed constantly (McDowell & Newell, 1987; Bowling, 1991, 1995; Wilkin, Hallam & Doggett, 1993; Jenkinson, 1994; Johnston et al., 1995; Cabeza & Kingstone, 2001).

Questionnaires are an essential tool for the diagnosis of chronic mental conditions such as dementia (for example, the Iowa Dementia Test, Mini-Mental State Examination), mental disorders (for example, the General Health Questionnaire, GHQ-12, Minnesota Multiphasic Personality Inventory, Beck Depression Inventory), pain (for example, McGill Pain Questionnaire), anxiety (for example, State-Trait Anxiety Inventory) and neuropsychological deficits (for example, Wechsler Memory Scale, Bender-Gestalt Visual Motor Test). In the study of intelligence and personality, some of the best known psychologists have been those responsible for questionnaires designed to measure the dimensions or factors of personality or intelligence (the Eysenck Personality Inventory (EPI); Cattell's '16PF'). Some of the best-known questionnaires have been produced following **factor analysis**, a way of enabling items that are measuring the same thing to be grouped and scored together on a sub-scale of the overall instrument. The techniques used by Cattell, Eysenck and others to create such classic measures 50 years ago remain useful today for the design of new measures for clinical and health research.

THE ESSENTIAL CHARACTERISTICS OF THE QUESTIONNAIRE

Questionnaires vary according to objectives, content, question format, number of items, and in their **sensitivity** or **responsiveness** to change.

Questionnaires may be employed either in cross-sectional or longitudinal studies. In prospective longitudinal studies the same measures are taken from a number of groups of participants on a number of occasions and the principal objective will be to statistically evaluate the differences that occur between groups across time. When looking for changes over time, the responsiveness of a questionnaire to clinical and subjective changes is a crucial feature. Longitudinal studies comparing the effect sizes obtained from different questionnaires have found large between-questionnaire differences in the impression of improvement, stability and deterioration gained (Fitzpatrick et al., 1992). Thus, a combination of a questionnaire's content, sensitivity and size, together with its psychometric properties of reliability and validity, influence a questionnaire's selection for a particular study.

Guides are available to advise users on making a choice between appropriate measures (Bowling, 1991, 1995). These guides are extremely useful in planning research projects as they include details on the content, scoring, validity and reliability of dozens of questionnaires for measuring all of the major aspects of psychological well-being and quality of life, including disease-specific and domain-specific questionnaires and more generic measures. It is important to ensure that the content of a specific questionnaire includes the characteristics that are of interest to a particular investigation. A disease- or domain-specific questionnaire may not have been developed with the same purpose in mind that you may have in designing your study.

Portfolios of measures for use in health psychology and clinical psychology research have also been published (Johnstone et al., 1995). These portfolios are useful, if a mixed blessing. On the one hand, they provide a convenient toolbox for the novice investigator who can play 'lucky dip' and hopefully find a questionnaire that is applicable to a study of immediate interest. On the other hand, the questionnaires are of mixed quality and their very convenience can lead to a lazy, opportunistic approach to data collection. As time runs out in the planning stage, compromises may be made, and the measures in the portfolio may influence the research question, rather than the other way around – the 'tail wagging the dog'. There may be a strong case for using commercially published, less accessible, and more costly questionnaires because, in specific instances, they may actually be psychometrically superior. Under copyright law, these questionnaires may not be reproduced and users are warned by the producers not to photocopy them, forcing the payment of fees, sometimes of several pounds per copy for a few pages of printed material. In other instances, lesser-known but more specific instruments, that are not available in the portfolios, may be required. You may be able to use an existing questionnaire for the variables you want to measure, and then supplement this by adding extra items of your own. Finally, there may be simply no escaping the fact that *no* existing measure is suitable for your planned research, and you will need to take the plunge and develop your own measure. The latter decision should not be taken lightly, however, because designing a new measure can be a challenging, time-consuming task.

There are some essential characteristics that should be considered in selecting or designing a questionnaire: your objectives, type of respondents, the content, question format, number of items, reliability, validity and sensitivity to change.

Objectives

The investigator must ask from the very outset: what is it that I want to know? The answer to this question will dictate the selection of the most relevant and useful questionnaire. The most important aspect of questionnaire selection is therefore to *match the objective of the study with the objective of the questionnaire*. For example, are you interested in a disease-specific or broad ranging research question? When this question is settled, you need to decide whether there is anything else that your research objective will require you to know. Usually the researcher needs to develop a specific block of questions that will seek vital information concerning the respondents' socio-demographic characteristics, which can be placed at the beginning or the end of the main questionnaire. When you have addressed all aspects of the research question, it is necessary to check that the scoring system used is compatible with the analyses you have in mind, for example, does it produce continuous or categorical data? Then it is necessary to be assured that the reliability, validity and sensitivity of the questionnaire have been adequately evaluated.

Type of respondents

When the issues above have been addressed, the research team can move on to assess the *appropriateness* of the instrument for the study population and its *acceptability* to the group under study. These matters are essential, and the final assessment of acceptability will be aided by a pilot study with a small number of representatives typical of the respondents who are expected to participate in your main study. The instrument can be fine-tuned following the feedback from the pilot sample. For example, the font size may be too small for people who are older or who have visual impairments, the instructions may be unclear, or the consent form insufficiently concise. For members of ethnic minorities or refugees, it may be necessary to produce the questionnaire in different languages, which will have implications for the validity, reliability and sensitivity of the questionnaire (see below). Note that a questionnaire may be reliable and valid for one population but not another. For example, a questionnaire designed to measure health status in cancer patients may be insensitive to smaller variations in health status in a general population sample.

Questionnaire content

One of the easiest and most practical ways of assessing a person's feelings, attitudes and behaviours is to ask them, either in interview or self-administered questionnaire. **Self-reports** are therefore a primary means of obtaining psychological data. Self-reports are related to the processes of *introspection* and communication, which are controversial in psychology because they may be affected by all kinds of subjective and social processes that are difficult to measure and control. Self-reports are often combined with objective measures of behaviour taken by direct observation or by using neurodiagnostic techniques, such as fMRI, PET scan, CAT scan, P300, EEG, biofeedback, electromyogram or other psychophysiological methods of brain imaging. (The latter techniques are beyond the scope of this book; a useful source is Cabeza & Kingstone, 2001.)

The fact remains that many of the processes that clinicians are interested in are subjective experiences and so it is practically impossible to avoid the use of the self-report. For example, feelings of pain, depression, anxiety, stress, coping, recovery, energy, fatigue, wellbeing, satisfaction, social support, self-esteem and self-efficacy are all subjectively defined experiences, which can only be assessed by self-report. Thus the century-long debate in psychology about the use of self-reports as data has had little bearing on the everyday necessity of using such data in health care diagnosis, assessment and research. However, there is a serious concern about the best ways of obtaining such data in the most reliable, valid and sensitive fashion. Examples of content from some important and frequently used questionnaires are given below.

Questionnaire content may vary from the highly generic (for example, 'how has your health been over the last few weeks: excellent, good, fair, poor, very bad?') to the highly specific (for example, 'have you had any arguments with people at work in the last two weeks?). The items may all be different ways of trying to measure the same thing, or there may be a variety of scales and sub-scales for measuring different dimensions or variables within a single instrument. When the data are to inform decisions that are both serious and complicated, for example, the diagnosis of mental illness, it is necessary to use an instrument like the Present State Examination (Wing, 1992) administered after professional training and combining interview methods with computerised scoring.

Question format

Most questionnaires contain a series of questions intended to assess aspects of the respondent's socio-demographic, psychosocial and health/clinical status. The questions are obtained from a variety of sources including other questionnaires, qualitative data from interviews, discussions or focus groups with the population of interest, or even the author's imagination. When constructing new questions it is important to use simple, everyday language rather than abstract, theoretical or technical jargon. Questions should always avoid ambiguity, making leading suggestions or presumptions about the respondent, double-barrelled statements and double negatives. Questions may be closed or open-ended.

Closed questions may be asked in a variety of forms; for example, as *yes/no* or *yes/no/don't know* questions; *Likert scales* usually with three, five or seven categories ranging in order of frequency from 'never' through 'sometimes' to 'always', or agreement from 'strongly agree' and 'agree' through 'neither agree nor disagree' to 'disagree' and 'strongly disagree' (Likert, 1952); *rating scales* with 1–5, 1–7, 0–10, and 0–100 being the most common ranges in use; *visual analogue scales*, in which a line is provided for the respondents to mark the degree of belief, agreement or feeling they hold about a particular matter; or *diagrammatic symbols* such as 'smiley' or 'sulky' faces to represent levels of satisfaction or agreement (see Box 8.1).

Open-ended questions elicit qualitative responses and are a useful addition to any questionnaire or interview. Although they do not share the properties of reliability and validity, they have several advantages over closed questions. The answers will not be biased by the researcher's pre-conceptions as much as closed questions can be. The respondents are able to express their opinions, thoughts and feelings freely using their own words in ways that are less constrained by the particular wordings of the question. The respondents may have responses that the questionnaire designers overlooked. They may have in-depth comments that they wish to make about your study and the topics that it is covering that would not be picked up using the standard questions in the structured part of the questionnaire. Open-ended responses require extra coding in the analysis stage, do not always elicit very full responses, but often the results are well worth the extra effort.

Number of items

Questionnaires vary greatly in the number of items that are used to assess the variable(s) of interest. Single-item measures use a single question, rating or item to measure the concept or variable of interest. For example, the now popular single verbal item to evaluate health status shown in Box 8.1 above: 'During the past four weeks ... how would you rate your health in general? Excellent, Very good, Good, Fair, Poor.' (For a review of single-item measures of health status, see Idler, 1992.) Single items have the obvious advantages of being simple, direct and brief. The disadvantage is that one cannot calculate the reliability. Using a single item is like carrying out an experiment with just one response instead of collecting many responses to check that these are all similar and therefore reliable.

Multiple-item questionnaires often lend greater sensitivity, reliability and validity, and in general are psychometrically superior to single-item scales (for example, Bowling, 1995; Ware et al., 1993). Such questionnaires use a series of items to assess the same variable or concept, allowing the answers

Box 8.1   *Examples of different formats for questionnaire items*

Yes/no/don't know

During the past four weeks . . . would you say your health in general has been good?

Yes   No   Don't know

Likert scale

During the past four weeks . . . your health in general has been good.

| Definitely agree | Moderately agree | Neither agree nor disagree | Moderately disagree | Definitely disagree |

Verbal rating

During the past four weeks . . . how would you rate your health in general?

Excellent   Very good   Good   Fair   Poor

Numerical rating

During the past four weeks . . . how would you rate your health in general?

1   2   3   4   5

Diagrams + verbal rating + numerical rating

During the past four weeks . . . how would you rate your health in general?

Excellent   Very good   Good   Fair   Poor
1   2   3   4   5

Visual analogue rating

0 ————————————— 50 ————————————— 100

Open ended format

1) In general, how would you say your health has been over the past four weeks?

_____

_____

_____

_____

_____

_____

_____

(If you need more space, please turn over and continue writing on the other side. More paper can also be found at the end of this questionnaire.)

2) Is there anything else relevant to this topic that you would like to tell us, which has not been covered elsewhere?

_____

_____

_____

_____

_____

_____

to be summed or weighted along a single scale. Some questionnaires contain items measuring different factors or dimensions of a psychological state or trait and require careful scoring to ensure the items measuring the same variable are summed and weighted together in the correct combinations. Finally, batteries of instruments may be constructed which combine a large number of different measures, and perhaps interviews as well as questionnaires measuring several variables at the same time.

THE MEASUREMENT OF RELIABILITY, VALIDITY AND SENSITIVITY

Before a new questionnaire can be placed into general use, various checks must be made of its psychometric properties. The individual items must be screened for their reliability, face validity and acceptability by piloting the questionnaire on a sample of participants, and the psychometric properties of the questionnaire must be assessed in terms of its overall **reliability** and **validity**. Using factor analysis the associations between items can be identified to determine whether the items are measuring only one or more than one factor, variable or dimension. Another important characteristic that should ideally be investigated is the sensitivity or responsiveness of the questionnaire to changes over time or differences between groups of respondents from different backgrounds. I shall describe each of these three characteristics in turn.

Reliability

When we use a thermometer to measure the temperature of ice on three occasions, we would expect the values all to be 0 °C each time we took the readings. If the same thermometer produced values for the temperature of ice of −10 °C, 0 °C, and +10 °C on the three occasions, we would conclude that the thermometer is unreliable. Alternatively, if we have two identical thermometers and one gives a reading of +5 °C and the other a reading of − 5 °C, not only do we not know what to believe, we have no basis to accept the reading of either. We would be wise to discard such a thermometer because it would be unreliable and potentially very misleading. The same argument applies to psychological questionnaires. Reliability is inferred when an instrument consistently produces the same readings or values for the same observations every time they are made. Thus we would expect the distribution of questionnaire scores for the same sample of people to be the same on different occasions of testing, unless we have reasons to believe that the people have changed. Reliability is normally measured using correlation and therefore expressed as a decimal in the range 0.00–1.00. Four methods are commonly used to measure the reliability of a question-naire: internal consistency, alternative form, split-half and test-retest reliability.

Internal consistency or *homogeneity* is measured by correlating the scores on each item with the total scores on the remainder of items, an index known as **Cronbach's alpha** (Cronbach, 1951). A value of alpha in the range +0.70 to 0.90 is considered good, or if in the range +0.50 to 0.70 adequate. It is a good procedure to screen all items for their internal consistency before doing anything else, then any deviant items can be removed prior to carrying out further studies of reliability using one or more of the other criteria below.

Alternative form reliability is measured by developing two comparable versions of the new questionnaire and administering them to the same group of individuals. If the questionnaires are indeed measuring the same area and are reliable, the two sets of scores will correlate together highly positively, with a correlation in the region of +0.70 to 0.90. In practice, this form of reliability is seldom used because only rarely are two versions of the same instrument available.

Split-half reliability is measured when we have a method for dividing the items on a questionnaire into two equal sets, say by taking odd and even numbered items, and scoring the totals or averages of the odd and even sets independently. Again, we can use correlation to investigate whether the two halves of the questionnaire appear to be measuring the same area, in which case, once again, the correlation will be in the range +0.7 to 0.9.

Test-retest reliability is measured by administering the questionnaire to the same sample on two occasions and correlating the two sets of scores. There may be carry-over effects due to respondents memorising their scores, and inflating their own consistency, and there could be other possible means by which the first administration affects the second. Normally a period of several weeks is allowed between administrations to try to block such carry-over effects but this can never be assured.

Validity

Imagine that you (or a physicist colleague) developed a new device for measuring the temperature of liquids. You, or your colleague, would want to be sure that the new device actually did measure temperature and not something else, such as pressure. Your new device would therefore have to be tested alongside a tried and trusted, existing temperature-measuring device, such as a glass and mercury thermometer. Both the new and the old instruments would be employed to take readings in a number of fluids at different temperatures. If the readings from the new instrument were highly positively correlated with the readings from the old instrument, we would be willing to accept that the new instrument was providing a valid measurement of temperature. This is what is meant by the term 'validity'.

The evaluation of the validity of psychological measures follows the same logic and procedure as in the temperature example just described. For example, if we have devised a questionnaire intended to measure stress, we can validate the measure using a more established measure of stress – but of course we can never have an objective method or 'gold standard' that we can use, or we would not need to develop a new measure! (Unless we wanted to develop a shorter or quicker measure or one that is less dependent on experts to administer.) This has led to a wide variety of methods for establishing validity that all depend, in one way or another, on mixtures of confidence, theory and intuition.

Content validity is the simplest and most intuitive form of validity assessed by comparing the questionnaire items with the professed objective of the questionnaire. Do the former collectively represent the construct or variable that the questionnaire has been designed to measure? Is there something missing, or are there some items that go beyond the construct and are therefore superfluous? Do the items appear to be measuring what the questionnaire is designed to measure? Does the questionnaire have *face validity*?

Criterion validity is the most mathematically precise and rigorous form of validity because it uses the correlation between scores on the new questionnaire and scores on existing measures as a criterion or index of the validity of the new questionnaire. Concurrent validity is assessed when the new and old measures are administered to the same people, one immediately after the other. Predictive validity is obtained when the new measure can be used to make predictions about experience or behaviour at some time in the future.

Construct validity is the most generic and complex kind of validity and it cannot be achieved until a large body of evidence has been collected concerning the whole pattern of relationships between the measure of interest and other kinds of measures based on a theoretical analysis of the constructs concerned and how they may be empirically related. This type of validity is not likely to be of much use for the novice investigator who is establishing the validity of a new questionnaire. It may take years, or even decades, before the construct validity of a questionnaire can be established. However, this is the most important kind of validity. If you claim that your new instrument is measuring stress, then your questionnaire scores should be related in a meaningful and predictable way with those processes that theoretical analysis of stress postulates are the antecedents and sequelae of stress. The construct itself must first be given a precise conceptual and theoretical meaning and, as is the case for stress, this itself can be the most crucial problem for the test designer. The golden rule is: *be clear about your constructs before you construct your questionnaire.*

Sensitivity

Sensitivity, or *responsiveness*, refers to the capacity of a questionnaire to measure changes over time, even when the changes are small in size. Sensitivity is particularly important in longitudinal designs where the success of the entire study depends upon one's ability to detect differences in the extent of changes between the various treatment groups. Three methods have been suggested for calculating the sizes of change, all of which divide the change from time 1 to time 2 by an estimate of the precision of the instrument (Hevey & McGee, 1998). One way of measuring responsiveness is to convert the change that an instrument measures into an effect size, in other words, the change in means between baseline and follow-up divided by the baseline standard deviation (Hevey & McGee, 1998; Kazis, Anderson, & Meenan, 1989). An even better way is the standardised response mean (SRM) that controls for the individual variation in change by dividing the change in mean scores by the standard deviation of the individuals' change scores (Katz et al., 1992). A third measure, the 'responsiveness index', divides the change in mean scores for improved patients by the square root of twice the mean square error (another measure of variation) for stable patients (Guyatt, Walter & Norman, 1987). Sensitivity is the 'proof of the pudding' as far as having a psychometrically approved instrument is concerned. If the instrument is reliable and valid, but insensitive to change, it will not be a very useful indicator of health outcomes in studies measuring change. The instrument will be too 'blunt' to measure anything that is interesting in a clinical or health setting, especially if you are interested in detecting change. A good instrument is not only both reliable and valid, but it must also be sensitive to change.

Box 8.2   *Criteria for selecting and designing questionnaires*

- Specify your objectives in terms of the key variable(s) that you want to measure and select a questionnaire designed to measure the variable(s).
- The instrument should be as brief as possible and to the point.
- If necessary supplement the existing instrument with additional questions before designing a new scale.
- Designing a new questionnaire is a major enterprise requiring a series of processes that will take much time and effort.
- Be clear about your constructs before you construct your questionnaire.
- Questionnaires should use simple, plain, everyday language.
- The questionnaire content and administration should be ethical and user-friendly, and avoid exposing the respondents to embarrassment, trauma or fatigue.
- The questionnaire should be piloted on a sample from the study population to ensure the administration and scoring are manageable and acceptable to all likely participants.
- Special care must be taken to ensure that the instrument is readable and comprehensible especially if people from different educational backgrounds, age groups and ethnic minorities are included.
- Good evidence of the questionnaire's reliability, validity and sensitivity must be available before it can be used in a major study.

THE ESSENTIALS OF THE SURVEY METHOD

In clinical and health research we often want to explore the beliefs, knowledge, experience or behaviours of groups or categories of people. For example, we may want to know how drug users' perceptions of themselves and their families differ from those of non-users, or to better understand the experiences of patients receiving specific kinds of treatment, or to compare the **quality of life** (**QoL**) and mental health of people in different occupations. The survey will be the method of choice for many of these types of study.

The survey method, whether using interviews, questionnaires or some combination of the two, is versatile, and can be applied equally well to research with individuals, groups, organisations, communities or populations to inform our understanding of a host of very different types of research issues and questions. Normally a survey is conducted on a sample of the **study population** of interest (for example, people aged 70+, women aged 20–44, teenagers who smoke, carers of people with dementia, family members of people with a diagnosis of schizophrenia). Issues of key importance in conducting a survey, which are discussed in turn below, are: the objective(s); the mode of administration; the method of sampling; the sample size; the preparation of the data for analysis.

The objective

Throughout this book we have emphasised the importance of having a clear idea in mind about the objective of a piece of research before starting it. Research is an inquiry or exploration into new territory, which can be both exciting and enjoyable, akin to a journey by an explorer or adventurer (see also Willig, 2001).

A bit like the navigator exploring the unknown, we must have a very clear idea about *why* we are doing our study (the theory or policy behind the research), *what* we are looking for (the research question), and *where* we intend to look (the setting or domain). We must also decide *who* will be in the sample (the study sample), and *how* to use the tools we have at our disposal (the specific procedures for applying the research methods). However, we must not be so desperate about finding the answer to our quest that we impose a pre-determined answer on whatever we discover, even when it isn't really there, akin to Columbus discovering 'India' by sailing west to Central America. We have to be cautious that our procedures do not generate any self-fulfilling prophecies.

A research project can only ever succeed if the objective is clearly in focus, and if it is achievable within the constraints of the time and assets available. This point may seem obvious, but our experience of supervising many projects suggests that *lack of clarity about purposes and objectives* is one of the main stumbling blocks for the novice investigator to overcome. This is particularly the case when carrying out a survey, especially in a team of investigators who may have varying agendas with regard to the *why?*, *what?*, *who?*, *where?* and *how?* questions that must be answered before the survey can begin. The essence of the survey is that it lends itself to data collection on a wide variety of themes and topics. The research team (and surveys usually are carried out by teams) therefore has the scope to seek data on a large range of topics and, as a consequence, there is a danger of becoming overwhelmed. In the end, the value of the survey will be limited by the team's capacity to collect, analyse and disseminate their data within the time and resources available. Therefore any survey must be well focused, carefully time-tabled and efficiently managed (see Chapter 2).

Except for their use in market research or other commercial applications, using surveys as fact-finding exercises in the absence of policy or theory is a temptation that should be resisted. *Decide in advance what it is that you want to know and why you need to know it, then design a survey that will give you that information.* The more specific and well defined the question, the more likely it is that a satisfactory answer will be obtained. This applies as much to surveys as to any other kind of research. Being clear about your objective(s) enables everything else in your study to follow logically. It will be assumed in what follows that you are in the fortunate position of having clear objectives (the *why?* question) and a set of questions that you want to ask (the *what?* questions). Now you will need to decide *how* to administer the questions, *whom* to include, *where* to carry out your survey, and last but by no means least, *how many* people to include in your sample. These issues are discussed below.

Mode of administration

The main modes of administration are: face-to-face interview, telephone interview, group self-completion, postal self-completion and the internet. These modes may also be used in combination.

Face-to-face interviews are the preferred mode of data collection in health surveys. This procedure is preferred because there are fewer missing data, and the response rate is higher.

Telephone interviews are second best after face-to-face interviews as far as obtaining fully completed sets of responses is concerned, but they have the advantage of being efficient and economic. This is particularly the case if the interview is brief, say five minutes or less. A technique that is proving useful is random digit dialling, which gives a random sample of the telephone-using population.

Self-completion questionnaires are best employed when the issues being surveyed are easy to describe but hard to answer, for example, when the topics are sensitive or require anonymity. If the topic is a sensitive one, for example, concerning alcohol or drug use, or sexual experiences, then respondents will generally feel more comfortable with a self-completion method, either in a group setting or via postal survey.

Group settings are commonly employed in studies carried out in schools, colleges, universities or work places. The respondents can complete their answers anonymously and more honestly, with less fear of stigmatisation or embarrassment, placing the completed questionnaire in a plain brown envelope or collection box when they have finished.

Postal surveys are one of the most economic modes of administration. Simplicity must be a key feature both in the instructions and the questionnaire itself. The response rates tend to be lower; it is also possible that the forms will not be completed by those intended, and that there will be a relatively high percentage of spoilt or incomplete returns.

Internet surveys enable large numbers of people to be invited to participate very economically but gaining a high enough response rate to produce a sample that is representative is almost impossible. *Intranet* (internet communication within a single organisation) has the possibility of producing high response rates especially if senior managers endorse the survey and encourage responses from employees.

Method of sampling

Next you need to decide *who* will be the sample for your survey and also *where* you will carry it out. The first issue that needs to be addressed is the definition of your study population. In other words, which population of people is your research question about? And how specific can you be about the definition of this population? On the whole, the more clearly you specify your population the better, for example, people diagnosed with non-reactive depression. However, the study population can also become too specific, for example, left-handers diagnosed with non-reactive depression with alcoholic mothers and non-drinking fathers employed in the military services. In such cases, a sufficiently large sample will be difficult to locate.

The sample for any survey should represent the study population as closely as possible. In some cases, the sample can consist of the entire study population, for example, every pupil in a school, every student at a university, every patient in a hospital. More usually, however, the sample will be a random selection of a proportion of the members of a population, for example, every tenth person in a community, or every fourth patient admitted into a hospital. This method is called **simple random sampling (SRS)**. The exact proportion of the study population that must be recruited into the study must be calculated by estimating the necessary sample size (see below). For example, the sampling fraction might be $1/10$th, $1/5$th or $1/4$th, meaning that 10 per cent, 20 per cent or 25 per cent respectively of the study population would be selected using a completely random method.

A variation on SRS is **systematic sampling**. In this case the first person in the sampling frame is chosen at random and then every nth person on the list from there on, where n is the sample fraction being used.

The sampling method may require a number of strata or clusters, instead of simply a fixed proportion by random selection. For example, in a community household survey, random selection of addresses will always tend to yield a sample biased towards older people, because they are more likely to be at home when the researcher calls. In **stratified sampling** the population is divided into groups or 'strata' and the groups are randomly sampled, but in different proportions so that the overall sample sizes of the groups can be made equal, even though they are not equal in the population (for example, the 40–59, 60–79 and 80–99 age groups in a community sample, or men and women in a clinical sample). These groups will therefore be equally represented in the data. Another sampling technique is **multi-stage cluster sampling**. For example, in a stress survey in an organisation, with different numbers of staff in different branches, rather than randomly selecting people from all branches it could be more practicable to sample from branches that are considered typical of the organisation as a whole, for example, 3 of 6 small branches and 5 of 10 large branches. Each branch, or 'cluster', is seen as a microcosm of the organisation as a whole. In some cases there may be a hierarchy of levels within each of the clusters selected.

Other methods include non-random sampling of six kinds: convenience samples, most similar/dissimilar samples, typical case samples, critical case samples, snowball samples and quota samples. All have their advantages and disadvantages, and the decision about what method of sampling to employ is a crucial one as far as the interpretation of findings is concerned. For a helpful guide on sampling, see Henry (1990).

If the study population is the general population, the sample is normally drawn using a **sampling frame**, a file or register of population members, for example, an address or postal file kept by the national postal service, electoral register, population register or telephone directory. Health interview surveys are best conducted using a sample of addresses/ households, taking into account the fact that an address may contain more than one household, sometimes very many (for example, a hostel for homeless families, or a student hall of residence divided into flats). In such cases it is necessary to use a special selection procedure to generate the choice of household(s) within each address, for example, the middle household when households are listed alphabetically according to the surname of the oldest household member.

All such sampling methods are biased; in fact there is no perfect method of sampling because there will always be a category of people that any sampling method under-represents. In the case of the four methods above these will be the homeless, those not registered to vote, those who did not complete a population registration form (for example, because they are travellers or wish to evade surveillance), and those who do not rent a telephone connection (including a high percentage of people with low socio-economic status) respectively. Electoral registers include only people who are at least 18 years old and who have nationality of the country.

In any survey it is necessary to maximise the proportion of selected people who are recruited. If a large proportion of people refuse to participate, the sample will not represent the population, but will be biased in unknown ways. As a general principle, surveys that recruit at least 70 per cent of those invited to participate are considered representative. However, this is an obviously arbitrary rule and one should always aim for the maximum possible recruitment rate. If the study population is a category of patient, for example, all patients admitted into hospitals A, B and C with a diagnosis of non-reactive depression, it will be necessary to maximise the proportion of selected patients who are recruited into the study. For example, if the three hospitals admit 100, 150 and 200 such patients a year respectively (a total of 450), and if you estimate that you require a sample of 90 patients for your study, you would need to estimate the number of patients who will agree to participate following any exclusions after the completion of your explanation and consent procedures. You may also set inclusion/exclusion criteria that mean that some of the potential participants will be excluded from your study. Novice investigators are frequently optimistic in making such estimates and their studies can flounder badly as a result.

It can readily be seen that a conflict exists between the scientific need to recruit a high proportion of patients to obtain a representative sample on the one hand, and the ethical need to provide fully informed consent and allow people not to participate or to drop out on the other. Finally, you would want to ensure that a similar proportion of patients are recruited in each of the three hospitals in the above example to prevent a biasing of the results in some way because of differences between the three hospitals. Inevitably sample selection and recruitment involve a difficult balancing act. In the above example, let us assume that you estimate that 80 per cent of patients who are invited into the survey agree to participate. This is above the threshold value for a representative sample of 70 per cent. To obtain 90 altogether you need 20, 30 and 40 from hospitals A, B and C respectively, that is, one in five or 20 per cent of new admissions. If only 80 per cent of invitees agree, however, you will need to invite 25, 38 and 50 patients respectively from the 3 hospitals into your survey, in other words a total of 113 patients.

All methods of sampling require skill, judgement and, one has to admit, a degree of good luck if one is to obtain a truly representative sample of the study population. A low recruitment rate is the biggest bugbear of any survey study, because you often have no way of controlling or predicting it. Recruitment can be raised by offering incentives, for example, lottery tickets, shopping vouchers or cash payments. However, it may be impossible, or considered unethical, to offer such incentives. In some settings it may prove very difficult to obtain voluntary participation of a sufficient proportion of people to gain a satisfactory sample.

The sample size

The sample size is a key issue for any survey. The variability of scores obtained from the sampling diminishes as the sample size increases. So the bigger the sample, the more precise will be the estimates of the population scores, but the more the survey will cost. Larger samples mean spending more time and effort on data collection, leaving less time and effort for data coding and preparation, data analysis, report writing and dissemination.

The proportion P of the population Q to be selected is chosen on the basis of the required sample size N. N may be determined in two ways: (a) according to the efficiency or error rate (E_1) that your team or your sponsors are prepared to tolerate in your estimates of the true population values; (b) alternatively, if you are comparing two or more sub-samples (for example, women vs men), it is necessary to use power analysis (Cohen, 1988; Lipsey, 1989; see Chapter 10) by making an estimate of the effect size E_2 of a difference D between mean scores of two sub-samples in your survey. Thus the computation of the ideal sample size N is part of a chain of decisions that can be written as follows:

$$E_{(1 \text{ or } 2)} \longrightarrow N \longrightarrow P \longrightarrow Q$$

This chain of reasoning may be illustrated by a case in which we agree to accept an error rate E of 5 per cent of the true population percentage.

Suppose you want to know the percentage of people in the general population who live in fear of being mugged in their local neighbourhood. Your question might be worded as follows:

> Do you ever fear being mugged or robbed on the streets in your neighbourhood? YES/NO

Let us suppose that previous surveys suggest that the true figure for the proportion saying 'Yes' (p) is 70 per cent, and for the proportion saying 'No' (q), 30 per cent. Then the minimum sample size can be calculated using the formula:

$$3.84 \times \frac{p\ q}{n} < 25$$

Thus n can be computed as follows:

$$n > \frac{3.84}{25} \times 70 \times 30$$

$$n > 323$$

The figures 3.84 and 25 are threshold values to ensure that the sample size is sufficiently large to provide an error of no more that 5 per cent from the true value.This sample size of 323 will give an estimate of the true figure, which we have already assumed is in the vicinity of 70 per cent, within 5 per cent of the true population figure. However, the above formula assumes that the list of population members is so large that its size is not significantly reduced by randomly drawing the previous names from the list. All it really tells us is that there is a 95 per cent chance of obtaining an estimate that is within 5 per cent of the true population value. Sampling is a technical issue about which any survey team may well take specialist statistical advice. Useful guides on sampling and survey design have been published by Dixon and Carr-Hill (1989), de Vaus (1991), Fowler (1993), Henry (1990) and Moser and Kalton (1971). These source books also contain formulae and tables for calculating n for varying values of p and E in different circumstances that apply in specific cases.

ILLUSTRATION OF A SURVEY USING INTERVIEWS AND QUESTIONNAIRES

Context

The author was commissioned by the Director of Public Health of Blooms-bury and Islington Health Authority to carry out a health and lifestyle survey in 1990. The aims of the survey were to collect baseline health status information in the years 1990 and 2000 and to inform policy development within the district's purchaser and provider units, local authorities and associated organisations. The survey development team consisted of staff members from the departments of public health of the two participating health authorities and other staff with an interest in health needs assessment and service evaluation.

The objectives

The objectives were: (a) to assess health status, beliefs, attitudes to health-related issues, and current health service utilisation for a representative sample of the population of Bloomsbury and Islington, two inner city districts in London. (b) to identify specific issues of service provision and disease prevention for more detailed study; (c) to make comparisons with national and regional data on a number of key parameters, such as alcohol consumption, prevalence of smoking and health status; (d) to provide the basis for focused, qualitative, in-depth studies on sub-samples of the population (for example, the elderly, refugee groups and ethnic minorities) towards the development of more effective programmes.

Sampling and design

A multi-stage sampling method combining simple random sampling, systematic sampling and cluster sampling was used. The sample frame consisted of all identifiable addresses lying within each square kilometre within the district boundaries. A grid map was compiled which merged the Postcode Address File used by the Royal Mail with the co-ordinates from the National Ordnance Survey map of the Bloomsbury and Islington districts. The sample was generated by a computer program that selected 1 in every 25 residential addresses for each square kilometre on the district map. At each selected address the interviewer ascertained the number of households, selected one at random, then randomly selected one adult from within that household for the study. Thus, there were four stages of sampling as follows:

Stage 1: divide the district into 1 sq km squares.
Stage 2: create a list of addresses in each square and randomly select every 25th address in each square using the Postcode Address File as the sample frame (systematic sampling).
Stage 3: create a list of households living at each address and randomly select one household at the address (simple random sampling).
Stage 4: create a list of adults in the household and randomly select one adult at the address (simple random sampling).

The fieldwork was conducted between September 1990 and May 1991. This was a difficult period for household surveys because an unpopular Poll Tax had been introduced earlier that year and residents were wary of callers. Interviewers were postgraduate students in the social sciences who were trained and paid to carry out the work. It was agreed to aim at a sample of 1400, 0.75 per cent of the adult population. Of 2003 contacts made, 1411 people agreed to participate giving a response rate of 70.4 per cent, which, under the circumstances, was satisfactory.

The interview schedule

Major content areas were agreed by the survey development team, who designed and developed interview questions and searched for relevant questions from similar surveys conducted nationally or locally. Such questions were screened for their local relevance and where appropriate improved or amended. It was agreed that the total interview time should not exceed one hour on average. From a provisional set of 250 questions, a final set of 90 questions was agreed and piloted. A listing of the major areas covered by the interview is listed in Box 8.3.

Box 8.3   *Topics covered by the health and lifestyle survey (Marks & Chipperfield, 1993)*

Interview schedule:

Attitudes to and knowledge about health and healthy behaviour
Health status – acute and chronic illnesses
Weight and height
Diet
Exercise
Alcohol consumption
Smoking
Drug usage (prescription, over-the-counter, herbal, etc.)
The environment
Social support
Accidents
AIDS/HIV
Women-only section (breast, cervical screening, etc.)
Private medical insurance
Health service utilisation (including hospital, GP, screening, paramedical)
Use of complementary practitioners
Demographic questions (ethnic origin, language, religion, housing, employment, education, other people in the household)
GP satisfaction

Self-completion questionnaire: the Nottingham Health Profile

Measures of: lack of energy, social isolation, physical mobility, sleep disturbance, emotional reactions and pain

---

The questionnaire

In addition to the interview, it was decided to administer the Nottingham Health Profile or NHP (Hunt, McKenna & McEwan, 1989). This instrument was originally designed as a QoL measure for clinical samples rather than for the general population. However, the NHP covers 6 health areas of potential significance for the assessment of community health status using a relatively small number of questions (38) and it is therefore a convenient survey tool. Population norms exist for the NHP, it is short and simple and is one of only a few measures of perceived health then developed for use in Europe (Bowling, 1991). The authors of the NHP have published a review of how they developed the scale, evidence on reliability and validity, the NHP items, and a user's manual (Hunt, McEwan & McKenna, 1986; Hunt, McKenna & McEwan, 1989). The distributions of scores are highly skewed. However, there is evidence that, in spite of this skewing, the NHP is sensitive to change (Bowling, 1991). The instrument measures perceived health status by asking yes/no responses to 38 sets of statements of 6 health dimensions according to whether the statement applies to them 'in general at the present time'. Relative weights based on scaling are applied to the items giving scores of 0–100. Examples of NHP items are:

- I'm tired all of the time
- I have pain at night
- Things are getting me down
- I take tablets to help me sleep

Data preparation

Interview and NHP data were transferred to coding sheets and entered into a single data file for analysis using SPSS. A series of exploratory data analyses enabled all data to be 'cleaned' (by removal of recording and coding errors) and entered prior to the data analysis.

Results

In consultation with the health authority, which employed a research health psychologist to carry out the data analysis, the data were analysed and tabulated to create a large variety of findings that could be used by the health authority as baseline data on health status of the population, to inform policy and to enhance service provision in areas of greatest health need (Marks & Chipperfield, 1993). Further in-depth qualitative studies were also planned.

Of methodological interest was the strong relationship between reported health status and NHP scores. Interview question 33 asked:

> Over the last 12 months, would you say your health has on the whole been good, fairly good, or not good?

A highly significant relationship existed between answers to this single question and scores on the six NHP variables.

The strength and consistency of this association across all six of the NHP measures suggest that, for many practical purposes, the NHP can be substituted with a single-item self-reported health status measure of the kind quoted above (Bowling, 1991, 1995; Idler, 1992; Jenkinson, 1994; Marks & Chipperfield, 1993). The research team must ask themselves, do I need a whole questionnaire, or will a single question do? Any study must aim to make the most effective and efficient use of the resources available to meet the study objectives.

SUMMARY

Questionnaires, interviews and surveys are some of the most useful tools in the health care researcher's toolbox. We have described the essential aspects of designing and selecting questionnaires for clinical and health research. The reasons for using instruments that are reliable, valid and sensitive have been explained, and we introduced ways of measuring these. The essential features of carrying out a survey have also been described, and these have been illustrated by an example of a health and lifestyle survey carried out in a city district.

Box 8.4   *Designing and conducting a survey*

1 Clarify your research objectives, your research question: *what* do you want to know?
2 Decide *who* your study population is, *what* your sampling frame will be, and *where* you will carry out the survey.
3 Develop a sampling method that will give you the most *representative* and *random sample* in the most *efficient* manner.
4 Decide *how* to collect your data: by interview, questionnaire or a combination of the two.
5 Develop an interview schedule that is as *clear, simple, comprehensive* and as *brief* as possible.
6 Select, or design, a questionnaire that is *reliable, valid* and *responsive* (see Box 8.2).
7 Consult with all relevant *stakeholders* about your design, sampling method, instruments and procedures *before* you begin.
8 *Pilot* and fine-tune your procedures.
9 Prepare your data for analysis by using coding sheets, *exploratory plots* and *tables* to deal with errors and missing data.
10 *Focus* on your research question at all times – and keep an open mind!

RECOMMENDED READING

Bowling, A. (1991). *Measuring health*. Buckingham: Open University Press.
Bowling, A. (1995). *Measuring disease*. Buckingham: Open University Press.
De Vaus, D.A. (1991). *Surveys in social research* (3rd edn). London: Allen & Unwin.

REVISION QUESTIONS

1 What is meant by the: (a) sensitivity; (b) reliability; (c) validity of a questionnaire?
2 What are the advantages and disadvantages of open-ended vs closed-ended questions?
3 How many different methods for measuring reliability can you describe?
4 How many different methods for measuring validity can you describe?
5 What are the different options for obtaining survey data?
6 Describe four different methods of survey sampling.

9 ANALYSIS OF QUESTIONNAIRE AND SURVEY DATA

David Clark-Carter and David F. Marks

AIMS OF THIS CHAPTER

(i) To discuss factors to consider when choosing the most appropriate method of analysis.

(ii) To describe the basics of using SPSS.

(iii) To discuss missing data and their treatment.

(iv) To define and compare parametric and non-parametric statistics.

(v) To introduce the general linear model.

INTRODUCTION

Questionnaires and surveys are widely used tools in psychology and health care. Knowing how to analyse questionnaire and survey data is therefore essential for researchers in clinical and health psychology. Perhaps the first question any researcher will ask in carrying out a study is: *how will I analyse my data?* or, more plainly, *which test shall I use?* It is an unfortunate fact that the novice researcher tends to collect his or her data first and worry about the analysis afterwards. More seasoned researchers will anticipate the analysis while at the design stage. An ounce of foresight is worth a pound of hindsight when collecting and analysing data of any kind. In fact, with the wisdom of hindsight, many studies have to be redone in modified form or extended rather dramatically because the study lacked power or the data were not suitable in some other way.

A number of factors determine the type of analysis which can be conducted: the design of the research, the type of the data and, even when a choice has been made as to what appears to be the most appropriate statistical test, the data have to be checked to see whether they fulfil the requirements of the chosen test.

Designs

One basic property of research designs is how often each individual participant provides data. On the one hand, in the case of **within-participants**

designs (also known as cross-over, paired, repeated, dependent or related measures designs, or, if a measure is taken on a number of occasions, longitudinal designs) a given person contributes more than one data point. An example of a within-participants independent variable (IV) would be a survey of attitudes concerning the use of sunscreen before and after a campaign to raise awareness of skin cancer. On the other hand, if a comparison is being made between conditions and each person is measured only once then we have a **between-groups design** (also known as unpaired, independent or unrelated groups design). An example of this design would be a study making a comparison of patient satisfaction with their therapy among the different patients of two different hospitals. Finally, it is possible to have a combination of the two designs where one or more variables are within-participants, while others are between-groups, which would be a mixed design. An example of a mixed design would be a study comparing males and females (the between-groups IV being *gender*) to investigate their drinking behaviour before and after an alcohol awareness campaign (the within-participants IV being *stage in the campaign, before vs after*). The relative merits of these different designs are explored in Chapter 10.

Types of data

Since the era of Stevens (1951) psychologists have become aware of issues over the level of measurement of their data. This is an important issue but it has sometimes meant that they have ignored why it is important and have used it in a way not recognised by statisticians to choose which type of statistical test to employ. Stevens identified four levels of measurement – nominal, ordinal, interval and ratio. Nominal data are data that are fitted into categories, another name for it being 'categorical' data; for example, the variable of hair colour could have the categories ginger, auburn and blonde. Nominal data can be coded with numbers such as 0 = ginger, 1 = auburn and 2 = blonde but these numbers do not signify anything about the order of the categories, as shown by the fact that we could just as easily have coded auburn as 0, blonde as 1 and ginger as 2.

As the name suggests, ordinal data have an inherent order or rank. For example, in a queue to see a GP someone is first, someone second and so on. Here we could code the first person as 1, the second as 2, and so on and the numbers would tell us information about the order. However, if we wished to recode the data it would make little sense to use numbers that lost the order. Nonetheless, although the coding tells us the order, it doesn't tell us about the time spent waiting for each individual patient. Thus, unless the doctor sticks to an incredibly exact schedule we cannot say that the second person will be seen three minutes after the first and the third person will be seen three minutes after the second person and so on. This type of information is called an interval scale.

An example of interval data is a patient's temperature. We can say that a person A with a temperature of 39 °C has a temperature which is 1 °C above person B with a temperature of 38 °C and that B, in turn, has a temperature that is 1 °C above person C whose temperature is 37 °C. We can also correctly deduce that A has a temperature that is 2 °C above C. Thus we not only know that the first person has a temperature that is higher than the second and third persons, we can also say by how much it is higher. Clearly we could not make these inferences with ordinal data such as the order in a queue.

Data on a ratio scale can be seen as the most informative because they contain one more element than interval data, a true zero, representing the complete absence of the characteristic being measured. An example of a ratio measure could be pulse rate. The advantage of a ratio measure is that we can talk of the ratios of two measures on that scale. Thus someone with a pulse of 70 beats per minute has a pulse which is double that of someone with a pulse of 35. We cannot make the same statement with an interval measure. Assuming that you found someone with a temperature of 20 °C we would not be able to say that his or her temperature was half that of someone with a temperature of 40 °C. If you doubt this, note what happens to the figures when we convert from Celsius to Fahrenheit. The colder person now has a temperature of 68 °F while the hotter person has a temperature of 104 °F.

Having made these distinctions between the different levels of measurement, what is more important is what the data are being used to indicate. Thus the early French psychologist Binet was using a measure of reasoning ability but he treated it to indicate a nominal distinction – capable of being taught in a 'normal' school or not. Body temperature is often used more like an ordinal scale to indicate dangerously low, low, in the normal range, high, dangerously high. Similarly income, which can be seen as a ratio measure, is more likely to be used as an ordinal scale. Clearly a £1000 raise to someone with an income in the millions has a very different value compared to someone on £10,000 a year. Accordingly, we need to think of the use to which we are putting a measure rather than its strict surface properties.

Before introducing particular forms of analysis, it is helpful to discuss the statistical package SPSS.

USING SPSS

Fortunately the days of doing statistics by hand are gone. We now have powerful statistical packages available for our PCs and Macs. One of the most widely used by psychologists is a suite of computer programs called the **Statistical Package for Social Sciences** or SPSS. The full version of the name explains why the output from the package may include information that psychologists don't normally use but which may be of use to econometricians or other social scientists.

The current versions of SPSS present the researcher with two initial windows in which to work: a *Data* window and a *Variable* window. The latter is used for giving details about the variables in the data. Thus here, among other things, the variable is given a name, a label (its fuller name used in output), how missing values are to be coded and, for categorical data, what the categories are and by what numbers they will be coded. The initial variable name is restricted in a number of ways: it can only be of eight characters, it can't contain certain characters, such as commas, and it cannot have spaces in it. Hence, it may be desirable to give it a fuller name (or label) which will make clearer in tables and the like to what it refers. In the Variable window it is also possible to tell SPSS what code is going to be used when a score for a participant on a given variable is missing. A number that is outside the range of possible values for the variable is chosen for this purpose. Thus, if the variable were age then 999 could be used. However, if the variable were salary per month then you would have to use a different figure that was beyond the possible range (999,999 perhaps, unless Bill Gates is in your sample!).

In the Data window you enter the values for each person on each of the variables. Like many statistical packages, SPSS assumes that every data point in the same row comes from the same person, or, what in SPSS jargon is called a 'case'. Therefore, in a between-groups design, for each IV, there will have to be a category column that shows each person's group (A, B, C, etc.). We recommend entering data in their original form. By this we mean, rather than forming totals for a scale, enter all of the scores on each of the questions that make up the scale, even if the scoring has to be reversed. Within SPSS, data can be recoded, means for a number of columns computed, or transformations made automatically.

Once the data are ready for analysis, the most frequently used menus will be *Analyze*, for both descriptive statistics – including the creation of tables – and inferential statistics, and *Graphs* for visual exploration and reporting of the data.

Whenever you ask for an analysis or a graph, a new window will open – the *Output* window. The menus that accompany the three windows are not all the same. Therefore, you may need to change to a different window in order to be able to gain access to certain menus.

As items are selected from menus to set up, for example, an analysis, SPSS writes the equivalent of a computer program. There are some aspects of analyses, for example particular options, which are not available via the menus. However, in SPSS's syntax language it is possible to use such options. If, instead of clicking on OK to get SPSS to carry out the set of commands that you have selected via the menus, you click on *Paste* then a *Syntax* window will be created. By entering the Syntax window it is possible to add to the program directly and so access other options. The *Help* menu can be used to find out what options are available with particular analyses. Once a Syntax window has been created it is possible to obtain the required analysis either by running the entire contents of the window or by selecting desired bits of it – as long as they form a meaningful program for SPSS. Some analyses are only available via creating a

Syntax window. In addition, syntax commands can be used to perform analyses that are from earlier versions of SPSS but are no longer available via menus.

Data exploration

Before applying any inferential tests to data it is important that they are explored descriptively. This has a number of advantages: it can give us a feel for the data, it can show us whether we have made mistakes in entering the data into the computer and it can tell us whether the data comply with the assumptions of the inferential test which we had originally chosen.

There are two basic forms of description that we can use – numerical and graphical. Each is important and would be useful to include in a report of research. However, for space reasons, journals often specify that you can use one or the other but not both. Numerical summaries of the data provide exact values but leave the reader having to do a lot of work in order to get a feel for what is going on. The most informative way of displaying a set of scores is by making a graphical display of the entire distribution (see below).

Numerical descriptive statistics   These tend to be separated into measures of central tendency such as the mean, the median and the mode, and measures of spread or dispersion such as the range, inter-quartile range, standard deviation and variance.

At this level we are going to assume that you are aware of how most of these are calculated and that anyway you are likely to be using a computer to do the calculations. Instead we will look at some possible pit-falls with their use and interpretation. Firstly, the mode can sometimes be a particularly useless measure, for example, if we are looking at people's salaries and, in a sample of 100 people whose annual salaries range from £6,000 to £100,000, all but two people (with salaries of £100,000) have different salaries from each other, then the mode will be £100,000, which is hardly a central or typical figure. It may also be the case that there is no mode because everyone has a different salary. In both cases it would be better to put the salaries into ranges and find the modal range. Secondly, the mean can misrepresent the data. One of the authors attended a course (not run by psychologists) that involved groups discussing and then rating various concepts on five-point scales. For reasons which weren't made clear, the means were taken of the ratings of the different groups. The groups' ratings were diametrically opposed on most things, which meant that the means suggested total agreement at three for most issues. This demonstrates the need for a measure of spread to accompany a measure of central tendency as it can show how diverse the scores were. Finally, there is a danger, having assigned numbers to nominal data, of treating the numbers in the same way as for other data. Thus it is possible to say that the mean smoking status was 1.45 because non-smoker has been coded as 1 and smoker coded as 2. Nominal data should only be used to produce summaries such as frequencies – for example, out of a sample of 110 people, 60 were non-smokers and 50 were smokers – or, as percentages – for example, 54.54 per cent were non-smokers and 45.45 per cent were smokers.

A distinction, which is made by statisticians, and one that we will return to later, is between a statistic and a **parameter**. In this context a parameter is the equivalent of a summary statistic such as the mean but for the whole population from which your sample has come. Typically statisticians have denoted parameters by letters from the Greek alphabet, for example while M denotes the mean in a sample (the statistic), μ (mu) denotes the mean for the population (the parameter).

Confidence intervals   One useful statistic, which hasn't been used as much by psychologists as it could be, is the **confidence interval**. However, its use is being strongly encouraged by the APA (American Psychological Association, 2001a) and has been a standard practice in journals such as the *British Medical Journal* for many years. It provides a range of possible values that the parameter is likely to have. Thus if we know the mean cholesterol level in a given sample, the confidence interval would tell us within what limits the cholesterol level is likely to be for the population from which the sample was taken. Confidence intervals are expressed as being at a particular percentage of confidence. Thus the typical confidence interval is at the 95 per cent confidence level. What this means is that if we were repeatedly to take a sample of the same size from the same population and then calculate the mean for that sample and the confidence interval for the mean in the population, then on 95 per cent of occasions the confidence interval would contain the value of the mean in the population. More ways in which the confidence interval can be useful will be shown below.

Odds ratios   Another statistic which is underused by psychologists but which is widely used by the medical profession (and also in gambling!) is the **odds ratio (OR)** (see Chapter 10). To get to the odds ratio we have to go via probability and then **odds**. Marks and Sykes (2002) compared the effectiveness of a standard government campaign to stop smoking (controls) against a cognitive behaviour therapy programme tailored for smokers (CBT). A follow-up survey of smoking behaviour was conducted 12-months after the treatment. The output from *Crosstabs* in SPSS looks like this (Table 9.1).

We can see that 23 out of the 116 CBT group had ceased to smoke while 93 continued to smoke. Thus, in the CBT group, the probability of being a non-smoker was $^{23}/_{116}$ or 0.198 and the probability of continuing to be a smoker was $^{93}/_{116}$ or 0.802. The odds, in the CBT group, of being a non-smoker relative to being a smoker were $^{23}/_{93} = 0.247$. Using the same reasoning, the odds, for controls, of being a non-smoker relative to being a smoker were $^{6}/_{98} = 0.061$. The odds ratio of the likelihood of being a non-smoker for those treated via CBT versus that for the controls is the odds for

Table 9.1   *Smoking * group crosstabulation*

| | | Group | | |
		CBT	controls	Total
Smoking	quit	23	6	29
	continue	93	98	191
Total		116	104	220

the CBT condition divided by the odds for controls: 4.039. Thus CBT was four times more effective than the standard intervention.

An odds ratio of 1 would show that there is no difference in the odds for the two groups; greater than 1 shows that those in the CBT are more likely than controls to quit smoking and less than 1 would have shown that controls were more likely to cease smoking than those in the CBT group. It is possible to calculate a 95 per cent confidence interval for an odds ratio (obtainable in SPSS), which for the ratio of odds for CBT versus controls is between 1.57 and 10.36. As the 95 per cent confidence interval does not cross 1.00, this suggests that, in the population of smokers, there would be a real difference in the ratio of odds for quitting and continuing to smoke among those treated by CBT and controls. Thus we see that the confidence interval puts the result into context.

Graphical descriptive statistics

Tukey and others (Cleveland, 1985; Tukey, 1977) have long argued for the benefits of graphical exploration of data. This has recently been emphasised by the APA's task force (Wilkinson, 1999). There are at least two benefits of this approach which are not provided by tables of summary statistics. They can show peculiarities in the data and they can present an easily compre-hended impression of what is going on in the data. On the one hand, a frequency plot (or histogram) of the data for a single level of an IV can show possible outliers or a skewed distribution. On the other hand, a graph that shows the mean or median of each level of an IV, complete with a measure of spread for each level, can encapsulate results for the study in a way that a table of figures cannot.

Nonetheless, we have to be aware of the dangers of graphical presen-tation. One danger is that the person trying to understand what the picture is trying to tell them is unfamiliar with the conventions of that type of picture. This is a problem that is frequently seen in conference presen-tations. The person presenting the data has devised his or her own way of presenting the data or is using conventions that are little known to the audience. However, she or he fails to spend a reasonable amount of time talking the audience through what the results show.

A second danger is of a false impression being created by the picture. If the axis of the graph that is denoting the values on the dependent variable

(DV) only shows a range of scores close to those found in the study then a small difference can appear much larger than it really is. Computer programs such as SPSS will automatically select such a foreshortened range. However, it is possible to countermand this and extend the range. Imagine that we are interested in seeing whether or not an important factor which controls craving among cigarette smokers who wear a patch is the presence of the patch not the fact of its containing nicotine. We give one group a placebo patch and one an active patch. After a period we get participants to rate their craving for tobacco. Figure 9.1 shows an error bar graph, with standard deviations, which suggests that the two groups have a markedly different mean.

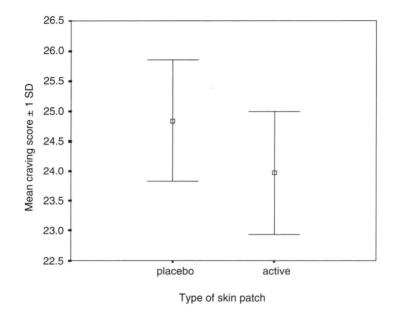

Figure 9.1   *An error bar graph comparing craving scores for placebo vs nicotine patches*

However, the impression is exaggerated by the way that SPSS has truncated the craving scale so that it just encompasses the range of the data that we are displaying. If we alter the scale to include zero we find a somewhat different picture (Figure 9.2).

There are three other useful exploratory graphical displays that are less well-known than the histogram. Firstly, there are **box-and-whisker plots**, which look at medians and other percentiles within the data and allow simpler comparisons between distributions. Secondly, the **stem-and-leaf plot** can give actual data values on the equivalent of a histogram, again providing more specific information than a histogram. Finally, the **normal quartile-quartile plot** can be more useful than the histogram in trying to

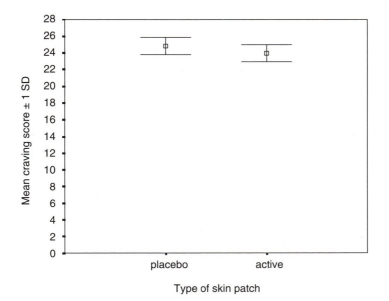

Figure 9.2   *An error bar graph comparing craving scores for placebo vs nicotine patches with zero included in the craving axis*

judge whether data are normally distributed when looking at a small number of data points.

The box-and-whisker plot   Imagine that we have taken a measure of depression from elderly people in the community and in care homes. The following box-and-whisker plot, in Figure 9.3, which was created in SPSS, tells us a number of things about the two distributions.

The rectangular boxes tell us where the middle 50 per cent of scores were (the inter-quartile range), from the score 25 per cent from the bottom (the 25th percentile) to the score 25 per cent from the top (the 75th percentile). The thick line within the box shows where the 50th percentile (the median) was. From these we can see that the scores from those in care homes are more widely spread and that the median lies more centrally in the community sample, thus suggesting less skewed data in that group. The bars that are perpendicular to the boxes (the whiskers) extend 1.5 times the height of the box above and below the box, where possible. As you can see the lower whisker in the care home sample cannot extend beyond zero as that is the lowest score on the scale. Specific cases have been highlighted by the computer. Those whose case numbers are shown next to circles lie between the end of the whisker and another whisker length. They are described as **outliers**. Those whose case numbers are next to asterisks are beyond two whiskers length from the edge of the box and are described as **extreme cases**.

In certain situations it may be safe to omit a small number of extreme cases from the analysis, but this decision should not be taken lightly, and it

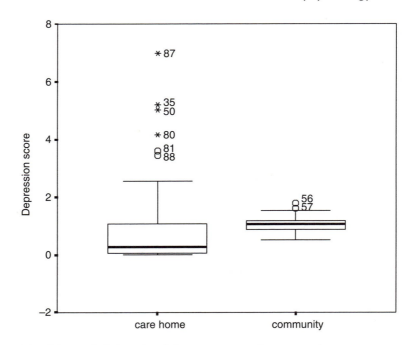

Figure 9.3   A box-and-whisker plot of depression scores for two samples

is a fact that must be recorded in your report of the results. The safest tactic is to run the analysis with and without the extreme cases present to investigate the influence that omitting these scores has on the final outcome.

Stem and leaf plots   The following plot, in Table 9.2, has been obtained via SPSS for the data from people in care homes.

Table 9.2   Care home stem-and-leaf plot

Frequency	Stem-and-leaf
44.00	0.00000000000000000000000000000000000011111111111
11.00	0.22222223333
7.00	0.4444555
8.00	0.66677777
3.00	0.999
5.00	1.00011
6.00	1.222223
3.00	1.445
1.00	1.6
1.00	1.9
0.00	2.00
3.00	2.233
2.00	2.45
6.00 extremes	(>=3.4)

The first column tells the reader how many cases were in a particular range of scores. Thus, 44 people gave scores in the range 0 to 0.1. In this example the stem is telling us the value before any decimal place, while the figures in the leaf provide the first decimal place of a given score. Thus we can see that there were three people with scores in the range 2.2 to 2.3, with one person scoring 2.2 and two people scoring 2.3. In this plot, extremes encompasses those which are more than one-and-a-half times the inter-quartile range above and below the inter-quartile range. The plot confirms the impression given by the box-plot that the data are heavily skewed (in this case a positive **skew**).

Normal quartile-quartile plots   This plot is one of a family in which the data points are plotted against the values that they would have if they conformed to a particular distribution, in this case the normal distribution (Figure 9.4). If the data do conform to the assumed distribution then they will lie on or close to the line that is superimposed on the graph. Once again the data from the people in the care home can be seen as not conforming to a normal distribution.

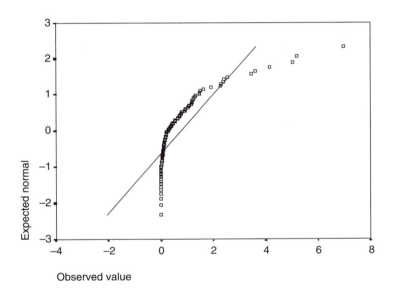

Figure 9.4   *A normal quartile-quartile plot of the depression scores of the care home sample*

On the other hand, the data from those in the community are much closer to being normally distributed (Figure 9.5).

Another way in which we need to explore data is to see the nature of any cases for which we do not have a complete set of data.

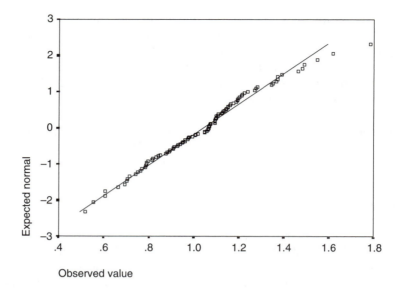

Figure 9.5 *A normal quartile-quartile plot of the depression scores of the community sample*

MISSING DATA AND THEIR TREATMENT

With questionnaires we often come across the problem that some participants haven't supplied us with data for some questions. The likelihood of having missing data is further increased if we have a longitudinal study because we may simply not be able to trace people on subsequent occasions. This leaves us with a dilemma. On the one hand, we want to include as many participants as possible to maintain as much statistical power as possible (see Chapter 10). However, analysing data that contain missing values can produce its own problems. The first thing we should do is check that there is not something about the participants for whom we have incomplete data that distinguishes them from those for whom we have complete data. For, if this were the case and we simply dropped those without complete data from further analysis we would be producing a biased sample. SPSS provides a facility called Missing Values Analysis (MVA) that allows the comparison of those for whom we do not have full data with the rest of the sample. Thus we might find that those with missing data were older than those with full data.

There is no simple solution as to how to deal with missing data because it depends on the pattern of missing data and the sample size included in your study. The most straightforward situation is where those with missing values do not differ from the others and there is a reasonably sized sample. In this situation cases with missing values can be dropped from the analysis. Rather than delete the cases from the database, the computer can be told to ignore them from a given analysis; in SPSS this is called **listwise deletion**, meaning that if just one data point is missing for a given person from one of the variables to be included in the analysis then that person will not be included in an analysis which entails that particular variable. Alternative ways of dealing with missing data have their own problems. SPSS also allows you to do what is called **pairwise deletion** in such analyses as correlation. The effect of this option is to take a person's data out of any analysis for which he or she has missing data on either variable in the pair. Thus, in looking at the correlations between a number of variables, the correlations would be based on slightly different samples depending on who is missing data from which variable.

The methods we have described so far for dealing with missing data have involved dropping participants from some or all of the analysis. However, there is another approach: to substitute the missing data in some way. The approach that you can choose in SPSS is to replace the missing data with the mean for the variable. This has the advantage of not losing participants from the analysis but it has the disadvantage of homogenising the scores on that variable by placing people artificially at the mathematical centre of the distribution. It is not a good idea to use this method if more than a small proportion, say 1 to 5 per cent, of data are missing.

Once the data have been explored, it is possible to decide whether the test that was originally chosen is appropriate. This requires further checking of the data and especially the shape of the data's distribution.

PARAMETRIC AND NON-PARAMETRIC STATISTICS

Statistical tests are frequently separated into two types – **parametric tests** and **non-parametric tests**. The former, which includes the t-test, assume among other things that the population from which the data have come has a **normal distribution**. The latter, sometimes also called **distribution-free tests**, do not make such assumptions. However, they do have their own assumptions about the nature of the data.

One mantra that has guided some psychologists is the **robustness** of parametric tests. Robustness means that the tests will cope with violations of their assumptions and still generate a probability that is accurate. This is only true to a certain extent. To illustrate the point let us start with a particular test – the between-groups t-test. This test is attempting to see whether the means of two conditions differ. The ability to detect such a difference will be thrown by differences in the shape of the distribution of the two conditions and the amount of variability that there is within each of the distributions. Two of the assumptions of the test are that both sets of scores (in the population) are normally distributed and that the variances of the two sets of scores are the same (in the population); this latter is usually referred to as **homogeneity of variance**.

Whether the test is robust to violations of these assumptions depends on a number of factors: firstly, the number of assumptions which are violated – if more than one assumption is violated then the test will be less robust; secondly, the sample size – the smaller the sample size, the less robust the test; thirdly, the degree of the violation of the assumption – the greater the skew, particularly if the distributions are different for the two sets of data, the less robust the test; the greater the disparity in variances between the two sets of data, the less robust the test. In addition, the greater the difference in sample size for the two groups the less robust the test. If we ignore the strong form of the mantra about robustness, as we have to for the results of our statistical analysis to make any sense, then we need some guidelines; fortunately they exist. The first thing we should do is to try to have balanced designs, in other words, have equal numbers of participants in each condition. Secondly, thanks to a mathematical phenomenon called the central limit theorem, if we have at least 40 participants in the study then the data should be robust to the problem of skew (as long as the distributions aren't extremely skewed or skewed in opposite directions and as long as skew is the only problem).

Some measures have been devised to evaluate skew and heterogeneity of variance (lack of homogeneity of variance). The problem is that those that provide a probability are themselves subject to the same laws of statistical power as any other test (see Chapter 10). Accordingly, with a small sample they can be under sensitive and with a large sample they can be over sensitive. In reality, the most direct method of checking the shape of a distribution is by simple visual inspection. For heterogeneity of variance, opinions vary as to how robust tests are. Nonetheless, a common piece of advice is that, as long as sample sizes are the same and the distributions are approximately normal, then as long as the larger variance is no greater than four times the smaller variance then the data have sufficient homogeneity of variance. However, if the sample sizes are unequal then the larger variance should be no greater than two times the smaller variance.

If the assumptions of a test are being violated then there are possible ways around the problem. One solution is that data can be transformed in such a way that skew can be improved. Advice exists as to which transformations can be tried for which pattern of skew (see Clark-Carter, 1997a; Howell, 2002; Tabachnick & Fidell, 2001). Some transformations can also help to solve heterogeneity of variance.

In the case of the between-groups t-test, SPSS automatically provides two versions of the test: one assuming equal variances (the standard t-test) and one not assuming equal variances (sometimes known as Welch's t). If the data do not have sufficient homogeneity of variance then report the results of Welch's t and make clear that this is what you are doing. In the case of ANOVA (see below), although there is an equivalent F-test of Welch's t for non-homogeneous data, SPSS, below version 11, does not calculate this. See Clark-Carter (1997a), Howell (2002) or Myers and Well (1991) for details of how to calculate Welch's F.

Non-parametric tests, such as the Mann-Whitney U test (an equivalent of the between-groups t-test), have fewer restrictions on their use than their parametric equivalents. However, it is a myth that they have no assumptions. The Mann-Whitney U test can be affected by severe skew and large differences in variances between the groups.

In addition to issues over robustness, a statement that is frequently made about the relative merits of parametric and non-parametric tests is that the former have more statistical power (see Chapter 10). However, this is only true under certain circumstances: if the data fulfil all the assumptions of a parametric test then a parametric test *will* have more power than its non-parametric equivalent. If the data do not fulfil the requirements of the parametric test then the non-parametric test may have *more* statistical power.

One assumption which most statistical tests make, whether they be parametric or non-parametric, is that data from participants from the same level of the independent variable will be independent; that is, that they will not be influenced by each other. If this assumption is violated it can have a severe effect on the statistical conclusions which can be drawn. Thus, if you conduct a focus group and the participants rate something they have been discussing, for example, an aspect of health policy, then the data from the members of the group will not be independent. One way around this problem is to treat the mean for a given group as the data to be analysed rather than each individual member's data.

As the generations of SPSS have developed there has been a tendency to place a number of tests under the general heading of the general linear model.

THE GENERAL LINEAR MODEL

Tests that fall into this category include Analysis of Variance (ANOVA), Analysis of Covariance (ANCOVA) and their multivariate counterparts Multivariate Analysis of Variance (MANOVA) and Multivariate Analysis of Covariance (MANCOVA). Although SPSS does not so far include it in the menu for the general linear model, regression (multiple and simple) is also a member of the same family.

The basic principle of the **general linear model (GLM)** is that a person's score on the DV is formed by a combination of a constant, a value that accounts for the level/score which he or she had on the IV(s) and a measure of how that person differs from others treated in the same way (individual differences or error). The term 'linear' is used to denote the way in which the elements in the equation are combined.

Imagine that a study has investigated the efficacy of an approach to reducing smoking – CBT. The study also includes a control group. Thus the study has one IV – type of treatment – with two levels. The DV would be the number of cigarettes that a person smoked after a fixed period of treatment. The general linear model can be used to describe someone's score within a one-way between-groups ANOVA:

Predicted number of cigarettes
= a constant + a coefficient × code for condition participant was in   *(Eqn 1)*

Clearly the better the model the more accurately it will predict the number of cigarettes a person will smoke and the smaller will be the difference between the predicted and actual number of cigarettes smoked. This difference is the error (sometimes called the residual).

If we call the number of cigarettes y, the constant b_0, the coefficient b_1 and the code for the condition the participant was in x, then equation 1 can be expressed as:

$$y = b_0 + b_1 \times x$$ *(Eqn 1a)*

This may be recognised as the equation for a straight line (or as an equation relabelled so that b_0 is c and b_1 is m so the equation becomes y = c + mx or even y = mx + c).

How well parts of the model fit the data is usually assessed statistically by a ratio of an estimate of the variance attributable to an IV and the variance attributable to individual differences (error or residual). This ratio is the F-ratio.

You may have noticed that equation 1a is the same as would be seen in a simple regression. An extension of that equation would denote the results of a multiple regression, an ANOVA with more than two levels or a multi-factorial ANOVA. The similarity between the way in which an ANOVA and a regression can be described further reflects the fact that they are both examples of the GLM. Note that the output you get from a statistical package for a regression will include a summary table for the analysis of the variances involved, including an F-ratio. Another similarity between regression and ANOVA is the **effect size** that can be derived from each (see Chapter 10). In ANOVA we have η^2 (eta-squared), while in regression we have R^2. Both are describing the proportion of variance in the DV that is explicable in terms of the IV(s) in the model. The full extent of the statistical techniques that are subsumed under the GLM can be found in Tabachnick and Fidell (2001). A useful and more detailed treatment of data analysis using SPSS can be found in Foster (2001) or Kinnear and Gray (2000).

Follow-up analysis to GLM

There are a number of designs where an initial analysis merely answers the question whether conditions differ significantly. If that initial analysis is significant then further analysis has to be conducted to identify, more precisely, the source of that significant result. We will discuss three such designs: the first situation is when a variable has more than two levels; for example imagine that researchers have compared groups which have been given three therapies against arachnophobia – relaxation, flooding and systematic desensitisation – and a control group. The measure they take is skin conductance when presented with a model of a spider on a table. A second situation is when there is more than one IV with levels which are categorical; for example in an investigation of depression in those with chronic pain, one IV is type of pain – with the two levels chronic pelvic pain (CPP) or chronic backache – the other IV is whether the participants have a diagnosis for the pain – with the two levels diagnosis and no diagnosis. The third situation is when there is more than one DV; for example, if in the first design in addition to measuring skin conductance we measured heart rate and took self-report measures of stress and arousal.

The first design would normally be analysed using one-way ANOVA; one-way because there is only one IV. Here the null hypothesis which is being tested is that the means for all the levels of the IV are the same. Statistical significance merely suggests that they are not all the same but it does not tell us which particular levels are statistically different. More specific comparisons between the different conditions need to be made to find out which groups differ significantly.

Comparisons

Comparisons (also known as **contrasts**) can take a variety of forms. However, they all share one feature, which is that if there is more than one of them in the set (or family) then there is an increased danger of making a **Type I error** (wrongly rejecting a null hypothesis) unless an adjustment is made to the alpha level to compensate. The degree to which alpha has to be adjusted depends most critically on the number of contrasts that are going to be conducted; the more that are conducted the greater the adjustment. The simplest adjustment is the **Bonferroni adjustment**, which involves dividing alpha by the number of contrasts to be conducted.

Paired contrasts

An example of a paired contrast would be an analysis that compared just the relaxation and the control groups. When there are three levels of the IV, there are three possible paired contrasts that could be conducted. As the number of levels of an IV grows so does the number of contrasts, but not in a linear fashion: with four levels there are six possible paired contrasts, with five levels there are ten. Clearly the more contrasts you do then the stricter the criterion you are setting yourself for achieving significance in each contrast. With three contrasts, using the Bonferroni adjustment, the alpha level becomes 0.017, with six contrasts it becomes 0.0083. Therefore, ideally, you want to keep the number of contrasts to a minimum. This can be done by planning the contrasts you are going to do before you collect the data. Why *before* the data are collected? Because as soon as they are collected you can get an impression of which contrasts might produce the biggest difference and that is like looking at all the possible contrasts and picking the ones which are most likely to be statistically significant.

Planned and unplanned contrasts

If you choose the specific contrasts in advance of conducting the study then they are described as planned or *a priori* contrasts. If you carry out all the possible ones then they are called unplanned, post hoc or even *a posteriori*. If you are planning your contrasts and you plan to do all the possible ones, then you have gained nothing, as the adjustment will have to be as great as if they were unplanned.

Bonferroni adjustment can be quite conservative when there are more than three levels of the IV. Statisticians have devised a number of different methods of adjusting the alpha level, which depend on the type of contrasts that are being conducted; SPSS offers a bewildering array of them. Choosing the best contrast test for each particular analysis is beyond the scope of this book; interested readers are recommended to look at Howell (2002) or Clark-Carter (1997a).

Multi-way ANOVA

We have seen above that the more levels of an IV there are in a design, the more follow-up analyses there will need to be to explore a significant result. The same situation holds for multi-way ANOVAs. Every extra IV in the design brings more potential results to be explored. In a design, such as the one described earlier, involving two IVs, and using a two-way ANOVA, there will be three null hypotheses tested: two for main effects and one for the **interaction**. The first null hypothesis is that the mean depression score of people with CPP does not differ from that of participants with chronic backache. This ignores the presence of the second IV (whether or not they had been given a definite diagnosis). The second null hypothesis tested is that those with a diagnosis will have the same mean depression score as those without a diagnosis (regardless of the type of pain they are suffering).

The final null hypothesis relating to the interaction is more complicated; it states that once the two possible main effects have been controlled for, there are no additional differences between groups that can be attributed to an interaction between the two IVs. An example of an interaction would be if people with CPP and no diagnosis were more depressed than those with CPP who had a diagnosis, whereas for the people with backache there was no difference in depression between those with and without a diagnosis. This interaction is shown in Figure 9.6.

Thus, with two IVs there are three effects that are being tested. With three IVs there are seven effects: three main effects, three two-way interactions and one three-way interaction. Hence it can be seen that introducing an extra IV into a design adds complexity to the interpretation of the results.

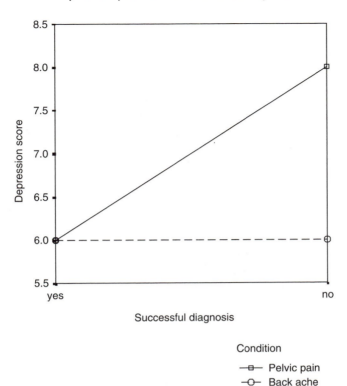

Figure 9.6   *Illustrating the interaction between successful diagnosis and type of diagnosis, chronic pelvic pain vs back ache*

The source of any significant effect will have to be found. If an interaction is found to be significant, then it can be explored using simple effects.

Simple effects

To give an example of **simple effects**, imagine that we have got a significant interaction between type of chronic pain and diagnosis group. We can analyse the data in two possible ways and the choice we make depends on our perspective on the research. We could consider each chronic pain group in turn and test whether a significant difference existed between those who had a diagnosis and those who didn't; each analysis would be testing a simple effect. Alternatively our simple effects could be tested by comparing depression levels, among those who had a diagnosis, between those with CPP and those with backache followed by testing whether, for those without a diagnosis, there was a difference between those with CPP and those with backache. Whichever route we decide to take, we have to adjust the alpha level to take account of the number of times (2) the analysis is being performed. In these two cases alpha would become 0.025.

MANOVA

The initial test conducted by MANOVA is of a very general null hypothesis: that the means for the levels of the IV do not differ on any of the DVs or any interaction between them. Thus, if the result is significant, there are two sets of follow-up analyses that may need to be conducted: to ascertain which levels of the IV differ and on which DVs they differ. There are a number of different follow-up analyses that have been devised to answer these questions but we will describe only two as they should be adequate for most situations; frequently they may need to be used in combination. One route is to run the equivalent of paired contrasts but across all the DVs: a series of MANOVAs but with only two levels of the IV each time. If any contrast is significant, then it needs to be followed up with a set of univariate contrasts: one for each DV. Thus, if the systematic desensitisation group of arachnophobics differs significantly from the control group in the multivariate contrast then these two groups will have to be compared for each of skin conductance, heart rate, stress and arousal in univariate contrasts.

The alternative route is to conduct a series of univariate ANOVAs (one for each DV) across the levels of the IV and then, if any of them is significant, follow it up with univariate contrasts.

One factor that guides one's choice of route is the amount of adjustment that it is necessary to make to alpha. In the above example there is one IV with four levels and there are four DVs. If unplanned multivariate contrasts are conducted, then there will be six of them and alpha will have to be adjusted to 0.0083. If univariate ANOVAs are conducted, then there will be four of them and so alpha will become 0.0125.

Box 9.1   *Exploring, cleaning and analysing quantitative data*

- Enter the data into SPSS ensuring that the variables are correctly named and the levels are correctly defined.
- If the data are continuous, check the data for outliers and extreme cases.
- Look for missing data and decide a method for dealing with them.
- Check the shape of the distribution: if normal use a parametric test; if non-normal, either transform the data or use a non-parametric test.
- Check the homogeneity of variance. If this is seriously lacking, then transform the data to make them more equivalent, use Welch's version of the test or use a non-parametric test.
- If you looking for a relationship between variables, then calculate correlation or regression.
- If you are looking for a difference between means use a t-test (two levels), ANOVA (more than two levels or more than one IV), ANCOVA (ANOVA but with one or more covariates), or MANOVA (multiple DVs).

SUMMARY

In this chapter we have introduced the techniques employed in the analysis of questionnaire and survey data from the viewpoint of a person using SPSS. While other packages are available, SPSS is a very commonly used and helpful suite of programs for clinical and health psychology researchers. We have described some of the principles that influence the type of analysis to be used, and also the preparatory work that needs to be carried out to explore, clean and prepare data prior to the analysis, including the problem of missing data. We have described some of the checks that are necessary to ensure that the assumptions of the statistical analysis are not contravened by the properties of the data. Finally, we have described the properties of the general linear model as an umbrella for analyses of variance, covariance, and regression, and shown how the initial analysis may need to be followed up in order to answer specific research questions.

RECOMMENDED READING

Clark-Carter, D. (1997). *Doing quantitative psychological research: from design to report.* Hove: Psychology Press.

REVISION QUESTIONS

1 What is meant by 'levels of measurement'? List four.
2 Why do we need to explore data before we analyse it? What are we looking for?
3 Describe three graphical methods of data exploration in SPSS.
4 What options does SPSS offer for the problem of missing data?
5 What is the general linear model?
6 What is a 'simple effect' and what is an 'interaction'? Draw a diagram to illustrate the difference.
7 If we have several dependent variables, how should we decide whether to carry out a series of ANOVAs or a single MANOVA?

---

10 INTERVENTION STUDIES: DESIGN AND ANALYSIS

David Clark-Carter and David F. Marks

AIMS OF THIS CHAPTER

(i) To explain the relative merits of different research designs for experimental and quasi-experimental studies that are typically used to evaluate interventions.

(ii) To describe hypothesis testing and other approaches to the analysis of quantitative data.

(iii) To describe the concept of the power of a test and its implications for research design.

(iv) To outline some general principles that guide the analysis and reporting of research.

INTRODUCTION

An important part of clinical and health psychology is the provision of interventions to improve the health and wellbeing of clients or patients. The empirical demonstration that such interventions are effective and cost-effective is therefore of key importance. Normally such evaluations compare a new therapy or treatment (T_N) with an older, more standard type of care (T_O). For example, is a new therapy for phobias more effective than a relaxation procedure? Or, is a new treatment for lower back pain more effective than rest and analgesics? The treatment conditions that are administered in an evaluation study are equivalent to the levels of an independent variable (IV) in a traditional experiment. The measure that we take of the participants' responses to a therapy (the dependent variable (DV) in a traditional experiment) is referred to as the **outcome measure**. The **efficacy** of a new therapy is evaluated by a trial carried out under ideal conditions with very tight controls of variables using an experimental design. It is the extent to which an intervention produces a beneficial outcome under ideally controlled circumstances. Efficacy is a measure of whether an intervention *can* work. **Effectiveness**, on the other hand, is evaluated by a trial carried out in a clinical setting and measures the extent to which an intervention produces a beneficial outcome under ordinary everyday circumstances. It is a measure of whether the intervention *does* work. **Cost-effectiveness** is evaluated by combining evidence of the cost of the different treatment approaches and information on how effectively they deliver desired improvements in health.

All designs have their advantages and disadvantages. The ideal design will demonstrate that an effective intervention *is* effective and will not allow the effectiveness to be masked by other factors. Equally it will not allow an ineffective treatment to appear effective due to factors other than the intervention clouding the picture.

WITHIN-PARTICIPANTS OR CROSS-OVER DESIGNS

The within-subjects design or, more correctly, **within-participants design**, sometimes also termed the **cross-over design**, is where the same people provide measures at more than one time and differences between the measures at the different times are noted. An example would be a measure taken before an intervention (pre-treatment) and again after the intervention (post-treatment). Such a design minimises the effect of individual differences as each person acts as his or her own control.

However, there are a number of problems with this design. Any change in the measure may be due to other factors having changed. For example, you may have introduced an intervention that is designed to improve the **quality of life** (**QoL**) among patients in a particular long stay ward of a hospital but the hospital has also introduced other changes which have had an effect on QoL, for example, a new set of menus introduced by the catering department. In addition, the difference may be due to some aspect of the measuring instrument. If the same measure is being taken on both occasions, the fact that it has been taken twice may be the reason that the result has changed. If, to get around this problem, a different version of the measure is used then the difference might be due to the difference in the nature of the measures and not the efficacy of the intervention.

A further problem is that a lack of difference in the measure between the two occasions doesn't tell you much; the intervention might have been effective in preventing things from worsening. In addition, if you are using a cross-over design to compare two or more treatments, then you have to be careful that the particular results you get are not an **artefact** of the order in which the treatments were given. It may be that there is a carry-over effect so that later trials show improvement as a result of practice or later trials could demonstrate poorer performance as a result of fatigue and these effects would have happened even if the treatment had remained the same. To counter such order effects one can use a baseline or 'washout period' before and after treatment periods. Also one can randomly assign people to different orders or, if one is interested in seeing whether order does have an effect, a more systematic allocation of participants to different orders could be employed: for example, if there are only two conditions participants could be alternately placed in the two possible orders, or if there are more than two conditions a Latin square design could be employed (see Box 10.1). Such systematic allocations as those shown in Box 10.1 allow us to test formally whether there is an effect of order.

Box 10.1   *Controlling for carry-over effects in cross-over designs*

Case 1a: measures taken of two therapies or treatments, A1 and A2:

Group 1 receives the treatments in order: A1 A2
Group 2 receives the treatments in order: A2 A1

Case 1b: measures taken of two therapies, A1 and A2, and repeated baseline periods B1, B2 and B3:

Group 1 receives the treatments in the order: B1 A1 B2 A2 B3
Group 2 receives the treatments in the order: B1 A2 B2 A1 B3

Case 2a: measures taken of three therapies, A1, A2 and A3. There are now six possible orders of administration of the three therapies as follows:

Group 1: A1 A2 A3
Group 2: A1 A3 A2
Group 3: A2 A1 A3
Group 4: A2 A3 A1
Group 5: A3 A1 A2
Group 6: A3 A2 A1

Case 2b: measures are taken of the three therapies and also of multiple baseline periods before and after each therapy period:

Group 1: B1 A1 B2 A2 B3 A3 B4
Group 2: B1 A1 B2 A3 B3 A2 B4
Etc. as for Case 2a above

Case 2c: the three therapies are applied to each of three groups following a design termed a Latin square. In this design, each therapy has an equal chance of appearing first, second or third as follows:

Group 1	Group 2	Group 3
A1	A2	A3
A2	A3	A1
A3	A1	A2

For further details see Clark-Carter (1997a) or Myers and Well (1991).

Between-groups designs

To solve some of the problems identified, it can be a good idea to use a between-groups design in which similar, matched groups of people are allocated to different treatment groups. If the measures are taken at one time then this is sometimes called a **cross-sectional design** as if we are applying our measures in one slice of time only, in contrast to a **longitudinal design** where the groups are tested at two or more time points. Cross-sectional designs are the most common because they are the least expensive in terms of time and resources. Longitudinal designs are among the most powerful designs available for the evaluation of treatments and of theories about human experience and behaviour, but they are also the most costly in terms of labour, time and money. **Prospective** longitudinal designs obtain data at different times planned in advance while **retrospective** longitudinal designs use data that have already been collected.

When we are comparing only treatment groups, a failure to find a difference between them on the outcome measure might be for one of three reasons: they are equally effective; they are equally ineffective; or they are equally harmful. For this reason, it is desirable that one of the groups is in fact a **control group**. The presence of a control group will help to show whether the treatments differ from no treatment.

However, there are serious ethical issues over the use of a control group. Not to treat someone can be seen as unethical. Nonetheless, if we really don't know what is an effective intervention then it is better to carry out the study and include a control group than to continue, in perpetuity, applying the ineffective treatment. Once we know which therapy *is* the most effective, we should offer this to members of the former control group. We may build this into the design of the study by having the former treatment group now not treated by returning them to the baseline to see what the longer-term effects of the treatment are once it has been ceased.

The choice of control group is also important. The very fact of being in a group that is receiving some attention may improve psychological well-being, regardless of what the actual attention is. Therefore, it is often a good idea to have a group whose members are receiving the same amount of attention as those in the true treatment group(s). This type of control is known as a **placebo control** (**group/condition**), controlling for the fact that treatment itself often has a non-specific effect on the client's wellbeing.

If all of the various groups' responses are measured on one occasion only – after an intervention – then we haven't really measured change. It could be that all groups, including the control group, have changed but from different starting positions, and a lack of difference between the groups at the end-point of the study could miss this. We can try to solve this problem by using a mixed design in which we measure all of the groups both before and after the treatment. However, we would be introducing some of the potential difficulties that were mentioned earlier for a within-participants design. For further designs that try to address these issues, see Clark-Carter (1997a) or Cook and Campbell (1979).

Randomised controlled trials

The 'gold standard' to which much research in psychology, medicine and health care aspires is the **randomised controlled trial** (**RCT**) in which participants are allocated randomly to one or more intervention conditions and to a control condition. The statistical tests that are available have as one of their assumptions that participants have been randomly assigned to conditions. However, when researchers move beyond the laboratory setting to real world clinical and health research, it soon becomes evident that the so-called gold standard cannot always be achieved in practice and, in fact, may not be desirable for ethical reasons. This may be a stumbling block for the acceptance and introduction of new therapies offered by clinical and health psychology. It is essential that the evidence base in evaluation of new treatments and programmes is broadened beyond that of the RCT (see Chapter 11).

We are frequently forced to study existing groups that are being treated differently rather than have the luxury of being able to allocate people to conditions. Thus, we may in effect be comparing the health policies and services of a number of different hospitals and clinics. Such a design is sometimes described as quasi-experimental in that we are comparing treatments in as controlled a manner as possible, but we have been unable for practical reasons to manipulate the IV, the policies, or allocate the participants ourselves.

The advantage of a randomised controlled trial is that differences in the outcome measure between the participants treated in the different ways can be attributed with more confidence to the manipulations of the researchers, because individual differences are likely to be spread in a random way between the different treatments. As soon as that basis for allocation of participants is lost, then questions arise over the ability to identify causes of changes or differences between the groups; in other words, the **internal validity** of the design is in question.

The possible threats to internal validity are numerous and we should try, whenever possible, to put safeguards in place to protect our designs from such threats. Typical threats to internal validity include the fact that: members of the different groups may accidentally differ systematically in respect to the outcome measure at the start (selection); in a mixed design, there could be different drop-out rates, which affect the nature of the samples at follow-up (attrition); or participants could be changing in some critical way regardless of the treatment they are receiving as a result of an unknown or uncontrolled factor (maturation).

Where to conduct the study

There is no ideal place to conduct a study. What you may gain in one respect in one study setting, you are likely to lose in another. A controlled environment such as a laboratory has the strong advantage that participants are in an almost completely standardised setting and so extraneous factors will not vary as much between the testing sessions with different participants. In this way, differences between treatment groups in the outcome measure are more likely to be due to the treatment itself rather than to something not taken account of. Also, by cutting out extraneous or confounding variables, known as artefacts or **confounds**, if a difference really exists, it is more likely to be picked up under these conditions. However, it may be impossible to generalise the results obtained in such a controlled setting to other settings; the treatment may show a significant effect in the laboratory but it may not occur or may be diminished to a trivial effect in a different, real-world setting; that is, the **external validity** of the design is threatened. In addition, it may not be possible, appropriate or ethical to conduct the study in such controlled conditions. A real-world setting such as a clinic, classroom, household or a community location, on the other hand, provides the study with **ecological validity** but reduces the investigator's ability to control extraneous influences or confounds that may mask the true effect of the intervention, or suggest an illusory, arte-factual effect that is not replicable here or elsewhere.

Measures

In psychology we are dealing usually with measures that are *indicators* of the things we actually want to measure. For example, we do not have a straightforward measure of stress in the same way that we have a measure of height. We have to rely on self-report – possibly via a questionnaire – or observation of some physiological measure, such as heart rate or skin conductance. For many reasons, our measures are very unlikely to be 100 per cent reliable; in other words, they will not provide the same score from occasion to occasion, even when all conditions have been held constant. In addition, their validity may be questionable; that is, they may not be measuring what we thought they were. We may see physiological measures as the nearest we have to an equivalent of a measure of height. However, they are notoriously problematic. As an example, heart rate has frequently been used as an indicator of psychological stress. However, heart rate is sensitive and can be affected by a large number of factors, only one of which may be psychological stress. Accordingly, it would seem sensible to try to take a number of measures of the same phenomenon to see whether an intervention has been effective.

Another reason for requiring multiple measures is that the phenomenon for which we are trying to measure change may be relatively vague, in the sense that there may be a number of factors that we want to evaluate. An intervention may improve a measure of QoL while not improving anxiety or depression. We would want to detect the improvement rather than dismiss the intervention as ineffective for want of having taken sufficient measures. This will be true of a cross-sectional study whereby if we had only one outcome measure at a time we would have to repeat the study for each measure, but it will be even more true for a longitudinal study as we don't want to have to start the whole study over again in order to include a new measure.

A further reason for taking multiple measures is that an effect may not be detectable within each single measure but may emerge through a combination of measures (in fact through their interaction). Accordingly, simply repeating the study but taking a different measure each time will fail to detect this.

Thus we have at least three reasons why multiple measures would be a good idea. However, this approach can lead to its own problems. By requiring participants to complete more questionnaires or be involved in more time-consuming measurement we are increasing the participants' burden and thus the likelihood that people will refuse to take part in the first place. In addition, in a longitudinal study we are increasing the likelihood that people will drop out because they find being in the study too onerous. Therefore, we need to have a compromise. In *any* study we need to ask ourselves why we are taking each measure, but it becomes even more crucial in these circumstances. A pilot study, which should always be conducted, becomes all the more critical so that we can time how long it takes for each measure, and do a cost-benefit analysis to decide what we can keep and what will have to go. This is another example where testing a clear theory is better than simply going on a **fishing trip**. This refers to the tendency of researchers, motivated to find any significant result, to employ every possible measure and analysis they can think of, a dubious enterprise that is destined to mislead, as we shall see below.

EVALUATING THE RESULTS OF RESEARCH

Despite the efforts of Cohen (1962) and others, psychologists, in common with those in other disciplines, have adopted a particular way to evaluate their quantitative research. However, sometimes the stages are not explicitly stated, obscuring the nature of what can reasonably be concluded from the process. When the process is made explicit, a null hypothesis (H_0) and a research (or alternative) hypothesis (H_1) are proposed. Then, once the data are collected, a statistical test is applied to help the decision about which hypothesis is the more tenable. The reasoning behind this process will be examined, and alternative and complementary approaches will be suggested.

Hypotheses

In the case of an experiment or quasi-experiment, a null hypothesis (H_0) usually, although not necessarily, states that there is no effect, or, in the case of correlation, that there is no relationship between two variables. An example of a null hypothesis for an experiment would be: *this therapeutic technique T_1 does not change anxiety levels*. An example for a correlation would be: *there is no relationship between amount of exercise taken and anxiety levels*. Notice that neither hypothesis contains words like 'significant' or expressions such as 'except by chance' as they are not part of these hypotheses; rather these refer to decisions about the hypotheses.

An alternative hypothesis (H_1) normally states that there is an effect or a relationship. Examples of alternative hypotheses which would match the above null hypotheses could be: *this therapeutic technique T_1 reduces anxiety*, and, *there is a relationship between amount of exercise and anxiety levels*. Beware of having an alternative hypothesis that states that *there is no effect or relationship* for reasons that will be explained later.

Thus in hypothesis testing we set up two hypotheses, only one of which can logically be true. Of course it would be very odd to devise a method to reduce anxiety that you predicted wouldn't be effective. The study of the method is carried out with the explicit aim of demonstrating that the method is indeed effective. The question then arises as to why we have a null hypothesis at all. This follows from the logic of hypothesis testing, which looks for evidence *against* the null hypothesis and treats this as evidence *for* the alternative hypothesis. This is because the inferential tests that we use only address the null hypothesis. In fact, under an earlier method of hypothesis testing, popularised by Fisher (1925), the null hypothesis was the only hypothesis. The notion of the alternative hypothesis was championed by Neyman and Pearson (1928).

Significance testing

Having collected the data we then run a statistical (or inferential) test. This test will provide us with a probability (p), the probability that the result we achieved has of occurring *if the null hypothesis is true*. This latter part is emphasised because what we are being provided with is a *conditional* probability, with the condition here being that the null hypothesis *is* true. Thus we are being told the probability that the result of our research could occur when the null hypothesis is true. What we have to decide is whether that probability is sufficiently low that we think our results do not support the null hypothesis. Purely by convention, a probability of 0.05 (5 per cent or 1 in 20), is normally taken as a cut-off point for deciding whether a result is statistically significant. This is usually referred to as the **significance level** or **alpha level** of our finding.

Accordingly, if our result, on the assumption that the null hypothesis is true, has a probability (p) level of 0.05 or smaller, then we have a significant result and we choose to reject the null hypothesis. In some situations, for example when a large number of tests are being computed, or when the outcome of a study is particularly important clinically, it is prudent to use an alpha level that is smaller than 0.05, for example, 0.01 or even 0.001. However, the significance level alone cannot be used to evaluate a finding. We also need to consider the sample size and effect size, as discussed below. The statistical significance of a finding does not necessarily equate with the importance of the finding.

Strictly speaking the probability we are given is not just for the result that we actually did achieve, but for all other possible results including those which are even less likely but are in line with our research hypothesis. This is because the alpha level represents a proportion of possible results lying in the tails of the distribution.

Directional hypotheses and the tail of the test

A further complication that can affect the probability is the way in which the alternative hypothesis is phrased. The hypothesis, *the therapeutic technique T₁ reduces anxiety levels,* is a directional hypothesis as it predicts the direction in which the results will go while a non-directional hypothesis, *the therapeutic technique T₁ will produce a change in anxiety levels,* merely predicts a difference. The first hypothesis clearly has not been supported if the anxiety levels actually increase after therapy, whereas such an outcome could still support the second hypothesis.

For certain statistical tests, such as the t-test, it is possible to test either a directional or a non-directional hypothesis. Statisticians have worked out the distributions of the frequencies of the results which could exist when the null hypothesis is true and for such tests these distributions are symmetrical, with half devoted to results which went in one direction and half to those which went in the other direction. Therefore, if we propose a directional hypothesis, we are predicting which half of the distribution our result will occur in whereas, if we have a non-directional hypothesis, then we are not predicting the half in which our result will occur. Thus, when we make a directional hypothesis, we are looking for the 5 per cent of results which are as extreme as or more extreme than our result, in line with our hypothesis, in one half of the distribution of results consistent with the null hypothesis. In other words, we are looking in one tail of the distribution and so the probability is described as a one-tailed probability and we have run a **one-tailed test**. However, if we have not predicted the specific direction of the result, then the 5 per cent of results are half in one tail of the distribution and half in the other tail and so, in this case, we have run a **two-tailed test**.

Care must be taken in interpreting a one-tailed probability. We may have a directional hypothesis but, if the result has gone in the opposite direction to the one we predicted, then the true one-tailed probability of our result has to be found by subtracting the probability given to us by the computer from 1. Therefore, if we were told that $p = 0.1$, the true one-tailed probability would be 0.9.

Type I and Type II errors

When we see the probability (p) of our result we make a decision – whether or not to reject the null hypothesis. As stated earlier, even if we choose to reject the null hypothesis, we know that our result *could* have occurred even when the null hypothesis is true with probability p. Therefore we could be making an error which is called a **Type I error**. It must be emphasised that we never know for certain whether the null hypothesis is true, only that when we reject the null hypothesis, we *might* be committing a Type I error.

A second kind of error may occur in using the hypothesis testing approach to statistical inference. This so-called **Type II error** occurs when we fail to reject the null hypothesis when it is false. Again, we never know whether we are committing a Type II error, but we can compute the probability that it might happen in any particular circumstance. Then we can take steps to keep this probability as low as possible.

To sum up the discussion thus far, our hypothesis testing procedure for making statistical inferences means that we are willing to accept a 0.05 (1 in 20 or 5 per cent) danger of committing a Type I error. There has been a recent emphasis on trying to quantify and so minimise the likelihood of committing a Type II error. This leads us to the concept of statistical power.

THE STATISTICAL POWER OF A TEST

The **power** of a test in a given study may be defined as the probability that we will successfully avoid committing a Type II error, in other words, the probability that we find an effect when an effect is there. Thus, the formula for power is:

Power = $1 - \beta$
where β is the probability of a Type II error.

A number of factors influence β and hence the power of a test. Among these factors are: (a) if the hypothesis is directional, then the test has more power; (b) certain statistical tests are inherently more powerful than others; (c) a within-participants design is more powerful than a between-groups design; (d) the better controlled a study, the less the variability within a condition, the greater the power; (e) the larger the effect size, the greater the power; (f) the larger the sample size, the greater the power. This last factor of sample size is the one that we can most easily control, once all other design features have been decided. Cohen (1988) and others have recommended that a minimal level of power to which we should aspire is 0.8. This implies that the chance of a Type II error is 0.2. However, 0.8 should not be seen as ideal. Ideally we will want to maximise the power to the highest possible level, to 0.9, 0.95 or 0.99 even.

Choice of sample size

During the design stage of a quantitative study it is important that the sample size is chosen on statistical grounds rather than purely arbitrarily, for convenience or on the basis that previous research used such sample sizes. Once all the design and hypothesis features have been decided we can use special power tables (Clark-Carter, 1997a; Cohen, 1988) to decide how many people we need in our study to give us that level of power. However, before we can compute the power of a study, we need to know one more element: the effect size.

Effect size

Statistical significance is so dependent on sample size that it cannot be used to compare the results of studies, unless they have used the same sample size. **Effect size**, on the other hand, is much less influenced by sample size and so is a more useful basis for comparison. In addition, Cohen (1988) has examined published research and provided a set of criteria for what constitutes small, medium or large effect sizes in the behavioural sciences for different measures of effect size. In this way the result of a particular study can be compared against such criteria to give it a context.

There can be seen to be at least three forms of effect size. For each type there is frequently more than one version. Here we are going to present what we see as the most easily understood and popular measures; interested readers can find alternatives in Cohen (1988) or Hedges and Olkin (1985). Firstly, there is the comparison between two conditions (for example, depression in those suffering from chronic pelvic pain – CPP – and those suffering from chronic back pain – CBP). In this case measures can be used to summarise how big a difference there is between the two conditions. When the measure is quantitative (on an ordinal, interval or ratio scale), such as a standard depression measure, then Cohen's d can be used where

$$\text{Cohen's d} = \frac{\text{mean for CPP} - \text{mean for CBP}}{\text{standard deviation}}$$

In words, d is the difference between the means of the two conditions expressed in standard deviation (SD) units using the standard deviation from the control condition when there is a control condition or the pooled standard deviation when there isn't a control condition. Cohen's guidelines for d are: a small effect is d = 0.2 (less than a quarter of a standard deviation), a medium effect is d = 0.5 (half a standard deviation) and a large effect is d = 0.8 (more than three-quarters of a standard deviation). When the measure is qualitative (categorical or nominal), then an increasingly popular measure is the **odds ratio** (see Chapter 9).

A second form of measure of effect size is of the size of a relationship. Thus, in the case of quantitative data, Pearson's product moment correlation coefficient, r, gives an idea of how closely two variables are related. In the case of multiple regression, the multiple correlation coefficient, R, tells the researcher how closely a set of independent or predictor variables are to a dependent, or to be predicted, variable. An equivalent measure of the effect when the measures are qualitative (categorical or nominal) is w, where

$$w = \sqrt{\frac{\chi^2}{N}}$$

χ^2 is the chi-square statistic, which is a typical inferential test for such data, and N is the total sample size. R, r and w have built-in limits that help their use as measures of effect size. All of them have maximum values of 1 and so the stronger the relationship the closer the statistic is to 1. In the case of r, the stronger the negative relationship between the variables the closer the statistic is to –1. In the case of w the sign is rather arbitrary because it depends how categories have been coded. Thus if a comparison of the genders were conducted, then coding males as 0 and females 1 would produce a w of the opposite sign to the one which would be produced if males were coded as 1 and females as 0. For all three statistics, the closer they are to 0 the smaller the relationship. Cohen has suggested that an r (or w) of 0.1 is a small effect size, while 0.3 is medium and 0.5 is large.

The third form of effect size (which is strongly linked to the second) is the proportion of variance in one variable that can be controlled (or, as some still say, accounted for) by the variance in one or more other variables. Thus in the case of bivariate correlation (where the relationship between two variables is being analysed), if the study was looking at the relationship between locus of control and anxiety and found that the relationship between the two was r = 0.5 then r^2 would tell us that the proportion of variation in anxiety that can be controlled (or explained) by the variation in locus of control is 0.25 (or 25 per cent). This also tells us how much of anxiety is not controlled by locus of control (1 – 0.25 or 0.75, or 75 per cent). In multiple regression R^2 can be interpreted in the same way as r^2, except that there is more than one predictor variable. Cohen's guidelines for R^2 are just under 0.02 for a small effect, 0.13 for a medium effect and 0.26 for a large effect.

In the case of studies looking at the difference between more than two conditions, it is possible to report the proportion of variance in the dependent variable that is explicable in terms of the differences between the conditions, one measure of this is eta-squared (η^2). Thus, if we extended an earlier hypothetical design so that we were comparing the depression scores of those with CPP, those with CBP and those with rheumatoid arthritis we could say how much of the variation in scores could be attributable to the differences between these three groups. Although Cohen doesn't use eta-squared, guidelines have been derived from the measure he does employ for this type of design (see Clark-Carter, 1997a). Cohen would see an η^2 of 0.01 as a small effect size, 0.059 as a medium effect and 0.138 as a large effect.

The only effect size mentioned above which is not available in SPSS is d. R, R^2 and r are routinely reported. Eta-squared (or a modified version of it) can be requested as an option when doing ANOVA, ANCOVA, MANOVA and MANCOVA. In the case of w, this can be found by asking for phi or Cramer's phi (shown as Cramer's V in SPSS) when doing contingency table analysis.

Although three different types of effect size have been presented here, they can be converted into a standard form for the purposes of meta-analysis (see Chapter 11).

Calculating power and sample size

As mentioned earlier, there is a close link between statistical significance, effect size and sample size in a study. So close is the link that two studies with exactly the same result in terms of effect size can lead to totally different results in terms of statistical significance simply because of the differences in sample size in the two studies. Accordingly, to ignore the issue of what is a sensible sample size to employ is an ethical issue. For if you recruit so few people to take part in your study that it is highly likely that the result will be non-significant, then you have wasted your participants' time as well as your own. Similarly, if you study far more people than is necessary to achieve statistical significance then you are wasting many people's time as well. That is why ethical committees expect applicants to have carried out a power analysis to determine their sample sizes prior to submitting the study for ethical approval (see Chapter 2).

As Cohen (1988) and others point out, if we don't take statistical power and effect size into consideration, then all that inferential statistics are telling us is whether we used an adequate sample size for the given effect size; a study with a large effect but a small sample size may be non-significant while another study with a small effect but a large sample may prove to be significant.

As mentioned earlier, we need to know an effect size in order to choose a sample size. At first this may seem paradoxical because if we knew the effect size we probably wouldn't be doing the research. What we need to do is estimate the effect size or state the smallest effect size in which we would be interested. We can use previous relevant research to find out what effect size we are likely to find. In the absence of such information we can decide, for example, that we are only interested in detecting a significant result if the effect is at least a medium effect. Now, having chosen a test and an effect size we can find out what sample size would give us the desired level of power. As an example, let us return to the comparison of CPP and CBP patients. If we are interested in detecting a medium effect size ($d = 0.5$) as statistically significant and we have a non-directional research hypothesis, then, for a between-groups t-test, we will need 64 people in each group in order to achieve the recommended level of power of 0.8.

Unconventional research hypotheses

The problems with having a research hypothesis that is the equivalent of a conventional null hypothesis were alluded to earlier. Now that we have explained issues surrounding statistical power we can tackle this issue more fully. Imagine the research hypothesis is that there will be no difference between two therapies. Even if the difference is large (that is, there is a large effect size), if the test has low power because we use an inadequate sample size, the result is likely not to be statistically significant and so we might falsely conclude that there is no difference. Cohen has argued that to cope with such a research hypothesis it would be necessary to make power as large as 0.95. In this way our beta level (β, the likelihood of making a Type II error, which is 1 – power) becomes the same size as our alpha level. In order to arrive at the appropriate sample size to provide us with that level of power, we would still have to decide on an effect size that we considered sufficiently small that it would not be an important effect in the context of our research.

The result of this approach is that we can be forced to use very large sample sizes; for example, if we were to run a between-groups t-test with a two-tailed probability and we decided that an effect size of d = 0.1 (one tenth of a standard deviation difference between the conditions) is sufficiently small, then we would need a total sample size of 3150 to achieve power of 0.95. Typically sample sizes, and thus statistical power levels, in psychological studies have been much smaller than in epidemiological studies. This has had some unfortunate consequences. Too large a proportion of studies published in reputable psychology journals have lacked statistical power (for example, see reviews by Clark-Carter, 1997b; Cohen, 1962). It is necessary for psychological studies to give the consideration of power in study design a much higher priority than has been the case traditionally.

The traditional method of hypothesis testing, described earlier, which is a standard procedure in psychology, means that when researchers run a statistical test to find the significance of their result, they are determining *the probability with which the outcome could have occurred if the null hypothesis were true*. Although often misinterpreted, it is what is termed a **conditional probability** – the probability of the outcome *given* that the null hypothesis is true. In fact this isn't the information that we are generally interested in knowing. What we really want to know is *how likely is it that our research hypothesis is true, given the new evidence that we have obtained*. Yet the standard methods of statistical inference do not provide this information.

The conventional approach to hypothesis testing is sometimes described as a **frequentist** or **classical approach**. However, there has long existed an alternative approach, known as the **Bayesian** or **subjectivist approach**, which, under certain circumstances and assumptions, can provide the answers that we want. This technique is called Bayesian statistics after Rev. Thomas Bayes (1702–61) who is credited with demonstrating a mathematical relationship that in itself is perfectly innocuous but which has been applied in what frequentist statisticians see as a controversial way.

Bayesian statistics

Thomas Bayes described a very interesting relationship known as Bayes' theorem that enables the researcher to determine the probability that her or his research hypothesis is true given the new data. For this theorem to work, we need to know the simple (non-conditional) probabilities of the null hypothesis and of the research hypothesis, and the conditional probabilities of the result we achieved given the null hypothesis and the result we achieved given the research hypothesis.

The problem with this approach lies in the fact that we usually do not have an objective method for estimating the simple probabilities. A controversy arises when Bayesians argue that we can use subjective probabilities or degrees of belief to arrive at these *prior* probabilities. Bayesian statistics are based on the idea that we never start a piece of research in complete ignorance. We will always have an opinion or subjective probability about the truth of our null and research hypotheses. These prior opinions can be directly measured in the form of betting odds or indirectly as degrees of belief on a probability scale. Thus we might believe that H_0 has a probability of 0.1 and H_1 a probability of 0.9, giving a prior odds of 9 to 1.

Defenders of the Bayesian approach point out that the seeming objectivity of the classical approach is in fact illusory. Rather than enter into the controversy, which has raged since long before psychologists adopted the classical approach, a perfectly non-controversial use that can be made of Bayesian methods will be described. For further discussion, interested readers are referred to Howson and Urbach (1993).

When we are trying to diagnose a condition in a particular person, we can be helped by knowing the prevalence of the condition, from which we can derive the simple prior probabilities that a person will have the condition and the probability that the person will not have the condition; *prior* in the sense of prior to having tried to make the diagnosis. If a test exists to diagnose the condition, part of the information which the user wants to know is its accuracy – how many correct and how many incorrect diagnoses does it make. These provide us with the conditional probabilities of how likely a person is to be diagnosed as having the condition when they have that condition (correct positives – the test's *sensitivity*) or when they haven't got the condition (false positives), and how likely they are to be diagnosed as not having the condition when they have got it (false negatives) or when they haven't got it (correct negatives – the test's *specificity*). With this information we can test a given person and alter our judgement about the likelihood that the person has the condition given the result on the test.

One way of writing Bayes' theorem is:

$$\Omega_1 = L. \ \Omega_0$$

where Ω_1 is the **posterior odds**, L is the **likelihood ratio**, and Ω_0 is the **prior odds**.

The likelihood ratio (L) is the likelihood of obtaining a positive diagnosis (D) given that the person has condition C, or P(D/C), divided by the likelihood of obtaining a positive diagnosis given that the person does not have C, P(D/not C). As an example, let us say that the prevalence in the community tells us that the probability of a person having C is 0.2 and therefore the probability of their not having it is 0.8. These facts produce prior odds (Ω_0) of 0.2/0.8 or a 1 in 4 chance (0.25). Let us assume that we are going to use a test which is known to diagnose people as having the condition when they have got it on 95 per cent of occasions (and so produces false negatives on 5 per cent of occasions) and diagnoses them as having the condition on 35 per cent of occasions when they haven't got it (false positives) and therefore correctly diagnoses people who have not got the condition on 65 per cent of occasions. The value of L for this test is therefore $^{95}/_{35} = 2.714$. When someone is diagnosed as having the condition we can use Bayes' theorem to find that the posterior odds (Ω_1) that they have the condition are as follows:

$$\Omega_1 = \frac{95}{35} \times \frac{1}{4} = \frac{95}{140} = 0.678$$

Since $\Omega_1 = P(C/D)/1\text{-}P(C/D)$, this means that the probability that the person has C given the diagnosis P(C/D) is 0.404 and the chance that they do not have the condition is 0.596. Using a similar argument, if they are diagnosed as not having the condition, then Bayes' theorem tells us that the probability that they do have the condition is 0.02 and the probability that they don't have the condition is 0.98. From these calculations we can see that a negative result on the test is very informative while a positive diagnosis is less so. It would be necessary to get the false positive rate down to 23 per cent before the probability of having the disease given a positive diagnosis would be above 50 per cent. The accuracy of our diagnostic tool could also be further enhanced by knowing the prevalence figures for the sub-groups of the population based on gender, age, etc. The calculations above suggest that we may place more confidence in a diagnostic test than is warranted by the evidence.

PRESENTING RESULTS

Once we have explored our results and run statistical tests on them, we need to decide how to present the results in a way that will make them most understandable. A review of articles that are published in journals shows that the quality of reporting of studies varies enormously. The American Psychological Association (2001a,b) has produced guidelines for the way in which results should be reported in the light of the recommendations of a task force (Wilkinson, 1999).

Descriptive stats

It should be routine to report appropriate descriptive statistics. These should be linked to the statistical test that has been employed. Thus, in the case of a parametric test such as the t-test, it would be usual to report the means and SDs of the outcome measure for each condition. In the case of non-parametric tests, such as the Mann-Whitney U test, it is best to include the median as well, as the test compares medians rather than means.

In the case of correlation, it is useful to include details of means and SDs for each of the measures as these allow the reader to see where on the scale your participants are scoring. A correlation coefficient on its own will not tell the reader this information. Thus if we are looking at the relationship between Locus of Control and QoL, knowing that the relationship is r = 0.35 does not tell the reader whether the particular sample is generally high, low or average on either of the two measures.

When you only have one or two means and SDs then the recommendation is that you include these details in brackets in a sentence that describes the results rather than in a table. However, when you have such information for a number of measures then it is a good idea to put the information in a table. Where possible, make tables self-contained so that the reader doesn't have to refer to the rest of the report to understand what they are being told in the table. Label aspects of the table clearly so that it is easy to understand what the numbers refer to and what units they are in. Give tables clear, self-explanatory titles but ones that are not too long.

As with tables, graphs should be made as self-contained as possible. Axes should be labelled, including details of the nature of the measurements. Thus, it is not enough to label an axis as Stress; if it is heart rate, the axis label should say so and indicate what the numbers refer to. There should be a clear title that tells the reader what the IV(s) and DV(s) are. Remember that if you are presenting error bars around means then the reader needs to be told what type they are and, where appropriate, how many multiples of them. Thus you could be showing SDs, standard errors of means (SEMs), or **confidence intervals (CIs)**, and in the case of the first two, the bars could extend to one SD or SEM either side of the mean, or it could be two or more SDs or SEMs. There may be circumstances in which it is not possible to make a table or graph self-contained, in which case, tell the reader, as part of the key to the figure or table, that details may be found in the text.

The results of statistical tests

Now that the analysis is likely to have been carried out on a computer, some of the detail that it is recommended that authors report would appear to be from an earlier age. Nonetheless, they do allow the reader to check that aspects of the results are likely to be correct because they are consistent. Thus, you should report the type of test employed and on what – mentioning the IV, its levels and the outcome measure, where appropriate. For example: *a between-groups t-test was used to compare the depression scores of the therapy and control groups*. You should state what you found in words, including whether the result was significant and the direction, when there was a difference. For example: *the relaxation group had significantly lower depression scores than the control group*. Finally, provide the statistical evidence of your conclusion: *($t_{(11)}$ = 2.53, p = .014, one-tailed test)*. Note that you need the symbol for the test – t – the degrees of freedom (where applicable), the value of the test, the probability and, where applicable, the tail of the test. In the case of tests which either don't have degrees of freedom, such as most non-parametric tests, or chi-squared tests that have degrees of freedom which aren't linked to the sample size, report the sample size as well.

Notice that the number of decimal places are kept to two or three. There is no point in going beyond this as this is sufficient to make the necessary judgements. Notice also that the probability level has been reported as an exact figure rather than as p < .05. Some approaches to hypothesis testing would argue that the latter format is all that is necessary. However, it is not very informative; stating that p < .05 would be true when p = .000001. Computers provide the exact probability so you might as well report it. If the reader prefers to use the p < .05 approach then he or she can easily make the conversion. If it is necessary to rely purely on probability tables, then we recommend a bracketing system, which shows where the probability lies; for example .05 > p > .01 (the probability is less than 0.05 but greater than 0.01).

Sometimes the computer output will show a probability of 0.000. This is relatively meaningless as the probability is never truly zero. In such circumstances it is more accurate to replace the last zero with a 1 and write p < .001. Sometimes you will see values in a computer output along the lines of 2.57E-5. This is in 'scientific' code. It means that the number is either small, as in the example where the last 5 is preceded by a negative sign, or the value is large if the last digit(s) are preceded by a positive sign. Results should not be reported like this. It is possible to get SPSS to provide the number in normal decimal format and that is how it should be reported.

If a standard statistical test has been carried out, then there is no need to report the type of software used. However, if a less usual technique is used, or one where the results of statistical packages can differ, for example **structural equation modelling**, then one should report not only the software used, but also the particular version. If a less usual version of a test has been used, then readers should be informed. For example, if the data have been analysed using the version of the between-groups t-test that does not assume equal variances, then this should be stated and the reason(s) given. If the alpha level has been adjusted to take account of multiple testing, then this should be explained, including the method employed (for example, the **Bonferroni adjustment**) and what the adjusted level is.

Effect sizes

As part of the reporting of the statistics, the appropriate category of effect size for the test employed should be stated. Remember that because there is more than one effect size category for each type of test, it is necessary to say which effect size is being reported; for example, d = 0.35. It is worth giving the effect size a context. We recommend a statement along the following lines: *according to Cohen's (1988) classification, the effect size lies between a small and a medium effect*. If many versions of the same test are being reported, then it is better to put them in a table rather than as part of the text.

SUMMARY

In this chapter we have outlined the main research designs for experimental and quasi-experimental studies that are typically used to evaluate interventions in clinical and health psychology. The advantages and disadvantages of cross-sectional, between-groups and within-participants designs were compared. The principles of hypothesis testing and other approaches to the analysis of quantitative data were outlined, and some of the logical peculiarities of the approaches were pointed out. We have described the concept of the power of a test and, in the light of its implications for research design, argued for more use of the power concept in the design of research. Finally, we have suggested some points to improve the analysis and reporting of quantitative research in clinical and health psychology.

SUGGESTED READING

Clark-Carter, D. (1997). *Doing quantitative psychological research: from design to report*. Hove: Psychology Press.

REVISION QUESTIONS

1 What are the differences between 'efficacy', 'effectiveness' and 'cost-effectiveness'?
2 What is a 'cross-over' or 'within-participants' design?
3 What are the essential features of a randomised controlled trial?
4 Differentiate between a Type I and a Type II error.
5 What is the power of a test? Why is power important? What can be done to increase power?
6 What is meant by 'effect size'?
7 What is meant by 'Bayesian statistics'? How does the Bayesian approach differ from the classical approach?

11

SYNTHESISING EVIDENCE: SYSTEMATIC REVIEWS, META-ANALYSIS AND PREFERENCE ANALYSIS

David F. Marks and
Catherine Marie Sykes

AIMS OF THIS CHAPTER

(i) To describe the rationale for systematic reviews and their advantages and disadvantages.

(ii) To describe how to carry out a systematic review.

(iii) To describe how to carry out a meta-analysis.

(iv) To discuss the problem of integrating quantitative and qualitative evidence.

(v) To describe preference analysis, a method for combining effectiveness, economic and qualitative evidence into a single decision.

(vi) To describe an example of a systematic review.

INTRODUCTION

We have seen in earlier chapters that quantitative research is viewed by its most committed advocates as providing a 'window on reality', a way of obtaining an accurate description or 'reflection of reality'. Qualitative research on the other hand talks about social construction and interpretations of 'realities' in the plural. We turn now to one of the most fundamental issues in health care, the question of combining and integrating evidence from different sources. Every time a person makes a decision it is necessary to synthesise information of many different kinds, including both quantitative and qualitative elements. For example, in treating patients a doctor must integrate the relevant pieces of her or his knowledge about anatomy, physiology, microbiology, pharmacology and psychology, and also qualitative feedback received from previous patients about the treatments offered, and apply all of this knowledge together with current best evidence to the specific case. In planning a new service, a health service planner must synthesise evidence on economic costs, effectiveness and acceptability to patients. This chapter is concerned with methods for combining and integrating evidence in reaching conclusions and decisions in health care.

We begin this chapter with a discussion of the **systematic review**. A systematic review is an integration of evidence about an effect or intervention involving the summary of findings from a defined set of relevant and usable primary sources. What counts as relevant and usable is a matter for debate and judgement. Rules and criteria for selection of studies and for data extraction are negotiated by those carrying out the review. Publishing these rules and criteria enables such reviews to be replicable and transparent. Proponents of the systematic review argue that it is a way of integrating research that limits bias (for example, Mulrow, 1987).

The synthesis of research evidence has been discussed in psychology since the mid-1970s when Glass (1976) coined the term **meta-analysis**. From the late 1980s, research synthesis has been adopted by the medical sciences (Mulrow, 1987; Oxman & Guyatt, 1988). The foundation of the Cochrane Collaboration in the 1990s, an organisation that prepares and updates systematic reviews, was pivotal in establishing the systematic review as the method of choice for synthesising research in health care. The use of systematic reviews is now widespread and is strongly linked to evidence-based practice. A key concept in England's white paper, *The New NHS. Modern. Dependable* (Secretary of State, 1997), was clinical governance, which includes the implementation of best practice and the use of evidence-based interventions. Systematic reviews of randomised controlled trials (RCTs) are seen as the 'gold standard' for determining evidence-based practice.

In this chapter we provide a brief description of the processes involved in carrying out a systematic review. We illustrate the main processes with an example of a review and a reanalysis. After discussing systematic reviewing, we outline the technique of meta-analysis. Finally, we describe a method for combining information of different kinds into a single decision which we call **preference analysis**. For more detailed information, we recommend a report from the NHS Centre for Reviews and Dissemination (CRD) at the University of York (edited by Khan et al., 2001). A book edited by Egger, Davey Smith and Altman (2001) has an overview of recent research about factors that can bias systematic reviews. In this chapter, we follow closely the structure of the CRD report.

Knowing how to both carry out a systematic review and critically interpret a systematic review report are skills that health and clinical psychologists need to acquire. They are competences that enable the psychologist to integrate research findings with a view to making improvements in practice.

It has been estimated that over two million articles on biomedical research are published annually in over 20,000 journals (Mulrow, 1987). Even within a specialised field there could be hundreds or thousands of new papers each year, far too many to read and digest. Systematic reviews help to make this information more manageable, understandable and applicable. There are numerous other reasons why systematic reviews are considered useful in evidence-based practice. In total, Mulrow (1987) suggested nine advantages of systematic reviews:

1   Reduction and synthesis of multiple primary reports into digestible form.
2   Decision-makers, economists and policy-makers can use reviews to formulate guidelines.
3   Systematic reviews are an efficient technique that can, in principle, speed up health service improvements.
4   The generalisability of findings can be studied.
5   Consistency of findings can be explored.
6   Inconsistencies can be explained.
7   Systematic reviews can bring increased statistical power to collections of individual studies that may individually fail to show significant effects.
8   Increases in precision in estimates of risk or effect size.
9   Increased accuracy of estimates providing 'an improved reflection of reality'. (1987: 598)

In addition there is a tenth point: *a systematic review is an excellent method for gaining an in-depth understanding of a research field.*

Before summarising the procedures, we add a note of caution. Point 9 above is as clear and concise a statement of the realist view of science as one could hope to find. But, is the systematic review truly the unswerving road to reality that Mulrow and others have claimed? We have reasons to doubt it. Inevitably systematic reviews act like a sieve, selecting some evidence but rejecting other. To retain the visual metaphor, the reviewers act as a filter or lens; what they see and report depends on *how the selection process is operated.* Whenever there is ambiguity in the evidence, the selection process tends to operate in confirmatory mode, seeking positive support for a position or theory rather than disconfirmation. Therefore it is essential to be *critical and cautious in carrying out and interpreting* systematic reviews of biomedical and related topics. There is no question that systematic reviews have the potential to influence clinical and health psychology practice in many different ways.

To give three examples, systematic reviews of new pharmacological therapies to improve diabetes patients' quality of life, treat psychiatric disorders, or slow the progression of dementia would all be of great relevance to patient care. However, if we want to implement new practice as a direct consequence of such reviews, *we had better make certain that the findings are solid and not a mirage.* This is why study of the method itself is so important. Like all forms of knowledge, the results of a systematic review are the consequences of a process of negotiation about rules and criteria, and therefore cannot be accepted without criticism, debate and replication.

Now, to the main business of this chapter. The three stages in conducting a systematic review are:

Stage 1: Planning: defining the review topic and search parameters.
Stage 2: Reviewing: conducting the search using appropriate databases and sources.
Stage 3: Disseminating: summarising and disseminating the findings from the review.

These stages are described in turn.

STAGE 1 OF A SYSTEMATIC REVIEW: DEFINING THE REVIEW TOPIC AND SEARCH PARAMETERS

Assessing the need for a systematic review

A systematic review will take up a significant amount of time and effort. Before taking the plunge, it is wise to evaluate whether such a review is necessary and desirable. To avoid duplication, searches must be conducted to establish whether reviews or ongoing reviews are available. If there are no reviews or the available reviews are outdated or of poor quality, then updating an existing review, or carrying out a new review, is justified.

The best single source of systematic reviews is the Cochrane Library. The Cochrane Library contains the *Cochrane Database of Systematic Reviews (CDSR)*, the *Database of Abstracts of Reviews of Effectiveness (DARE)* and the *Health Technology Assessment (HTA)* database. DARE contains records of quality assessed reviews identified by highly sensitive searches carried out on *MEDLINE, CINAHL, BIOSIS, Current Contents Clinical Medicine* and *PsychInfo* since 1995.

Before starting work on a review, it is important to be aware of any relevant systematic reviews that may already be under way. This can be done by identifying key researchers in your chosen research area and finding out if they know of any systematic reviews that are currently being carried out. Other useful ways of identifying ongoing reviews are to consult the protocols in the CDSR, the titles of reviews in progress in the HTA database and the *National Research Register* (NRR).

A systematic review normally requires the skills of two or more researchers. If two or more people are to be involved, collaboration procedures need to be drawn up before the group commences working on the review. These procedures should include operational definitions of the inclusion criteria, the rules for making quality assessments, and procedures for negotiating any disagreements about inclusion and quality. The collaboration procedures also should include agreements about how often the review team will meet, and authorship arrangements of publications.

Assessing the viability of conducting the systematic review

Once the need for a new review has been established, you have to ask yourself whether you and/or your research unit have the time and resources to conduct the review. You will need to plan the work involved by looking at the scope of the literature on the topic. The time required to complete the review should be estimated. A timetable should be constructed with deadlines for when the various phases of the review are to be completed. Depending on its scope and complexity a systematic review could take anywhere between 6 and 24 months to complete. Systematic reviews can be quite costly. Two or more people will need to be involved in the review at various stages. There will be staffing or consultancy costs. Obtaining articles for the review can be costly. The cost of disseminating your findings should also be factored into your budget. You may decide that you need to seek funding to conduct the systematic review (see Chapter 2). If sufficient funds are available you or your organisation may decide to commission others to carry out the review by advertising in journals or web sites.

Developing a proposal for a systematic review

Key points are:

- The objectives of the review are clear and comprehensible.
- The methods to address the objectives are appropriate.
- The timetable is feasible.
- The review team is capable of undertaking the work.
- Dissemination will be fully carried out.
- The budget has been properly worked out and the necessary funds are available.

Developing a review protocol

A review protocol will need to be drawn up specifying the questions to be addressed by the review. The components of a protocol are summarised in Box 11.1. A summary of an actual protocol is given in the appendix to this chapter.

STAGE 2 OF A SYSTEMATIC REVIEW: CONDUCTING THE SEARCH USING APPROPRIATE DATABASES AND SOURCES

Having agreed the protocol, the next step is to carry out the review. A thorough search is needed to identify relevant studies for inclusion. Identified studies need to be assessed for quality and agreement on quality

---

Box 11.1   *Components of a systematic review protocol (Khan et al., 2001)*

- *Background*: describe why the review is needed.
- *Review questions*: state a clearly formulated question. Khan et al. (2001) define three health care issues that may be addressed. **Efficacy**: the extent to which an intervention produces a beneficial outcome under ideally controlled circumstances. Can it work? **Effectiveness**: the extent to which an intervention produces a beneficial outcome under ordinary day-to-day circumstances. Does it work? **Efficiency**: the extent to which the balance between inputs (costs) and outputs (outcomes) of interventions represents value for money. Are outcomes maximised for the given costs?
- *Search strategy*: identify relevant research, stating databases to be used and other sources, such as hand searches, along with the search terms.
- *Study selection criteria and procedures*: identify articles that help answer the review questions. The selection criteria define the population, interventions, outcomes and study designs of interest, and are applied to items found to make a decision about whether to obtain full copies. Once copies are obtained, apply the criteria and make decisions about inclusions.
- *Study quality assessment and study methodology*: draw up a list of criteria for assessing the quality of studies. Ideally, two or more researchers independently rate the quality of studies. Decide a cut-off score for inclusion in the review.
- *Data extraction strategy*: decide how to extract the data from the selected articles. Design a data extraction form.

---

is needed between two or more researchers. Once agreement for included studies has been made, agreement on data extraction is confirmed, and once all relevant and appropriate data have been extracted, the data can be analysed. It is essential that the researchers maintain good communication throughout the review by holding regular meetings.

The processes used in carrying out a systematic review should be replicable and transparent. Good documentation of the review is therefore essential. It is a good idea to keep a diary or notebook throughout the whole process, making entries each time that work is completed and giving reasons for any changes and amendments.

Identification of relevant studies

It is necessary to draw up a complete list of primary studies, both published and unpublished, relevant to the review question. A thorough search strategy is required, a strategy that is continually updated. A huge range of electronic databases is available to help with searches. It is important to have a good understanding of how to use the databases as articles can be missed by improper use of databases or inadequate search strategies. Also databases are incomplete and not completely up-to-date and so consulting databases alone is insufficient. A thorough search must also include searches in a number of other sources of relevant literature:

- Reference lists from primary and review articles.
- The 'grey literature' consisting of conference proceedings, books, dissertations.
- Unpublished reports.
- Hand searches in key journals.
- Consulting known researchers.
- The internet.

Once all the known articles on primary studies have been collected, one needs to make sure that they match the inclusion criteria.

Selection of studies

Only those studies that address the review question(s) must be included in the review, whatever their titles may be and wherever they were obtained. To minimise bias, predetermined written criteria must be adhered to. Once you have a list of potential studies, you need to obtain the abstracts, filter your list and check that the reasons you decide to include and exclude studies are within the written criteria. If the criteria appear faulty in some way, and you decide to amend them, you will have to go back to the beginning and review all of the articles again. Written rules of inclusion and exclusion are open to interpretation. Ideally, decisions should be taken independently by two researchers, and a measure of agreement obtained.

Study designs may be listed in an 'evidence hierarchy' intended to reflect the degree of control and, inversely, the amount of bias that is possible in studies using the designs:

1 RCTs.
2 Quasi-experimental studies (without randomisation).
3 Controlled observation studies:
   (a) cohort studies
   (b) case control studies.
4 Observational studies without control groups (cross-sectional studies).
5 Case studies.
6 Expert clinical opinion and the 'wise professor'.

Designs listed in 3 above are used in the field of epidemiology, currently engaging in some soul-searching about the lack of progress made in that discipline with systematic reviewing and meta-analysis (Dickersin, 2002; Egger et al., 2002). Qualitative studies are in a very ambiguous position in relation to the categories of information in the above hierarchy of evidence. We return to this issue in the final section of the chapter.

Study quality assessment and bias

Quality assessments can be used to determine a threshold quality score and to guide the final selection and interpretation of findings. It is inevitable that the studies that match your selection criteria will have a widely varying degree of quality. You will have to decide what constitutes a minimum quality level for research in the area of your review.

For example, in the review of studies of smoking cessation (see next section), biomarkers such as breath carbon monoxide readings were considered an important feature of research design because such readings validate self-reported smoking status. Quitting, and relapsing, smokers often are economical with the truth when asked about their cigarette consumption. A biochemical marker helps to keep them honest. Thus one study may rely on smokers' self-reports as evidence of smoking status, whereas another, otherwise equally well-designed, study may ask participants to confirm their smoking status by monitoring exhaled carbon monoxide levels. The outcome measures from the latter study would be considered more valid and therefore score more highly in a quality assessment. However, agreement must be reached between researchers carrying out the quality ratings over how quality criteria are to be interpreted. Rules tend to be interpreted differently by different people. For example, smoking cessation studies could be evaluated according to a criterion that biomarkers were used to confirm self-reported cessation status in at least 90 per cent of cases. Therefore, the researchers would have to negotiate what the term 'case' means. Does the criterion mean that biomarker confirmation is needed in 90 per cent of *all* participants or in 90 per cent of *those participants who gave a biomarker reading*? The latter is often a lower proportion of the total because not all participants necessarily contribute a biomarker reading.

The application of rules and criteria for evaluating quality are matters of judgement, and so which studies are included and excluded, and how studies are to be weighted in any pooling of the data, are subjective matters for the reviewers to resolve. End-users of the review must take these more subjective aspects into account.

Data extraction and monitoring

Data extraction involves the transfer of information from the **primary study** reports to the synthesised data set. As Khan et al. (2001) state: 'This can be a subjective process and is prone to error'. A specially designed data extraction form should be produced as a part of the review protocol (see above). Forms should be easy to use and not waste time by being overly complex to fill in. Data extraction is comparable to data collection in a primary study. To ensure 100 per cent accuracy and consistency across studies, it is important that every figure is checked and double-checked, by at least two people, otherwise the review findings will be erroneous and a lot of research effort will have been wasted. Primary data are sometimes published in multiple publications, especially in reviews or in serial publications in the case of longitudinal or follow-up studies. It is important that each unique dataset is extracted only once.

Data synthesis

Data synthesis can take two forms: tabulation or quantitative synthesis. In the former, the data from the primary reports are summarised as meaningfully as possible in a table with columns for each of the main characteristics of the studies, for example, authors, date, nature of sample, sample size, setting, intervention, outcome as an effect size and quality rating. An average effect size is obtained by weighting each study according to its perceived importance, based on its sample size, quality or some combination of the two. Only studies that are considered homogeneous with respect to the kinds of characteristics listed above can be weighted together into a single pooled effect. An example of tabulated pooling is given at the end of this chapter. Quantitative synthesis, or meta-analysis, is described in the next section.

Box 11.2   *Steps in carrying out a meta-analysis*

Step 1: convert the data into effect sizes.
Step 2: statistically pool the effect size data into a single estimate.

STAGE 3 OF A SYSTEMATIC REVIEW: REPORTING AND DISSEMINATION

The report and recommendations

If a review is to have any chance of making some impact on practice, it must be disseminated widely and effectively. There are various formats and audiences for a review. A dry and lengthy report might be appropriate for a dissertation or funding body, but would be completely unsuitable for busy health care managers who may or may not be persuaded to implement the review findings. For the latter group a report must be both credible and persuasive with a simple 'take-home' message, for example: 'Stop prescribing drug X; prescribe therapy Y instead, because it is five times more effective.' One of the most common ways of disseminating a systematic review is to write up the review for publication in a peer-reviewed journal. This is considered the most prestigious form of dissemination in the academic world. You will need to identify which journal you think will have the most impact. Then follow that particular journal's rules for submission. Unfortunately many journals do not provide guidance for authors of systematic reviews. This can make publication a risky and lengthy process and it might take one to two years for the review to appear.

In the meantime, it is worth disseminating your results using other methods. It is rare for the results of a review to be simplified and put into lay terms. Often the end-user and patient groups most relevant to a review are excluded from seeing the findings. We would like to encourage you to find creative ways to make your results reach a wider audience. This could include giving a presentation at support groups or associations, sending a summary of your results to an internet group, or preparing a press release of your results. You may also like to think about obtaining funding to prepare eye-catching material to present the results in a user-friendly way.

The title of the report should be informative but concise. Long titles do not attract the reader's attention. The title should be a true reflection of the results, perhaps using a declarative style such as: 'Psychological therapy for smokers is 10 times more cost-effective than simple advice.'

The abstract or executive summary may be the only text that is read by many readers. Readers need to be able to rapidly judge the quality of the review and of the findings. This section should be clear, have a limited amount of technical language and use a language that is accessible to most professionals.

The review protocol can be followed to guide the writing of the main text of the report. The review questions should be clearly stated. The review methods should be described in detail so that the review can be repeated or extended. The report should be as clear and as applicable as possible.

The discussion is an important part of the text in drawing the work together. There should be a statement of the main findings of the review. Importantly, you need to express awareness of the strengths and weaknesses of the review. Put your review in the context of other reviews, considering any differences in quality and results. Describe the direction and magnitude of the effect observed in summarised studies along with the applicability of the findings of the review. End the discussion with recommendations and practical implications for clinicians or policy-makers. Finally, add a conclusion that states any unanswered questions and implications for future research. Whatever format you choose for the publication of a review, the reader should be able to judge the validity and the implications of the findings.

Getting evidence into practice

Ideally, the results of every valid systematic review would rapidly be put into practice. For various reasons this does not happen. There is even evidence that findings from systematic reviews will not always be effective in practice. What can work (efficacy) may not work in practice (effectiveness). For example, Law and Tang's (1995) review concluded that brief verbal interventions involving simple advice were effective. Yet a recent study suggests that the brief verbal interventions have been shown to be ineffective (Hajek, Taylor & Mills, 2002). This does not mean that systematic reviews cannot play a significant role in the development of good practice. We just do not think anybody should develop an uncritical acceptance of the findings from systematic reviews. Critical appraisal of the methods used in systematic reviews is as vital as for any other method.

Systematic reviews of observational studies

Until recently there has been a fairly rigid insistence, at least in medical circles, that RCTs are the only acceptable source of evidence on effectiveness (Dixon-Woods & Fitzpatrick, 2001). For example, a *British Medical Journal* editorial stated: 'Only randomised controlled trials allow valid inferences of cause and effect. Only randomised controlled trials have the potential directly to affect patient care' (Altman, 1996). That view is still dominant, but there is increasing interest in the idea that other kinds of evidence including observational studies and qualitative methods can also be used in systematic reviews. This is due to the fact that carrying out RCTs in some areas (for example, health promotion and public health programmes) is often not feasible or is unethical.

The literature suggests that systematic reviews using observational studies are more easily distorted by confounding and selection biases than reviews of RCTs. The results of observational studies may appear very precise but they can be spurious as a result of these problems. For example, Egger, Davey Smith and Schneider (2001) discuss the evidence linking smoking with suicide from four prospective studies of middle-aged men, including the cohort of 390,000 men in the Multiple Risk Factor Intervention Trial (MRFIT). A dose-related increase in risk of suicide with number of cigarettes smoked per day is apparent in the data. Although this relationship is strong enough to be assumed to be causal, the association seems implausible (unless one assumed that the failure to quit after repeated attempts makes one suicidal). It seems more plausible that the association is based on a third common causal factor in the form of the predisposing psychosocial characteristics of people who both smoke and commit suicide (for example, depression). In other instances, systematic reviews of observational studies may yield plausible but equally spurious associations. When observational reviews are compared to RCT reviews the results may go in opposite directions, for example, the 'protective' effect of beta-carotene intake on cardiovascular mortality in observational studies became an increased risk factor when studied in RCTs (Egger, Davey Smith & Altman, 2001). The dangers of bias in systematic reviews are therefore higher when observational studies are reviewed.

One of the main challenges for evidence-based practice is the *illusion of certainty* created by the belief that systematic reviews produce evidence of best practice. Steps are needed to improve the quality of systematic reviews. It is also necessary to recognise the potential contribution of different forms of evidence beyond RCTs. The complexities of integrating knowledge from different study designs remain a significant challenge (see below).

Box 11.3   *Summary of steps in a systematic review (CRD report, Khan et al., 2001)*

Stage 1: planning the review

Step 1: identification of the need for the review.
Step 2: preparation of a proposal for a review.
Step 3: development of review proposal.

Stage 2: conducting a review

Step 4: identification of research.
Step 5: selection of studies.
Step 6: study quality assessment.
Step 7: data extraction and monitoring progress.
Step 8: data synthesis (tabulation or meta-analysis).

Stage 3: reporting and dissemination

Step 9: the report and recommendations.
Step 10: getting evidence into practice.

META-ANALYSIS

Meta-analysis is a set of techniques that enable the findings from primary studies to be statistically integrated and accumulated. Ideally the results section of every new study report would include a cumulative meta-analysis showing the results of the study as a single point in the cumulative pool of evidence concerning the effect being studied. There is no fixed or correct way of carrying out a meta-analysis. Each analysis is to some degree tailored to the specific circumstances. It is possible to divide the process into steps. The first three steps overlap completely with those described for systematic reviews above: (1) define the research question; (2) carry out a literature search; (3) extract the relevant data.

The next steps apply specifically to meta-analysis: (4) the data extracted from the primary studies must be converted into a common statistic or metric for the meta-analysis. This metric is normally a measure of effect size. This provides an index for the strength or importance of the relationship between two variables, or of the outcome of an intervention. Two of the best-established procedures are those developed by Glass (1976) and Hunter, Schmidt and Jackson (1982), the latter being an extension of the former.

For a series of studies involving two groups or conditions, Glass proposed an effect size statistic, δ, delta, as follows:

$$\delta = \frac{\text{mean of the experimental group} - \text{mean of the control group}}{\text{standard deviation of the control group}}$$

Cohen proposed a statistic, d, that is very similar to Glass' δ except that the standard deviation is pooled across both groups (see Chapter 10). Hedges' adjusted g measure is a version of Cohen's d adjusted by correcting for small sample bias. Hunter, Schmidt and Jackson (1982) used the Pearson Product Moment Correlation, r, as the expression of effect size. Their approach makes corrections for sampling error, study differences in errors of measurement, range restrictions, instrument validity, and computational, typographical and transcription errors.

Step 5 is to combine the individual effect size estimates from primary studies into a single pooled measure of the effect size. Different formulae are based on different assumptions about the nature of the effect, principally about whether the true effect size is assumed to be fixed (that is the same) or random across the different studies. A formula is used that combines the individual effect sizes by calculating a weighted average according to the precision of each estimate assessed using its standard error. It is important to state the confidence interval for any estimate of effect size (see Chapter 10).

A range of commercial and public domain software for meta-analysis is available. The free software is usually DOS-based and less user-friendly while the commercial software are generally Windows-based (further details may be found by consulting Sterne, Egger & Sutton, 2001).

Rosenthal (1979) contributed the concept of the **file drawer problem** which concerns the probability that there is a relatively large number of unpublished studies that have less significant results than the published studies: 'the journals are filled with the 5 per cent of studies that show Type I errors, while the file drawers back at the lab are filled with the 95 per cent of studies that show nonsignificant (e.g., P>0.05) results'. This concept is otherwise referred to as **'publication bias'**. There is good evidence that the bias is real (Dickersin, 1997; Sterling, 1959; Sterling, Rosenbaum & Weinkam, 1995) although the reluctance to publish non-significant results lies as much with authors as with editors. Even if the unpublished studies can be traced, whether the unpublished data should be included in systematic reviews and meta-analyses is a difficult question to answer. Unpublished studies may not only produce more non-significant results, they may be poorer in quality, and some may also be commercial in nature. It has become a standard practice in presenting meta-analyses in psychology journals to calculate the size of the file drawer that would be necessary to cancel out the obtained effect size.

CAN QUALITATIVE AND QUANTITATIVE EVIDENCE BE COMBINED?

We began this book by discussing ontology (what there is to be known, in other words, what reality is) and epistemology (how knowledge can be obtained). We focused on the *realism/constructivism debate* (see Chapter. 1). We argued that subjectivity is seen as pure, rational thought, internal to the individual and separate from the body. The rational mind is viewed as the vehicle with which we can seek to understand and control a mechanical, physical world. The researcher's task is to attempt to obtain accurate information about objective physical reality by maximising the precision of our observations and ensuring that error and bias are eliminated. Subjective distortions of reality may also be introduced by us as researchers and, in psychology, by human participants, and these potential sources of bias must also be minimised. These principles are illustrated further in our example of a systematic review at the end of this chapter.

In turning to the possibility of integrating qualitative evidence into systematic reviews we are facing an obvious dilemma. On the one hand, there is the realist idea that there is a single objective reality to be observed, if only the nuisance factors of error and subjectivity can be eliminated. On the other, there is the post-realist idea that all knowledge is subjective and negotiated. Surely we cannot have it both ways? Or is there perhaps a third way enabling integration of knowledge from different epistemological sources?

Firstly, we must ask how the idea of having a synthesis of research that is systematic can be achieved with qualitative evidence. It is manifestly true that synthesis of qualitative data is not only possible, but that it is the essential process in carrying out a qualitative study. It is the process of synthesis that makes a collection of stories, discourse or interviews intelligible in the context of the participants' experience that defines the collection as data for a research study. If within-study synthesis is possible, there can be no reason in principle why across-study synthesis should also not be feasible. The key issues here are comparability and transparency. The processes used to generate the data should be the same and they should be replicable across different sites and in different contexts (Deeks et al., 2001).

Secondly, if we can solve the problem of integrating qualitative data, then is there also a possibility that qualitative evidence can be integrated with quantitative evidence in making decisions about health care? In fact this question is academic because this integration of knowledge occurs continuously in both everyday life and professional practice. As far as the world of health care is concerned, the combination of qualitative, subjective knowledge in the form of clinical judgement is constantly being integrated with more objective, factual information emanating from the professional community using research and good practice in every decision and action. The challenge is to design a method that will allow synthesis to happen in a way that is transparent, systematic and replicable. To date, that has not been possible.

PREFERENCE ANALYSIS

As we have seen above, health care decisions require a mixture of evidence of different kinds, both quantitative and qualitative. Yet we have no means of doing this formally. A further necessary ingredient in the messy mix of information and activities that constitutes health care decision-making is **economic evaluation.** Economic evaluation of alternative courses of action is becoming the key consideration in making health care decisions (Drummond et al., 1997). Yet, in spite of its pivotal importance, economic evaluation normally occurs alongside, or in parallel with, systematic reviews of effectiveness, *not as an integral part of the systematic review itself.* This situation is inelegant and unsatisfactory because, sooner or later, cost and the effectiveness must be brought together into a single decision about whether or not an intervention should be included in services. Attempts to integrate effectiveness with cost data are hampered by theoretical problems that health economists are struggling to solve (for example, Vale et al., 2000).

To add to these difficulties, no way has yet been found for effectively giving voice to patients' preferences about the quality of interventions, in spite of the fact that patients are literally at the sharp end of receiving them. This is where the special contribution of qualitative methods comes into play, because they are designed to explore the phenomenology, construction and articulation of lived experience. Yet the outputs of these methods are difficult to blend with quantitative data. Nevertheless, quantitative methods can be used to attempt to measure subjective experience through the use of questionnaires and rating scales. Ratings of pain, symptom severity, depression, anxiety, quality of life, side-effects and other clinical phenomena are capable of providing reliable and valid data on patient experience (Bowling, 1995). Qualitative ratings (i.e. ratings of qualities) can also be analysed in ways that produce interval, ordinal or ratio scales.

A new method for combining effectiveness, economic evidence about quality into a single decision is called 'preference analysis' (Marks, 2003). This method enables us to integrate evidence into a single preference score by using a simple formula called the **preference theorem**. This is modelled on Bayes' theorem, a way of integrating subjective probabilities in a single formula for adjusting beliefs (see Chapter 10). In Bayes' theorem there is no limit to the amount or kind of evidence that can be combined. The preference theorem operates in a similar manner, except that instead of entering only probabilities into the equation, costs and preferences are entered as well. Then it is possible to compute a **preference index** (π) that tells us how much a new treatment is preferable to a control treatment, usually standard care. The likelihood ratios of Bayes' theorem are replaced by preference ratios, one for each type of evidence: (a) effectiveness ratios from RCTs, systematic reviews or meta-analyses; (b) efficiency ratios from economic evaluation of treatment costs; (c) acceptability ratios from measures of patient perceptions of the acceptability of the treatment, including any side-effects or other problems.

The preference adjustment process has three stages: (1) setting the initial preference values; (2) carrying out systematic research to gather evidence of three kinds, on effectiveness, costs and acceptability; (3) computing the revised preference values in the light of the new evidence.

Imagine that we are planning a study providing evidence (E) about a new intervention, T_N. We are interested in comparing T_N with the standard treatment T_O. The three steps are as follows:

Step 1: before we begin the investigation, it is necessary to assign a value to our prior preference for T_N relative to T_O (π_0). This is a value on a ratio scale of the extent to which we currently prefer T_N to T_O. For example, if we have no reason to prefer T_N over T_O, $\pi_0 = 1$. If we already have the opinion that T_N is overall twice as good as T_O we put $\pi_0 = 2$. To avoid building our initial biases into the equation, the most conservative and even-handed value of π_0 is 1.0.

Step 2: we carry out our investigation and gather the best possible evidence on the relative effectiveness, costs and acceptability of T_N and T_O. This analysis will include RCT evidence of effectiveness, economic evaluation of costs and evidence from the end-users (patients or public) on their preferences.

Step 3: the final stage is to calculate the impact of the evidence on the preference index. Three basic categories of data are: (1) evidence (E) from a systematic review or meta-analysis on the relative effectiveness of T_N compared to T_O ($E_N/E_O = R_E$); (2) economic evidence (C) about the efficiency, which is the reciprocal of the cost, of T_N relative to T_O ($C_O/C_N = R_C$); (3) Evidence about the acceptability (Q) of T_N compared to T_O ($Q_N/Q_O = R_Q$). The third ratio uses a quantitative score which can be derived from evidence about quality. Evidence from studies of the acceptability of the treatments is obtained from patients who have experienced the treatments.

The three kinds of evidence are integrated into a single decision using the preference theorem and decision rule (see Box 11.4).

The three kinds of evidence can be weighted equally or differentially. The procedures are systematic, transparent and replicable. A specific example of the use of the preference theorem is presented in Box 11.5.

Box 11.4   *The preference theorem (Marks, 2003)*

The preference, $_1$, of treatment T_N over treatment T_O is defined by:

$$\pi_1 = \pi_0 \cdot w_S \; R_E \cdot w_C \; R_C \cdot w_Q \; R_Q$$

where

> π_1 = the post-preference index for T_N relative to T_O
> π_0 = the prior preference index for T_N relative to T_O
> R_E = the ratio of the effectiveness of T_N relative to T_O
> R_C = the ratio of the efficiency of T_N relative to T_O
> R_Q = the ratio of the quality of patient experience of T_N relative to T_O

w_E, w_Q and w_C are the weights assigned to the three kinds of information E, C and Q.

If $\pi_1 > 1.0$, T_N is preferable to T_O

Box 11.5   *Using the preference theorem (Marks & Sykes, 2002)*

A treatment for smoking cessation, psychologist-led cognitive behaviour therapy, CBT (T_N), was compared to a standard, control treatment consisting of health promotion advice (T_O) in a RCT with a sample of 220 smokers. In order to use the preference theorem we need values for π_0, R_E, R_C and R_Q. Because no value for π_0 is available, we will set π_0 equal to 1.00. This assumes that no prior preference for T_N or T_O existed. The RCT results showed that, at 12-month follow-up, 19.8 per cent receiving CBT were abstinent compared to 5.8 per cent of the control group. Therefore **R_E = 19.8/5.8 = 3.41**. The unit costs of the CBT and control treatments were calculated to be £19.40 and £13.40 respectively. Therefore **R_C = 13.40/19.8 = 0.68** (efficiency = 1/cost). Quality ratings were not available from this study. However, the value for R_Q can be estimated from data collected in previous evaluations. Ratings of the overall quality of the CBT treatment are routinely obtained along a 5-point rating scale: excellent, very good, good, OK and poor. 85 per cent of participants rate the CBT treatment as excellent, very good or good. We estimated that 36 per cent of smokers receiving the control treatment give ratings in these categories. Therefore **R_Q = 85/36 = 2.36**.

Next we enter the estimates of π_0, R_E, R_C and R_Q into the theorem and assign values to the weights. In this case we will weight the three types of evidence equally, setting w_S, w_C and w_Q all equal to 1.0. Our preference π_1 for CBT over the control treatment, in light of the evidence above, is defined as follows:

$$_1 = _0 \cdot w_S \; R_E \cdot w_C \; R_C \cdot w_Q \; R_Q$$
$$_1 = 1 \times 1 \times 3.41 \times 1 \times 0.68 \times 1 \times 2.36 = 5.46$$

The CBT has a preference index of 5.45, indicating that it is 5.46 times better than standard care. The decision rule indicates that it would be rational to adopt CBT in place of standard care.

Box 11.6   *Steps in carrying out a preference analysis (Marks, 2003)*

Step 1: state an initial preference value concerning a new treatment, N, compared to an old treatment, O.
Step 2: carry out systematic research to gather evidence on effectiveness, costs and acceptability.
Step 3: compute the revised preference value using the preference theorem.

The preference theorem offers a potential solution to a fundamental problem in evidence-based health care: how to make a single decision based on evidence on effectiveness, efficiency and acceptability. Its use is summarised in Box 11.6. However, whether the complexities and variety of patients' attitudes to treatments can really be adequately represented by a single value in an equation remains open to debate, and the reliability and validity of the procedures for transforming evidence on quality into quantitative ratings are not yet fully established.

AN EXAMPLE OF A SYSTEMATIC REVIEW AND A REANALYSIS

Law and Tang (1995) carried out a systematic review of RCTs concerned with the effectiveness of interventions intended to help people stop smoking. The review covered a wide range of therapeutic procedures including nicotine replacement therapy, doctor's advice, acupuncture, hypnosis and psychological interventions. We are concerned here with the section of their review that dealt with group sessions led by psychologists. The outcome measure they employed was the point abstinence rate at six months. The effectiveness of an intervention was assessed by subtracting the abstinence rate in the control group from the abstinence rate in the treatment group. The mean effectiveness score for psychologist-led therapies was 0.7 per cent (95 per cent CI: −4.3–5.7). The abstract stated that psychological interventions were not cost-effective, yet no evidence on cost-effectiveness had been obtained by any of the primary studies. It was decided to carry out a reanalysis of Law and Tang's review for five reasons:

1   The literature search had not included the most important database for psychological studies, PsychInfo.
2   There were no quality assessments of the primary studies.
3   Errors were found in the data extraction.
4   All kinds of different psychological treatments were mixed together including behavioural therapies in the form of aversive therapy and cognitive therapy.

5   The abstract stated that non-specific behaviour modification therapy is not cost-effective, yet the primary studies did not include any measures of cost-effectiveness.

These problems suggested that Law and Tang's systematic review could be flawed. Our search using PsychInfo identified four primary studies that Law and Tang had not included. We prepared a set of ten criteria for evaluating studies and independently evaluated all of the primary studies originally included by Law and Tang together with the four extra studies. Quality assessments were carried out independently by the two authors. The quality assessments were then compared. If the total scores for a study differed by more than two points, the score was considered a disagreement. There was a disagreement on four studies. The researchers discussed these studies until an agreement, or a difference of two points or less, was reached. The scores were then averaged. The median score was seven. Papers with a score of five and above were considered to be of sufficient quality to be included in the review.

Eight studies from Law and Tang's review were found to be methodologically flawed. Law and Tang had included trials that had compared one treatment with another, without a control group, reducing the effectiveness scores that were computed as the difference between treatment effects. Aversion therapy trials were included twice, distorting the results. In some studies, inappropriate controls were used, for example, placebo drug treatments.

The eight primary studies that were not considered suitable for inclusion on methodological grounds were:

1   Barbarin (1978): the therapy in this study was aversion therapy and counted twice in two different sections of the review.
2   Cottraux et al. (1983): this study used an unsuitable control. The placebo was a pharmaceutical intervention (lactose capsules) rather than a non-specific therapist-led treatment.
3   Fee (1977): aversion therapy was employed and counted twice in two different sections of the review.
4   Ginsberg et al. (1992): a pharmacological treatment, nicotine replacement therapy, was used as a control.
5   Lowe et al. (1980): there was no proper control in this study. All smokers received a psychological intervention – self-control procedures or covert sensitisation.
6   Raw and Russell (1980): there was no proper control condition in this study; it compared three treatments: support, cue exposure and rapid smoking.
7   Rosser (1984): this study did not have a group session as part of the control so it was in effect a self-help treatment and therefore not valid as a control condition.
8   Thompson et al. (1988): this study did not include any psychologist-led therapy and so is not relevant.

Table 11.1   *Reanalysis of trials of group sessions led by a psychologist: abstinence rates at 4–12 months follow-up[1] (Sykes & Marks, 2002)*

Trial		Intervention group		Control group		Difference
Authors/year	Quality rating	Quitters	%	Quitters	%	%
Delahunt et al. (1976) (6)[2]	5.0	*2/9[4]*	22.2	*0/13*	*0.0*	22.2
Elliott et al. (1978) (6)	6.5	9/20	45.0	3/19	15.8	29.2
Glasgow et al. (1981) (6)	7.5	6/30	20.0	*0/14*	0.0	20.0B[3]
Hall et al. (1984) (6)	8.0	26/65	40.0	20/70	28.6	11.4B
Mothersill et al. (1988) (12)	8.0	15/86	17.4	11/78	14.1	3.3
Jason et al. (1988) (4)	7.5	13/66	19.7	6/71	8.2	11.5
Owens et al. (1989) (9)	8.5	2/14	13.8	3/40	7.5	6.3
Richmond et al. (1993) (12)	8.5	33/98	34.0	5/34	15.0	19.0
Windsor et al. (1988) (12)	8.5	19/133	14.0	7/139	5.0	9.0B
Overall	**7.5**	**125/521**	**24.0[5]**	**55/478**	**11.5[5]**	**12.5[5]**
95% CI			16.2–34.0		3.5–17.4	8.1–21.1

1   Abstinence rates are based on intention to treat point prevalence.
2   The number in brackets is the follow-up period in months.
3   B indicates that biochemical markers were available for at least 90 per cent of the followed-up sample.
4   Italics show recomputation of errors in the review reported by Law and Tang (1995).
5   The overall means are weighted by sample sizes for each condition in the nine primary studies.

Table 11.1 shows the reanalysis of the effectiveness of psychologist-led group interventions for smoking cessation. This analysis excludes the eight unsuitable studies but includes four additional studies found by searching PsychInfo. The reanalysis also corrected errors found in the computation of effectiveness and weighted study outcomes by sample size. The overall effect size based on 999 smokers in 9 studies was 12.5 per cent (95 per cent CI: 8.1–21.1 per cent). This figure is totally different from the figure computed by Law and Tang.

This reanalysis shows how sensitive systematic reviews are to selection bias. A number of potential flaws have been revealed: (a) inadequate searches of the literature can omit important studies which, when they are included, can have a major impact on the overall effect size; (b) quality controls need to be employed in choosing which primary studies are included; (c) data extraction must be carefully checked to ensure that errors are not made in calculating the efficacy scores; (d) the abstract must not contain conclusions that do not follow from the review findings.

However rigorously conducted, systematic reviews remain open to interpretation. Different results will be found depending on the rules and criteria that are employed. In the example above, the 'lenses' used by the two review teams yielded two radically different reflections of reality. Reality is perceived differently with different lenses. Bias can never be eliminated, only negotiated, and the amount of bias in any particular review is not easily determined. Therefore the most useful reviews are transparent, replicable and applicable.

SUMMARY

Systematic reviews involve a set of procedures for making literature reviews transparent, replicable and applicable. They have the potential to provide useful information about the effects of interventions, concerning what works and what doesn't work. Meta-analysis integrates the evidence statistically into a single score. As with any other method, however, biases and errors may occur and caution is required in interpreting systematic reviews and meta-analyses. Also, systematic reviews and meta-analyses have been narrowly concentrated on RCTs and observational data. Evidence on patient experience and economic efficiency need to be combined with effectiveness data into a single decision process about alternative treatments. Preference analysis, a new method for generating a single preference index using all three sources of evidence, is described. Further research must establish the validity and practical utility of such methods for integrating evidence about health interventions.

RECOMMENDED READING

Books

Egger, M., Davey Smith, G. & Altman, D.G. (eds) (2001). *Systematic reviews in health care: meta-analysis in context* (2nd edn). London: BMJ Books.

Khan, K.S., ter Riet, G., Glanville, J., Sowden, A.J. & Kleijnen, J. (eds) (2001). *Undertaking systematic reviews of research on effectiveness. CRD's guidance for those carrying out or commissioning reviews*. CRD Report No. 4 (2nd edn). University of York: NHS Centre for Reviews and Dissemination.

Web sites

The CRD web site: http://www.york.ac.uk/inst/crd/srinfo.htm

The Cochrane Collaboration's Review Manager (Rev Man version 4.03): http://www.cochrane-org/cochrane/revma.htm

The Health Development Agency's web site:
http://www.hda-online.org.uk/evidence

National Research Register:
http://www.update-software.com/National/

The National Institute of Clinical Excellence NICE web site:
http://www.nice.org.uk/nice-web/

The web site for the book by Egger, Davey Smith & Altman (2001): http://www.systematicreviews.com

---

REVISION QUESTIONS

1 What advantages does a systematic review have over a conventional or 'narrative' review?
2 What are the main parts of a systematic review protocol?
3 What is meant by an 'evidence hierarchy'?
4 How does meta-analysis complement a systematic review?
5 What is meant by the 'file-drawer problem'?
6 How can effectiveness, efficiency and patient preference be combined in a single formula?

APPENDIX: AN ILLUSTRATION OF A REVIEW PROTOCOL

This appendix summarises the protocol designed for the reanalysis of a systematic review of psychological interventions used to aid smoking cessation described in the text (Sykes & Marks, 2002).

Background

There are over 120,000 smoking related deaths each year in England. In 1998 £60 million was pledged to invest in smoking cessation resources over three years. The focus of this money was providing free nicotine replacement therapy (NRT). Money was also spent on a campaign in the year 2000 entitled 'Don't give up giving up'.

Close inspection of the systematic review used to inform policy-makers about the efficacy of smoking cessation methods by Law and Tang (1995) revealed a flaw. Despite investigating the efficacy of psychological interventions, it failed to search a major psychological database (PsychInfo) thus ignoring a large amount of psychological evidence related to smoking cessation.

This systematic review will partially replicate Law and Tang's study but also search PsychInfo for studies in the same period. Errors in Law and Tang's data extraction will be corrected. Also Law and Tang did not assess the quality of the studies included in their systematic review. This reanalysis will include a quality assessment. To ensure comparability with Law and Tang, only studies up to 1995 will be included.

Review question

What is the efficacy of psychological interventions to aid smoking cessation in adults?

Search strategy

1   All the articles on non-specific behaviour modification led by a psychologist previously reviewed by Law and Tang will be rereviewed and the effect-size will be remeasured.
2   PsychInfo will be searched for psychological interventions to aid smoking cessation for articles from 1967–95.

Search terms   The following search terms were used to find articles in PsychInfo: smoking cessation/tobacco smoking +

a)   relaxation
b)   visualisation
c)   visualization
d)   imagery
e)   trigger
f)   positive reasons
g)   psychological
h)   behaviour therapy
i)   randomised controlled trial
g)   randomized controlled trial
k)   post-treatment follow-up
l)   follow-up study
m)   psychotherapy

Database   PsychInfo

Hand search   *Journal of Behavioral Medicine* 1990–95

Study selection criteria

Participants   Adults (>16 years of age) using a psychological intervention to aid smoking cessation irrespective of their interest in stopping smoking.

Interventions   Non-specific approaches: relaxation as an alternative to smoking, visualisation, idenitification of triggers, emphasis on positive reasons for stopping.

Outcomes   Cessation or significant reduction for at least six months verified by biological markers (carbon monoxide, thiocyonate or cotinine).

Study design   Randomised controlled trial.

Search procedure

CS will select studies for the inclusion into the review. Identified studies will be screened for suitability using the inclusion criteria by CS and DM. Both researchers are familiar with smoking cessation research.

Study quality assessment checklists and procedures

The quality of each study will be scored between 0 to 10, giving one point
for:

- adequate randomisation
- adequate participants (i.e. includes power analysis or over 100 participants in each group)
- biomarkers confirm self-reported cessation status in 90 per cent of cases
- suitable comparison interventions
- similar groups at baseline
- no other confounding intervention
- acceptable drop-out rate (25 per cent or less)
- motivation to quit measured
- reliable measurement techniques
- appropriate statistical analyses

The quality assessments will be done by CS and DM independently. CS
and DM will agree the definitions of the quality criteria. The delphi method
of achieving agreement will be used.

Data extraction strategy

A data extraction form will be used to obtain the necessary information
from the selected studies:

> *Data extraction form*
> General information
> Date of extraction:
> Study reference:
> Author contact details:
> Identification number in systematic review:
> Notes:

Study characteristics

Verification of study eligibility:

- participants
- intervention
- outcome
- design

Quality assessment score:

Methodology

Intervention:
Number of condition groups:
Duration of intervention:

Outcome

What was measured at baseline?
What was measured after the intervention?
Who carried out the measurement?

Analysis

Statistical analyses used:
Attrition rate:
Follow-up rates for each condition

Results

	Condition A (mean, SD)	Condition B	Condition C
Variable 1			
Pre			
Post			
Variable 2			
Pre			
Post			

Data analysis

When it is established that a meta-analysis is possible and appropriate, 3 choices will be decided:

1   Which comparisons will be made?
2   Which outcome measure will be used?
3   Which effect measure will be used to describe effectiveness?

GLOSSARY

Action research: a co-operative approach to research in which all the participants play an active research role in the research process, including: selecting the problem(s) to be addressed by the research; designing the study, which should include some form of intervention or *'change experiment'* intended to address the problem(s) identified; and analysing the outcome of the intervention; then putting the findings into practice to improve the situation.

Artefact: any type of methodological, statistical or measurement error that makes the results of a study unreliable, e.g. incomplete randomisation, imperfect sampling, poor controls or using inappropriate methods of analysis.

Bayesian or **subjectivist approach**: a method for statistical inference that uses subjective probabilities, which are revised in the light of new evidence, allowing the probability of a hypothesis to be directly assessed. The approach is an alternative to the *frequentist* or *classical* approach.

Between-groups design: a design that employs two or more independent groups of participants at least one of which is given a treatment or intervention and another of which may be a control condition.

Bias: a systematic or non-random error in a study caused by differences in selection, context, measurement or attrition between treatment groups.

Bonferroni adjustment: a method for adjusting the required significance level when multiple (N) statistical tests are carried out. The chosen alpha α level is divided by N so that the adjusted significance level, $P_a = \alpha N$. Thus, if the desired p level is 0.05, and 10 statistical tests are carried out, then, P_a, that must be obtained from the statistical tests would be $P_a = .05/10 = .005$.

Box-and-whisker plot: produced by the SPSS procedures Explore, or from the Graph menu, summarising the scores on a variable by displaying the median, and the 25th and 75th percentiles as a box representing the inter-quartile range. Bars are drawn that are perpendicular to the boxes (the whiskers) extending 1.5 times the height of the box above and below the box, where possible. Specific cases are highlighted. Those that lie between the end of the whisker and another whisker length are described as *outliers*. Those beyond two whiskers length from the edge of the box are described as *extreme cases*. The plot enables the statistical properties of a sample to be explored prior to testing.

Case study: a holistic study of a specific bounded system, which can be an individual, an event, an institution or a society.

Cash flow analysis: a systematic method for planning and recording the income and expenditure of a project over time, usually over monthly periods.

Change experiment: an intervention or change in practice introduced in an action research project to try to address a perceived problem. The change introduced is regarded as an experiment because its effects are monitored, analysed and discussed, and thus provide an opportunity to test the participants' theories about what the possible causes and solutions to a problem may be.

Clinical health psychology: seeks to relate psychological variables to biomedical conditions in order to understand, predict and control health processes, outcomes or *Quality of Life (QoL)*.

Clinical psychology: aims to reduce psychological distress and to enhance and promote psychological wellbeing by the systematic application of knowledge derived from psychological theory and data (Clinical Psychology, 2001).

Closed questions: questions used in questionnaires or interviews that allow only a limited set of responses for the respondent to choose among (e.g. yes/no/don't know; good/poor/bad). Can be referred to as 'multiple choice questions' or 'MCQs'.

Code/coding: the procedure of identifying and labelling recurrent features or patterns in a qualitative data set. This allows the researcher to systematically retrieve every instance of that feature or pattern for further analysis (e.g. counting occurrences of that code; comparing instances of that code; carrying out more detailed analysis of the coded segment).

Coding frame: the labels and definitions for the complete set of codes applied to a qualitative data set in a research project.

Coding sheets: specially designed forms for entering data from questionnaires or interview schedules prior to entry into a computer program data file. The aim of using the sheets is to reduce the errors that occur when data are inputted to a computer program data file.

Community psychology: an approach seeking to increase empowerment among lay communities to take greater control over health and health care (including research).

Conditional probability: the probability that a proposition, A, is true given that another proposition, B, is true, or $P(A/B)$; e.g. the probability of obtaining a difference between two means, A, of a certain size given that the null hypothesis, B, is true.

Confidence interval (CI): the interval around the mean of a sample that one can state with a known probability contains the mean of the population. For example, for normal distributions there is a 95 per cent probability that the population mean is within plus or minus 1.96 standard errors of the sample mean.

Confidentiality: maintaining confidentiality means not disclosing to others personal information that has been disclosed to you privately in your professional role. In the context of research, this means that access to identifying details of participants should be restricted to only those researchers who have to know this information in order to carry out the research project.

Confidentiality rules: in the context of a research team, rules designed to optimise confidentiality for the participants. The rules specify the types of information that have to be shared and with whom on a 'need to know' principle: who must, should, could and shouldn't know.

Confound: an uncontrolled, 'free-floating' or extraneous variable (x_u) that is associated with another variable that is controlled (x_c) but which has an influence on the outcome. For example, imagine a prospective longitudinal study carried out in an era when smoking only occurs in private. A Martian called Martina, who has never observed anyone smoking, divides a sample of human beings into two groups, those with yellow stains on their fingers (group A) and those without (group B). Martina records mortality over ten years and observes that group A has many more cancer deaths than group B. Martina concludes that yellow finger stains cause cancer.

Constant comparative method: the procedure of comparing the characteristics and context of each coded qualitative data segment with those of other instances of that code, and with instances of different codes. This procedure allows the analyst to identify the properties and relationships between codes.

Constructivism: an approach to attaining knowledge (or *epistemology*) that is based on the assumption that all our knowledge is constructed by our thoughts and/or activities.

Consultancy: a service to a client involving professional skills and expertise that address an issue or problem brought by the client.

Content analysis: a method of data analysis that involves categorising and quantifying the characteristics of qualitative data that are of interest to the researcher.

Continuous measures: observations that can take any value along a ratio or interval scale of measurement, as contrasted with observations that are discrete or categorical.

Contrasts: the testing of specific pairs of means in an analysis of variance. Contrasts may be planned or unplanned. Also known as 'comparisons'.

Control group: a group of study participants that are treated in an identical manner to the experimental (or treatment) group except for the delivery of the treatment. All variables other than the treatment are kept constant.

Cost-effectiveness (CE): the cost of producing one added unit of value in a desired health outcome with a particular treatment or intervention. Can be measured as a ratio of an estimate of the value of resources required (the costs) to achieve a particular desired health outcome. For example, an obesity intervention, TO, costs £500 per person to administer and 10 per cent of participants reach their goal weight within one year and maintain it for a second year, the desired health outcome. The CE of the intervention would be £500/0.10 = £5000. In other words, it would cost £5000 to help one obese patient to eliminate their excess weight and to maintain their new weight for the second year post-treatment.

Critical psychology: an approach that aims to analyse how *power*, economics and macro-social processes influence and structure health, health care, health psychology and society at large.

Cronbach's alpha: a measure of the consistency of the item scores in a questionnaire based on computing the average of the correlations of scores on each item with the total scores for the remaining items.

Cross-over design: a study design in two phases in which participants are randomly allocated to two treatments, T_1 or T_2, in phase 1 and then to the opposite treatment in phase 2. Group A receives T_1 first and T_2 second, while group B receives T_2 first and T_1 second. Also referred to as a *within-participants design*.

Cross-sectional design: a study design in which one or more groups of participants contribute data on a single occasion.

Cross tabulation: a method of analysing and presenting data that combines two or more levels on two or more variables showing how the responses to one question are related to responses to another (e.g. co-morbidity between patients who do or do not suffer from depression and/or anxiety).

Deconstruction: a form of discourse analysis that involves analysing or deconstructing the socio-political functions of linguistic terms, talk or texts, paying particular attention to value-laden dichotomies that create dominant and oppressed meanings (e.g. natural vs abnormal).

Deductive coding: the procedure of applying to a qualitative data set pre-existing coding categories that have been developed prior to data collection on the basis of theory or previous empirical research.

Discourse analysis: a blanket term used to refer to a wide variety of methods for analysing the social origins and functions of talk and text.

Discrete measures: observations that must fall into discrete categories along interval, ordinal or nominal scales.

Discursive strategies: the ways in which language is used to accomplish particular social actions, such as providing a socially acceptable justification for a claim that has been made, or constructing the object of talk in a particular light (e.g. as normal or good).

Distribution-free tests: statistical tests that make no assumptions about the population distributions. Also referred to as *non-parametric tests*.

Ecological validity: the degree to which the conditions of a study are similar to the conditions that would occur naturally in the expected setting or context for a procedure or intervention.

Economic evaluation: the comparative analysis of alternative courses of action in terms of their costs (resource use) and effectiveness (health effects).

Effectiveness: is evaluated by a trial carried out in a clinical setting and measures the extent to which an intervention produces a beneficial outcome under ordinary everyday circumstances. A measure of whether an intervention *does* work.

Effect size: the strength of an association between study variables and outcome as measured by an observed difference or correlation. Cohen's d and Pearson's r are the most popular indices of effect size in psychological studies. For more details, see Chapters 10 and 11.

Efficacy: is evaluated by a trial carried out under ideal conditions and measures the extent to which an intervention produces a beneficial outcome under ideally controlled circumstances. A measure of whether an intervention *can* work.

Efficiency: a concept that is related to cost effectiveness measures referring to the extent to which the balance between inputs (costs) and outputs (outcomes) of interventions represents value for money.

Epistemology: the theory of how it is possible to obtain knowledge.

Ethical committee: a committee normally consisting of experts and lay people who review research studies before they are carried out to ensure that the principle of informed consent is adhered to and that no harm will be caused to the participants.

Ethnography: a research tradition that involves seeking to understand the lifestyles and cultural meanings of others (for more details, see Chapter 7).

Exclusive coding: a coding system in which only one code can be applied to each segment of data.

External validity: the degree to which the results of a study are reproducible or replicable when applied in practice or generalisable to everyday life.

Extreme cases: scores that lie beyond two whiskers (three times the inter-quartile range) of the edge of the box in a *box-and-whisker plot*.

Factor analysis: a form of analysis of the correlations between questionnaire items that enables the items to be grouped together yielding 'factors' or 'dimensions'.

Field note: a qualitative verbal record made by an observer of what is observed while they are still in the 'field' or setting in which observation is taking place.

File drawer problem: the number of studies on a topic that are unpublished because the results were not statistically significant or the studies were of poor quality.

Fishing trip: a trawl among a sea of data using any readily available means of analysis as a net to catch as many desirable fish in the form of statistically significant findings as possible with no planned, theoretical reason for doing so.

Focus group: a group of people invited to meet for a discussion of a topic or set of issues introduced by a researcher or *moderator*.

Frequentist or **classical approach**: a method of statistical inference popularised by Sir Ronald Fisher and developed by J. Neyman and E.S. Pearson which calculates the probability that the data obtained in a study were sampled from the distribution described by the null hypothesis.

Functional: means serving a purpose, hence functional analyses focus on the purposes of words or actions.

Gantt diagram: a way of planning a project timetable in visual form that enables activities of different kinds to be started and completed in a logical and integrated sequence.

General Linear Model (GLM): the basic principle underlying analysis of variance, regression and related techniques that assumes that a person's score on the dependent variable is formed by a combination of a constant, a value which accounts for the person's score on the independent variable, and an error, a measure of how that person differs from others treated in the same way.

Grounded theory: a set of clearly defined procedures for inductively developing and verifying theory from qualitative data.

Health psychology: the application of psychological knowledge and methods to the study and improvement of health, illness and health care.

Homogeneity of variance: the assumption in parametric statistical inference that the variances of the distributions being tested are the same.

Hypothetico-deductive method: a commonly used approach (or dominant paradigm) in scientific research in which hypotheses are derived from theory and then tested empirically by carrying out experiments to determine whether the theory can accurately predict observed reality.

Inductive coding: the procedure of developing coding categories to describe and discriminate between features or patterns that can be discerned in a qualitative data set.

Interaction: the score on a dependent variable is affected by at least two independent variables so that one needs to know the person's score on both independent variables to estimate their score on the dependent variable.

Internal validity: the degree to which the results of a study can be attributed to the manipulations of the researchers and are likely to be free of bias.

Inter-rater reliability: the procedure of calculating the correspondence between the codes or ratings independently assigned to the same data by two different people. If both people assign the same codes to the same data segments then the coding or rating system can be considered to be reliable.

Interview schedule: the set of standardised questions and prompts that will be used in a series of research interviews.

Latent: a property of data that is not directly observable but can be inferred.

Leading question: a question that is phrased in such a way that it is likely to prompt a particular type of response; for example, the phrasing, 'Do you agree that the treatment is helpful?' makes it difficult for the respondent to state that the treatment was not helpful, because this requires the respondent to contradict the interviewer, which is socially awkward.

Likelihood ratio: the ratio of (a) the probability that new evidence would be obtained if a proposition is true to (b) the probability that the new evidence would be obtained if the proposition is untrue. In Bayes' theorem, the *posterior odds* $(?_1)$ is the product of the likelihood ratio (L) and the *prior odds* $(?_0)$.

Linking: the process of explicitly identifying patterns of association between coding categories.

Listwise deletion: if just one data point is missing for a given person from one of the variables in an analysis then that person will not be included in an analysis which entails that particular variable in SPSS.

Longitudinal design: a study design in which one or more groups of participants contribute data on two or more occasions or 'waves'; a longitudinal study can be prospective or retrospective.

Manifest: a property of data that is obvious and directly observable.

Memo: a record of the thought-processes of the researcher while undertaking a qualitative research project. Relevant material may include questions and hypo-theses suggested by the data, subjective experiences and intuitions (e.g. impressions of settings or participants), and the rationale for coding decisions.

Meta-analysis: the use of statistical techniques to combine the results of primary studies addressing the same question into a single, pooled measure of effect size, with a confidence interval.

Moderator: the researcher who facilitates a focus group discussion, by posing questions and presenting materials to the group for discussion, and by creating a social setting in which all participants are encouraged to contribute freely to the discussion.

Multi-stage cluster sampling: a method of sampling that selects sub-units within the study population (e.g. districts) from which other sub-units may be selected (e.g.

city blocks) and so on until reaching the level at which random samples can be drawn (e.g. individual household members).

Narrative: the use of the story form in talk and text to create a bounded, coherent, vivid account of a particular set of events from the perspective of the narrator.

Narrative content: refers to the actual substance (rather than the structure) of the narrative. For example, two narratives might share a common plot structure in which the narrator overcame obstacles to achieve success, but in one narrative the content of the story might be that the narrator overcame post-natal depression, while in the other the content might be that the narrator overcame obstacles to working with a disability.

Narrative strategy: refers to the use of narrative to accomplish social actions – a particular kind of discursive strategy. Because the narrative form conveys a powerful sense of subjective reality or 'being there' in the intended audience, it is a persuasive means of presenting the perspective on events that the narrator wishes to promote.

Narrative structure: refers to the essential characteristics of the story form, which consists of traditional roles, settings and storylines that are familiar to all members of the culture. These cultural resources are used to create a plot that gives meaning and coherence to a sequence of events over time, and to construct social identities for the actors in the narrative (including, crucially, the narrator).

Non-parametric tests: statistical tests that do not assume that the population distributions are normal. Also referred to as *distribution-free tests*.

Normal distribution: a distribution of scores that has the properties of the classical bell-shaped curve often observed in biological and social phenomena.

Normal quartile-quartile plot: a plot of scores against the values that they would have if they conformed to the normal distribution, enabling exploration of statistical properties of a sample prior to testing.

Odds: the ratio of the number of people in a group with an event or characteristic to the number without the event or characteristic. Thus, if there are 40 obese people and 60 non-obese people in a sample, the odds are 40/60 or 0.667.

Odds ratio (OR): the ratio of the odds of an event or characteristic in the experimental (intervention) group, T_N, to the odds of the event or characteristic in the control group, T_C. An OR of 1.00 indicates no difference between groups while, for desirable differences, a difference lower than 1.00 indicates that the intervention was effective in reducing the risk of that outcome. Thus if the intervention group contains 20 obese and 80 non-obese people and the control group contains 60 obese and 30 non-obese people, the OR = 0.25/2.00 = 0.125. Also referred to as a 'relative risk' (RR) ratio.

One-tailed test: a statistical test of a difference or association when the direction of the difference or association was predicted in advance.

Ontology: the theory of what things there are that can be known.

Open-ended question: a question that is open to many different kinds of answer rather than just a few limited responses, and therefore invites respondents to reply at length by talking about whatever seems relevant to them in any form or manner they choose.

Outcome measure: the measure used to evaluate the results of a study or trial.

Outliers: scores that lie in extreme positions along a scale of measurement, possibly because of anomalies of measurement; in SPSS scores that lie between the end of the whisker and another whisker length in a *box-and-whisker plot*.

Pairwise deletion: removal of a person's data from any analysis for which the person has missing data in *SPSS*.

Parameter: a value defining a population distribution, e.g. a population mean or variance.

Parametric tests: statistical tests that are based on the assumption that the population distributions are normal.

Participant observation: an approach to data collection by means of observation in which it is assumed that it is not possible for the observer to be completely detached and have no impact on what is observed. The observer may participate simply by being present as a researcher, and therefore influencing the setting, actors and process of research, or the observer may fully participate by taking part in the activities that are observed.

Phenomenology and Phenomenological methods: study of the content or essential characteristics of subjective experience and a varied and loosely defined set of interpretive, qualitative and theoretical methods designed for that purpose.

Placebo control group/condition: a control group which receives a set of conditions that appear the same as a set of treatment conditions when in fact they are completely general, e.g. in an alcohol study an orange coloured and flavoured drink with a trace of vodka smeared on the rim of the glass could be used in the placebo condition.

Posterior odds: the ratio of the probability of an event or proposition to the probability of the complementary event or proposition *after* new evidence has been produced. For example, immediately after England drew with Argentina 1:1, the first author evaluated his subjective probability for England to win the World Cup at 0.10, giving an odds of 0.10/0.90 = 0.11. Immediately after England beat Denmark 3:0, these odds were increased to 0.25/0.75 = 0.33. Finally, during the quarter final against Brazil, Michael Owen's goal increased the odds to 0.5/0.5 = 1.00, then Brazil's equaliser reduced the odds back to 0.33, and the odds plummeted practically to zero with Ronaldinho's 50-minute freak second goal lobbed over Seaman. At full-time, with no more goals scored, the final odds were zero, and Brazil went on to win the World Cup, beating Germany 3:0 in the final. Thus, supporting evidence is equivalent to goals for and increases the odds of winning, while disconfirming evidence is equivalent to goals against and reduces the odds.

Post-modern: a term coined by the French philosopher Jean-François Lyotard referring to a worldview that has emerged in the latter period of modern society from the 1960s. Post-modern thought questions the goal of modernity, which is to progressively achieve a rational understanding of and control over objective reality through an appeal to 'grand narratives'. Instead, post-modernism proposes that there are many different and valid ways of understanding or 'little narratives' of 'reality', and that these do not fall on a linear dimension of progressively more objective, rational and hence superior comprehension.

Post-positivism: an approach to obtaining knowledge (or *epistemology*) that assumes that although there is an objective reality we cannot ever achieve a pure unmediated knowledge of it. Nevertheless, our goal should be to try to progressively eliminate distortion and bias in our perceptions, and produce measurements and models that provide the most accurate approximation to reality that we can achieve.

Power (1): in a social context: 'a generalised facility or resource in the society' (Parsons, 1950); a multiplicity of specific, localised relationships which together constitute the social body so that '(w)here there is power, there is resistance' (Foucault, 1973).

Power (2): in the context of statistical inference, power refers to the degree to which a statistical test will lead to the rejection of the null hypothesis, that is, detect a genuine difference or association. The power of a statistical test depends on three parameters: the significance criterion, the sample size and the effect size (Cohen, 1969). Power is the complement of the Type II error.

Power analysis: in the context of statistical inference, a method for computing the necessary sample sizes for a study to have a good chance of detecting the expected results. For example, a power analysis enables one to compute the sample sizes necessary in a study to enable a 90 per cent probability of detecting a difference between two means at the 5 per cent level of significance.

Pragmatism: a philosophy that argues that there can be no objective, absolute criteria for what is true or good. Instead, we must use negotiated, local working definitions; what seems to work well for people in a particular context is 'pragmatically' true and good for that context, although it may not be true and good in other contexts.

Praxis: accepted practice or custom.

Preference analysis: a method for integrating effectiveness, economic and acceptability evidence into a single decision about an intervention, programme or service.

Preference index: a measure of the benefits of adopting an intervention computed by using the *preference theorem*.

Preference theorem: a formula for combining effectiveness, efficiency and experiential evidence into a single preference score.

Primary, secondary and tertiary health care: (primary) the attempt to eliminate the possibility of disease (for example, by immunization); (secondary) the attempt to alleviate worsening of a condition by making pre-symptomatic changes or by early detection; (tertiary) medical care which attempts to control and reduce the severity as far as possible of an already identified disease.

Primary study: a study that is relevant to a topic in a systematic review from which data may be extracted for synthesis in the review and possibly also meta-analysis.

Prior odds: applied to subjective probabilities, indicating the ratio of the probability (P) of an event or proposition to the probability (1-P) of the complementary event or proposition, P/(1-P), *before* new evidence is produced. For example, consider the probability that England could win the 2002 World Cup. Until the moment of the final whistle in the final game that England played, the probability could lie anywhere between 0.00 and 1.00. The first author's prior odds before a single match was played were around 1/20 = 0.050. Prior odds must be revised in the light of evidence to give the *posterior odds*.

Prospective: a longitudinal research design in which data are collected on at least two occasions, the first of which provides a baseline against which any changes on later occasions can be compared.

Publication bias: the bias among journals to publish reports of studies with statistically significant results and to reject reports of studies with non-significant results.

Public health psychology: an approach seeking to identify psychological variables predicting mental and physical health and health-promoting behaviours in the general population or in special population groups.

Qualitative methods: research methods that deliberately seek to investigate how context and interpretation (including those of the researcher) influence our experience and understanding of the world. This can be achieved by collecting contextualised data, often in real-world settings and in the natural language of participants, and encouraging reflection on the social and subjective processes influencing the interpretations that are constructed. The aim is not to identify universally applicable laws but to develop insights, which are meaningful and useful to particular groups of people, such as patients, participants in a study, or people in similar situations, health care workers, and/or other researchers.

Quality of life (QoL): an abstract concept with a multitude of different possible meanings and interpretations: (a) 'an individual's perception of their position in life in the context of the culture and value systems in which they live and in relation to their goals, expectations, standards and concerns' (WHOQOL Group, 1993); (b) what quality of life questionnaires measure; (c) if you are healthy, how well you feel; if you are unhealthy, how unwell you feel; or, perhaps, even a combination of the two.

Quantitative methods: these are research methods that are capable of generating data in numerical form suitable for testing quantitative laws and theories that are assumed to be universal to all human beings. The data produced by such methods have properties that permit the use of statistical hypothesis testing which is a method for choosing between hypotheses based on the results of experiments, *randomised controlled trials*, observational studies, or other similar methods.

Randomised controlled trial (RCT): an experimental design in which participants are randomly allocated either to a new intervention or treatment or to a control condition.

Realism: an approach to obtaining knowledge (an *epistemology*) that is based on the assumption that it is possible for us to make accurate observations of an objective, unchanging reality.

Referee: in the context of applications for funding, a person who is empowered to give an opinion about the quality, feasibility and applicability of a research study described in an application. In other contexts, referees are people asked to give opinions about job applicants, papers submitted for publication, or decisions in sports like football. Referees make decisions on the basis of evidence as they see it, thus involving a considerable degree of judgement and subjectivity.

Reflexivity: a self-conscious awareness and analysis of the ways in which the assumptions, activities and interests of the researcher are likely to have influenced the process and findings of the research.

Reliability: the ability of an instrument to generate a consistent set of scores for the same individuals or states measured on two or more occasions, when the conditions of administration are kept constant and there is no reason to expect the scores to change.

Responsiveness: the ability of an instrument to generate a change in score proportionate to a change in the individual or state being measured on two or more occasions, when the conditions of administration are kept constant and there is a reason to expect the scores to change. Also called *sensitivity*.

Retrospective: a research design in which data are collected on just one occasion, and participants are invited either to describe their current state relative to their state at a prior point in time (e.g. better or worse health), or to recall their previous state or experiences. The problem with this kind of design is that participants may not recall their previous state or experiences accurately, and their recall is often influenced by their current state.

Robustness: the degree to which a statistical test can function reliably when its assumptions do not hold.

Sampling frame: a list of all members of the study population, e.g. an electoral roll, postal register or telephone directory.

Saturation: the stage in a qualitative project when the data already analysed seem to provide the basis for a thorough and comprehensive description of a circumscribed phenomenon, and so analysis of further data from similar sources would be redundant as it is unlikely to reveal significant new information.

Self-presentation: the universal tendency of people to try to present themselves in particular ways in their talk and their responses to questionnaires, usually in order to conform with whatever characteristics are seen as normative or socially desirable, but sometimes in order to project a particular image of themselves (e.g. as more disabled or less anxious than they really are).

Self-reports: reports, descriptions or accounts of experiences given by people.

Semi-structured interview: a face-to-face method of qualitative data collection in which the researcher asks a small number of open-ended questions that invite the interviewee to talk at length about the topics of interest.

Sensitivity: see *responsiveness*.

Significance or **alpha level**: in significance testing, the alpha level is the probability at which the null hypothesis will be rejected. By arbitrary convention, the alpha probability level is set at a maximum or threshold value of 0.05, the probability at which it is regarded safe to infer that the null hypothesis is untrue.

Simple effects: the differences between means on independent factors in a statistical analysis.

Simple random sampling (SRS): a sampling method that gives every member of the study population an equal chance of being selected for the sample.

Skew: a measure of the degree to which a distribution is asymmetric, and has its median towards one end of the range of scores.

Splicing: the procedure of merging two or more sets of related coded data segments into a single set labelled with a single code.

Splitting: the procedure of making distinctions within a set of coded data segments to create two or more subsets labelled with different codes.

SPSS: see *Statistical Package for Social Sciences*.

Stakeholder: any person, body or organisation with a stake or interest in the process and/or outcome of a project. Relevant stakeholders in clinical and health psychology research might include the psychologists or health professionals who deliver a therapy, the patients who receive the therapy and the family members who support them, the representatives of public or private institutions who approve and fund the therapy, or the research, and so on.

Standard error (SE): a measure of the variation in sample that is related to the standard deviation (SD): $SE = SD/\sqrt{N}$, where N is the sample size.

Statistical Package for Social Sciences (SPSS): a popular and versatile statistical package for analysing quantitative data.

Stem-and-leaf plot: a way of plotting a distribution of scores in the Explore procedure of SPSS that is similar to a histogram but which plots the actual scores.

Stratified sampling: a method of sampling that increases the amount of data collected from groups that might be under-represented if simple random sampling is carried out, e.g. younger people, members of ethnic minorities.

Structural equation modelling (SEM): a method for analysing the relationships between observed variables using latent (unmeasured) variables. A specific form of SEM, 'path analysis', attempts to place observed variables in a causal chain, X causes Y, Y causes Z, etc. SEM is also referred to as 'covariance structure modelling'.

Structured observation: consists of making numerical counts or ratings of pre-defined features of data obtained by in situ or video-recorded observation.

Study population: the specific population of people who are relevant to the research question in a study.

Study quality: a measure of the quality of a study based on a set of criteria concerning study design and methodology that are used to assess the *internal validity* and *external validity* of the study findings.

Systematic review: a review of the evidence on a clearly formulated question that uses explicit methods to identify, select and critically appraise relevant primary research, and to extract and integrate data from the primary studies included in the review. *Meta-analysis* may also be used.

Systematic sampling: a method of sampling which selects every nth person on the list, starting with a randomly chosen person from within the first n positions on the list.

Thematic analysis: a method of qualitative data analysis that involves systematically identifying and describing themes or patterns in a qualitative data set.

Theoretical sampling: theoretical or 'purposive' sampling using theoretical grounds to determine which participants will provide the most relevant and useful data. It is employed in qualitative research, where the aim is not to obtain a statistically representative sample but to recruit participants who will provide valuable perspectives because of their unique or typical experiences or characteristics.

Time sampling: a procedure used in structured observation to systematically sample data at selected time-points (e.g. every morning and evening, or once every two minutes).

Transcription: a written verbatim (word for word) record of recorded speech.

Triangulation: a method of validating research that involves combining several different sources of evidence (e.g. using different data sources, investigators or methods).

Two-tailed test: a test of significance for a difference or association where no prediction is made about the direction of the difference or association.

Type I error: rejecting a true null hypothesis or falsely inferring the presence of a difference or an association when no such difference or association exists.

Type II error: failing to find a difference or an association when it exists. The higher the probability of a Type II error, the lower the power of a test.

Validity (1): in the context of research, validity concerns the extent to which a piece of research can be regarded as successfully accomplishing the central purpose of research, which is to extend our understanding of the world, including ourselves.

Validity (2): in the context of questionnaires, validity refers to the degree to which a questionnaire measures the construct(s) that it aims to measure.

Within-participants design: a study design in which all participants contribute data in all conditions. Special procedures are used to control carry-over effects. Also referred to as a *cross-over design*.

BIBLIOGRAPHY

Aldridge, D. (1994). Single-case research designs for the creative art therapist. *The Arts in Psychotherapy*, 21, 333–42.

Altman, D.G. (1996). Better reporting of randomised controlled trials: the CONSORT statement. *British Medical Journal*, 313, 570–1.

American Psychological Association (APA) (2001a). Health psychology. Division 38 webpages: http://www.health-psych.org/whatis.html

American Psychological Association (APA) (2001b). *Publication manual of the American Psychological Association* (5th edn). Washington, DC: American Psychological Association.

American Psychological Association (2002). Society of Clinical Psychology. Division 12 webpages: http://www.apa.org/about/division/div12.html

Anderson, G. (1998). Creating moral space in prenatal genetic services. *Qualitative Health Research*, 8, 168–87.

Arksley, H. & Knight, P. (1999). *Interviewing for social scientists*. London: Sage.

Atkinson, P. & Hammersley M. (1998). Ethnography and participant observation. In N.K. Denzin & Y.S. Lincoln (eds) *Strategies of qualitative inquiry*. London: Sage.

Balcazar, F.E., Keys, C.B., Kaplan, D.L. & Suarez-Balcazar, Y. (1998). Participatory action research and people with disabilities: principles and challenges. *Canadian Journal of Rehabilitation*, 12, 105–12.

Ballinger, C. & Payne, S. (2000). Falling from grace or into expert hands? Alternative accounts about falling in older people. *British Journal of Occupational Therapy*, 63, 573–9.

Ballinger, C. & Payne, S. (2002). The construction of the risk of falling among and by older people. *Ageing and Society*, 22, 305–24.

Banister, P., Burman, E., Parker, I., Taylor, M. & Tindall, C. (1994). Observation. In *Qualitative methods in psychology: a research guide*. Buckingham: Open University Press.

Barbarin, O.A. (1978). Comparison of symbolic and over aversion in the self-control of smoking. *Journal of Consulting and Clinical Psychology*, 46, 1569–71.

Barbour, R. & Kitzinger, J. (eds) (1999). *Developing focus group research: politics, theory and practice*. London: Sage.

Barbour, R.S. (2001). Checklists for improving rigour in qualitative research: a case of the tail wagging the dog. *British Medical Journal*, 322, 1115–17.

Barker, C., Pistrang, N. & Elliott, R. (1994). *Research methods in clinical and counselling psychology*. Chichester: Wiley.

Barlow, D.H. & Hersen, M. (1984). *Single case experimental designs: strategies for studying behavioral change*. New York: Pergamon.

Bartlett, D. & Payne, S. (1997). Grounded theory - its basis, rationale and procedures. In G. McKenzie, J. Powell, & R. Usher, (eds), *Understanding social research: perspectives on methodology and practice*. London: Falmer Press, pp. 173–96.

Bauer, M.W. (2000). Classical content analysis: a review. In M.W. Bauer and G. Gaskell (eds) *Qualitative researching with text, image and sound*. London: Sage, pp. 131–51.

Becker, G. (1997). *Disrupted lives: How people create meaning in a chaotic world.* Berkeley, CA: University of California Press.

Bennett, P. & Murphy, S. (1997). *Psychology and health promotion.* Buckingham: Open University Press.

Berelson, B. (1952). *Content analysis in communications research.* New York: Free Press.

Bevan, S. & Bevan, K. (1999). *Critical textwork: an introduction to varieties of discourse and analysis.* Buckingham: Open University Press.

Billig, M. (1985). Prejudice, categorisation and particularisation: from a perceptual to a rhetorical approach. *European Journal of Social Psychology,* 15, 79–103.

Billig, M. (1987). *Arguing and thinking: a rhetorical approach to social psychology.* Cambridge: Cambridge University Press.

Blaxter, M. (2000). Criteria for qualitative research. *Medical Sociology News,* 26, 34–7.

Bowling, A. (1991). *Measuring health.* Buckingham: Open University Press.

Bowling, A. (1995). *Measuring disease.* Buckingham: Open University Press.

Boyatzis, R.E. (1998). *Transforming qualitative information.* London: Sage.

British Psychological Society (2001). *The core purpose and philosophy of the profession.* Division of Clinical Psychology webpages: http://www.bps.org.uk/sub-syst/dcp/publications.cfm

Britten, N. (1995). Qualitative interviews in medical research. *British Medical Journal,* 251.

Brown, S.D. (1999). Stress as regimen: critical readings of the self-help literature. In C. Willig (ed.) *Applied discourse analysis: social and psychological interventions.* Buckingham: Open University Press.

Bruner, J. (1990). *Actual minds, possible worlds.* Cambridge, MA: Harvard University Press.

Cabeza, R. & Kingstone, A. (eds) (2001). *Handbook of functional neuroimaging of cognition.* MIT Press.

Cagnetta, E. & Cicognani, E. (1999). Surviving a serious traffic accident: Adaptation processes and quality of life. *Journal of Health Psychology,* 4, 551–64.

Capps, L. & Ochs, E. (1995). Out of place: narrative insights into agoraphobia. *Discourse Processes,* 19, 407–39.

Carrol, D., Davey Smith, G. & Bennett, P. (1996). Some observations on health and socioeconomic status. *Journal of Health Psychology,* 1, 23–39.

Chamberlain, K. (1999). Using grounded theory in health research: practices, premises and potential. In M. Murray & K. Chamberlain (eds) *Qualitative health psychology: theories and methods.* London: Sage, pp. 183–201.

Chamberlain, K., Stephens, C. & Lyons, A.C. (1997). Encompassing experience: meanings and methods in health psychology. *Psychology and Health,* 12, 691–709.

Charmaz, K. (1995). Grounded theory. In J. Smith, R. Harré & L. Van Langenhove (eds) *Rethinking methods in psychology.* London: Sage, pp. 27–49.

Charmaz, K. (2001). Grounded theory: methodology and theory construction. In N.J. Smelzer & P.B. Baltes (eds) *International encyclopedia of the social & behavioral sciences.* Amsterdam: Pergamon.

Chatoor, I., Ganiban, J., Harrison, J. & Hirsch, R. (2001). Observation of feeding in the diagnosis of posttraumatic feeding disorder of infancy. *Journal of the American Academy of Child and Adolescent Psychiatry,* 40, 595–602.

Clark-Carter, D. (1997a). *Doing quantitative psychological research: from design to report.* Hove: Psychology Press.

Clark-Carter, D. (1997b). The account taken of statistical power in research published in the *British Journal of Psychology*. *British Journal of Psychology*, 88, 71–83.

Cleveland, W.S. (1985). *The elements of graphing*. Monterey, CA: Wadsworth.

Clinical Psychology (2001) www.bps.org.uksub-syst/dcp/index.cfm

Cohen, J. (1962). The statistical power of abnormal-social psychological research: a review. *Journal of Abnormal and Social Psychology*, 65, 145–53.

Cohen, J. (1969). *Statistical power analysis for the behavioral sciences*. New York: Academic Press.

Cohen, J. (1988). *Statistical power analysis for the behavioral sciences* (2nd edn). Hillsdale, NJ: Lawrence Erlbaum Associates.

Consumers in NHS Research Support Unit (2000). *Involving consumers in research and development in the NHS: briefing notes for research*. Winchester: The Help for Health Trust.

Conway, S. & Hockey, J. (1998). Resisting the 'mask' of old age? The social meaning of lay health beliefs in later life. *Ageing and Society*, 18, 469–94.

Cook, T.D. & Campbell, D.T. (1979). *Quasi-experimentation: design and analysis issues for field settings*. Chicago: Rand McNally.

Cottraux, J.A., Harf, R., Boissel, J.-P., Schbath, J., Bouvard, M. & Gillet, J. (1983). Smoking cessation with behaviour therapy or acupuncture – a controlled study. *Behaviour Research Therapy*, 21, 417–24.

Creswell, J.W. (1998). *Qualitative inquiry and research design: choosing among five traditions*. London: Sage.

Cronbach, L. (1951). Coefficient alpha and the internal structure of tests. *Psychometrika*, 16, 297–334.

Crooks, D.L. (2001). Older women with breast cancer: new understandings through grounded theory research. *Health Care for Women International*, 22, 99–114.

Crossley, M.L. (2000). Making sense of HIV infection: discourse and adaptation to life with long-term HIV positive diagnosis. *Health*, 3, 95–119.

De Bruin, A., Picavet, H.S.J. & Nossikov, A. (1996). *Health interview surveys. Towards international harmonization of methods and instruments*. Copenhagen: WHO Regional Publications, European Series, No. 58. WHO.

Deeks, J., Khan, K.S., Song, F., Popay, J., Nixon, J. & Kleijnen, J. (2001). Data synthesis. In K.S. Khan, G. ter Riet, J. Glanville, A.J. Sowden & J. Kleijnen (eds) *Undertaking systematic reviews of research on effectiveness. CRD's guidance for those carrying out or commissioning reviews*. CRD Report No. 4 (2nd edn). University of York: NHS Centre for Reviews and Dissemination.

Delahunt, J. & Curran, J.P. (1976). Effectiveness of negative practice and self-control techniques in the reduction of smoking behaviour. *Journal of Counsulting and Clinical Psychology*, 44, 1002–7.

Denzin, N.K. & Lincoln Y.S. (eds) (1998) *The landscape of qualitative research theories and issues*. London: Sage.

De Vaus, D.A. (1991). *Surveys in social research* (3rd edn). London: Allen & Unwin.

Dey, I. (1993). *Qualitative data analysis: a user-friendly guide for social scientists*. London: Routledge.

Dickersin, K. (1997). How important is publication bias? A synthesis of available data. *AIDS Education & Prevention*, 9, 15–21.

Dickersin, K. (2002). Systematic reviews in epidemiology: why are we so far behind? *International Journal of Epidemiology*, 31, 6–12.

Dixon, P. & Carr-Hill, R. (1989). *The NHS and its customers. Booklet 2: customer feedback surveys: an introduction to survey methods*. York: Centre for Health Economics.

Dixon-Woods, M. & Fitzpatrick, R. (2001). Qualitative results in systematic reviews. *British Medical Journal*, 323, 765–6.

Doering, S., Katzlberger, F., Rumpold, G., Roessler, S., Hofstoetter, B., Schatz, D.S., Behensky, H., Krismer, M., Luz, G., Innerhofer, P., Benzer, H., Saria, A. & Schussler, G. (2000). Videotape preparation of patients before hip replacement surgery reduces stress. *Psychosomatic Medicine*, 62, 365–73.

Donmoyer, R. (1990). Generalizability and the single case study. In E.W. Eisner & A. Peshkin (eds) *Qualitative inquiry in education: the continuing debate*. New York: Teachers College Press.

Downie, R. & Calman, K. (1998). *Healthy respect: ethics in health care* (2nd edn). Oxford: Oxford University Press.

Drummond, M., O'Brien, B., Stoddart, G. & Torrance, G. (1997). *Methods for economic evaluation of health care programmes* (2nd edn). New York: Oxford University Press.

Edley, N. (2000). Analysing masculinity: interpretative repertoires, ideological dilemmas and subject positions. In M. Wetherell, S. Taylor & S. Yates (eds) *Discourse as data: a guide for analysis*. London: Sage.

Edwards, D., Ashmore, M. & Potter, J. (1995). Death and furniture: the rhetoric, politics and theology of bottom-line arguments against relativism. *History of the Human Sciences*, 8, 25–49.

Egger, M., Davey Smith, G. & Altman, D.G. (eds) (2001). *Systematic reviews in health care: meta-analysis in context* (2nd edn). London: BMJ Books.

Egger, M., Davey Smith, G & Schneider, M. (2001). Systematic reviews of observational studies. In M. Egger, G. Davey Smith and D.G. Altman (eds) *Systematic Reviews in Health Care. Meta-analysis in context*. London: BMJ Books. pp. 211-27.

Egger, M., Ebrahim, S. & Davey Smith, G. (2002). Where now for meta-analysis? *International Journal of Epidemiology*, 31, 1–5.

Eisner, E.W. (2003). On the art and science of qualitative research in psychology. In P. Camic, J.E. Rhodes & L. Yardley (eds) *Qualitative research in psychology: expanding perspectives in methodology and design*. Washington, DC: American Psychological Association.

Elliott, C.H. & Denny, D.R. (1978). A multiple-component treatment approach to smoking reduction. *Journal of Counsulting and Clinical Psychology*, 46, 1330–9.

Engel, G. (1977). The need for a new medical model: a challenge for biomedicine. *Science*, 196, 129–36.

Esplen, M.J. & Garfinkel, P.E. (1998). Guided imagery treatment to promote self-soothing in bulimia nervosa: a theoretical rationale. *Journal of Psychotherapy Practice and Research*, 7, 102–18.

Evans-Pritchard, E.E. (1940). *The Nuer*. Oxford: Clarendon Press.

Fabrega, H. (1990). The concept of somatization as a cultural and historical product of Western medicine. *Psychosomatic Medicine*, 52, 653–72.

Fee, W. (1977). Searching for the simple answer to cure the smoking habit. *Health and Social Service Journal*, 87, 292–3.

Feldman, M.S. (1995). *Strategies for interpreting qualitative data*. London: Sage.

Fetterman, D. (1998) *Ethnography step by step* (2nd edn). London: Sage.

Finucane, M.L., Alhakami, A., Slovic, P. & Johnson, S.M. (2000). The heuristic affect in judgements of risks and benefits. *Journal of Behavioral Decision Making*, 13, 1–17.

Fisher, R.A. (1925). *Statistical methods for research workers*. London: Oliver and Boyd.

Fishman, D.B. (1999). *The case for pragmatic psychology*. New York: New York University Press.

Fitzpatrick, R., Ziebland, S., Jenkinson, C., Mowat, A. & Mowat, A. (1992). The importance of sensitivity to change as a criterion for selection of health status measures. *Quality in Health Care*, 1, 89–93.

Fontana, A. & Frey, J.H. (1998). Interviewing: the art of science. In N.K. Denzin and N. Lincoln (eds) *Collecting and interpreting qualitative materials*. London: Sage, pp. 361–76.

Foster, J.L. (2001). *Data analysis using SPSS for Windows Versions 8-10. A beginner's guide*. London: Sage.

Foucault, M. (1973). *The birth of the clinic*. London: Routledge.

Foucault, M. (1989). *The birth of the clinic*. London: Routledge.

Fowler, F.J. (1993). *Survey research methods* (2nd edn). Newbury Park, CA: Sage.

Francis, C. (1999). *Ethics for psychologists: a handbook*. Leicester: BPS Books.

Gergen, K.J. (1985). The social constructionist movement in modern psychology. *American Psychologist*, 40, 266–75.

Giesbrecht, N. & Rankin, J. (2000). Reducing alcohol problems through community action research projects: contexts, strategies, implications and challenges. *Substance Use and Misuse*, 35, 31–5.

Ginsberg, D., Hall, S.M. & Rosinski, M. (1992). Partner support, psychological treatment, and nicotine gum in smoking treatment: an incremental study. *The International Journal of the Addictions*, 27, 503–14.

Giorgi, A.P. & Giorgi, B.M. (2003). The descriptive phenomenological psychological method. In P. Camic, J.E. Rhodes & L. Yardley (eds) *Qualitative research in psychology: expanding perspectives in methodology and design*. Washington, DC: American Psychological Association.

Gittell, R. & Vidal, A. (1998). *Community organizing. Building social capital as a development strategy*. Thousand Oaks, CA: Sage.

Glaser, B.G. (1978). *Theoretical sensitivity: advances in the methodology of grounded theory*. Mill Valley, CA: Sociology Press.

Glaser, B.G. (1999). The future of grounded theory. *Qualitative Health Research*, 9, 836–45.

Glaser, B.G. & Strauss, A. (1967). *The discovery of grounded theory*. Chicago: Aldine.

Glasgow, R.E., Schafer, L. & O'Neill, H.K. (1981). Self-help books and amount of therapist contact in smoking cessation programs. *Journal of Consulting and Clinical Psychology*, 49, 659–67.

Glass, G.V. (1976). Primary, secondary and meta-analysis of research. *Educational Research*, 5, 3–8.

Gold, R. (1958). Roles in sociological field observations. *Social Forces*, 36, 217–23.

Graham, K. & Chandler-Coutts, M. (2000). Community action research: who does what to whom and why? Lessons learned from local prevention efforts (International Experiences). *Substance Use and Misuse*, 35, 87–110.

Green, C. & Gilhooly, K. (1996). Protocol analysis: practical implementation. In J.T.E. Richardson (ed.) *Handbook of qualitative research methods*. Leicester: BPS Books.

Greenwood, D.J. & Levin, M. (1998). *Introduction to action research: social research for social change*. London: Sage.

Guba, E.G. (1979). The new rhetoric. *Studies in Educational Evaluation*, 5, 139–40.

Guba, E.G. & Lincoln, Y.S. (1998). Competing paradigms in qualitative research. In N.K. Denzin & Y.S. Lincoln (eds) *Strategies of qualitative inquiry*. London & Thousand Oaks, CA: Sage, pp. 195–200.

Guyatt, G., Walter, S. & Norman, G. (1987). Measuring change over time: assessing the usefulness of evaluative instruments. *Journal of Chronic Diseases*, 40, 171–8.

Haddock, G., Zanna, M.P. & Esses, V.M. (1993). Assessing the structure of prejudicial attitudes: the case of attitudes towards homosexuals. *Journal of Personality and Social Psychology*, 65, 1105–18.

Hajek, P., Taylor, T. & Mills, P. (2002). Brief intervention during hospital admission to help patients to give up smoking after myocardial infarction and bypass surgery: randomised controlled trial. *British Medical Journal*, 324, 87–9.

Hall, S.M., Rugg, D., Tunstall, C. & Jones, R.T. (1984). Preventing relapse to cigarette smoking by behavioural skill training. *Journal of Consulting and Clinical Psychology*, 52, 372–82.

Hall, W.A. & Callery, P. (2001). Enhancing the rigour of grounded theory: incorporating reflexivity and relationality. *Qualitative Health Research*, 11, 257–72.

Hammersley, M. & Atkinson, P. (1995). *Ethnography: principles in practice* (2nd edn). London: Routledge.

Hammersley, M., Gomm, R. & Foster, P. (2000). Case study and theory. In R. Gomm, M. Hammersley & P. Foster (eds) *Case study method*. London: Sage.

Happ, M.B. (2000). Interpretation of nonvocal behavior and the meaning of voicelessness in critical care. *Social Science and Medicine*, 50, 1247–55.

Hart, E. & Bond, M. (1995). *Action research for health and social care: a guide to practice*. Buckingham: Open University Press.

Hedges, L.V. & Olkin, I. (1985). *Statistical methods for meta-analysis*. London: Academic Press.

Henry, G.T. (1990). *Practical sampling*. Newbury Park, CA: Sage.

Henwood, K. & Pidgeon, N.F. (1994). Qualitative research and psychological theorizing. *British Journal of Psychology*, 83, 97–111.

Heron, J. (1996). *Co-operative inquiry: research into the human condition*. London: Sage.

Hevey, D. & McGee, H. (1998). The effect size statistic: useful in research outcomes research? *Journal of Health Psychology*, 3, 163–70.

Hickman, L.A. & Alexander, T.M. (eds) (1998). *The essential Dewey: pragmatism, education, democracy*. Bloomington: Indiana University Press.

Hodgson, I. (2000). Ethnography and health care: focus on nursing. *Forum: Qualitative Social Research*, 1. On-line journal, available at: http://qualitative-research.net/fqs/ 17.02.02.

Holland, K. (1999). A journey to becoming: the student nurse in transition. *Journal of Advanced Nursing*, 29, 229–36.

Hollway, W. & Jefferson, T. (1997). Eliciting narrative through the in-depth interview. *Qualitative Inquiry*, 3 (1), 53–70.

Hollway, W., & Jefferson, T. (2000). *Doing qualitative research differently: free association, narrative and the interview method*. London: Sage.

House, E.R. (1994). Integrating the quantitative and the qualitative. *New Directions for Program Evaluation*, 61, 5–11.

House, D.V. & McDonald, M.J. (eds) (1998). *Toward a psychology of persons*. London: Lawrence Erlbaum.

Howell, D. (2002). *Statistical methods for psychology* (5th edn). Belmont: Duxbury.

Howson, C. and Urbach, P. (1993). *Scientific reasoning: the Bayesian approach* (2nd edn). Chicago: Open Court.

Huberman, A.M. & Miles, M.B. (1994). *Data management and analysis methods*. London: Sage, pp. 428–44.

Hunt, S.M., McEwan, J. & McKenna, S.P. (1986). *Measuring health status*. London: Croom Helm.

Hunt, S.M., McKenna, S.P. & McEwan, J. (1989). *The Nottingham Health Profile user's manual* (revised edition). Manchester: Galen Research & Consultancy.

Hunter, J.E., Schmidt, F.L. & Jackson, G.B. (1982). *Cumulating research findings across studies*. Beverly Hills: Sage.

Huws, J., Jones, R. & Ingledew, D. (2001). Parents of children with autism using an email group: a grounded theory study. *Journal of Health Psychology*, 6, 569–84.

Idler, E.L. (1992). Self-assessed health and mortality: a review of studies. In S. Maes, H. Leventhal & M. Johnston (eds) *International Review of Health Psychology, Vol. 1*. Chichester: John Wiley.

Janis, I.L. (1958). *Psychological stress*. New York: Wiley.

Jason, L.A. (1997). *Community building. Values for a sustainable future*. Westport, CN: Praeger.

Jason, L.A., Tait, E., Goodman, D. & Buckenberger, L. (1988). Effects of a televised smoking cessation intervention among low-income and minority smokers. *American Journal of Community Psychology*, 16, 863–76.

Jenkinson, C.S. (1994). *Measuring health and medical outcomes*. London: UCL Press.

Joffe, H. (1999). *Risk and the other*. Cambridge: Cambridge University Press.

Joffe, H. & Bettega, N. (2003). Social representations of AIDS among Zambian adolescents. *Journal of Health Psychology* (forthcoming).

Joffe, H. & Haarhoff, G. (2002). Representations of far-flung illnesses: the case of Ebola in Britain, *Social Science & Medicine*, 54 (6), 955–69.

Johnston, M. (1986). Pre-operative emotional states and post-operative recovery. *Advances in Psychosomatic Medicine*, 15, 1–22.

Johnston, M., Wright, S. & Weinman, J. (1995). *Portfolio for health psychology*. Oxford: NFER-Nelson.

Katz, J.N., Larson, M.G., Phillips, C., Fossel, A. & Liang, M.H. (1992). Comparative measurement sensitivity of short and longer health status instruments. *Medical Care*, 14, 116–18.

Kazis, L.E., Anderson, J.J. & Meenan, R.F. (1989). Effect sizes for interpreting changes in health status. *Medical Care*, 27, Supplement, 178–89.

Kerr, J., Eves, F. & Carroll, D. (2001). The influence of poster prompts on stair use: the effects of setting, poster size and content. *British Journal of Health Psychology*, 6, 397–405.

Khan, K.S., ter Riet, G., Glanville, J., Sowden, A.J. & Kleijnen, J. (eds) (2001). *Undertaking systematic reviews of research on effectiveness. CRD's guidance for those carrying out or commissioning reviews*. CRD Report No. 4 (2nd edn). University of York: NHS Centre for Reviews and Dissemination.

Kidder, L.H. (1981). Qualitative research and quasi-experimental frameworks. In M.B. Brewer & B.E. Collins (eds) *Scientific enquiry and the social sciences*. San Francisco: Jossey-Bass, pp. 226–56.

Kinnear, P.R. & Gray, C.D. (2000). *SPSS for Windows Made Simple (Release 10)*. Hove: Psychology Press.

Kitson, G.C., Clark, R.D., Rushforth, N.B., Brinich, P.M., Sudak, H.S. & Zyzanski, S.J. (1996). Research on difficult family topics: helping new and experienced researchers cope with research on loss. *Family Relations*, 45, 183–8.

Knight, S.J. & Camic, P.M. (2003). Health psychology and medicine: the art and science of healing. In P.M. Camic & S.J. Knight (eds) *Clinical handbook of health psychology* (2nd edn). Toronto & Seattle: Hogrefe & Huber.

Kovacs, P.J. (2000). Participatory action research and hospice: a good fit. *The Hospice Journal*, 15, 55–62.

Krippendorf, K. (1980). *Content analysis: an introduction to its methodology*. London: Sage.

Krueger, R.A. (1994). *Focus groups: a practical guide for applied research* (2nd edn). Newbury Park, CA: Sage.

Kugelmann, R. (1999). Complaining about chronic pain. *Social Science and Medicine*, 49, 1663–76.

Kumar, S. & Gantley, M. (1999). Tensions between policy makers and general practitioners in implementing new genetics: grounded theory interview study. *British Medical Journal*, 319, 1410–13.

Kvale, S. (1996). *Interviews: an introduction to qualitative research interviewing*. Thousand Oaks, CA & London: Sage.

Kvale, S. (2003). The psychoanalytic interview as inspiration for qualitative research. In P. Camic, J.E. Rhodes & L. Yardley (eds) *Qualitative research in psychology: expanding perspectives in methodology and design*. Washington, DC: American Psychological Association.

Langer, L. (1991). *Holocaust testimonies: the ruins of memory*. New Haven, CT: Yale University Press.

Lansdown, R. (1998). Listening to children: have we gone too far? *Journal of the Royal Society of Medicine*, 91, 452–61.

Law, M. & Tang, J.L. (1995). An analysis of the effectiveness of interventions intended to help people stop smoking, *Archives of Internal Medicine*, 155, 1933–41.

Ley, P. (1988). *Communicating with patients. Improving communication, satisfaction and compliance*. London: Chapman & Hall.

Likert, R. (1952). A technique for the measurement of attitudes. *Educational & Psychological Measurement*, 12, 313–15.

Lincoln, Y.S. & Guba, E.G. (1985). *Naturalistic inquiry*. Newbury Park, CA: Sage.

Lipsey, M.W. (1989). *Design sensitivity: statistical power for experimental research*. Newbury Park, CA: Sage.

Lord, S.R., Sherrington, C. and Menz, H.B. (2001). *Falls in older people: risk factors and strategies for prevention*. Cambridge: Cambridge University Press.

Lowe, M.R., Green, L., Kurtz, S.M.S., Ashenberg, Z.S. & Fisher, E.B. (1980). Self-initiated, cue extinction and covert sensitization procedures in smoking cessation. *Journal of Behavioral Medicine*, 3, 357–72.

Lupton, D. (1993). Risk as moral danger: the social and political functions of risk discourse in public health. *International Journal of Health Services*, 23, 425–35.

Lykes, M.B. (2000) Possible contributions of a psychology of liberation: whither human health and human rights. *Journal of Health Psychology*, 5, 383–97.

McCann, J.J., Gilley, D.W., Hebert, L.E., Beckett, L.A. & Evans, D.A. (1997). Concordance between direct observation and staff rating of behavior in nursing home residents with Alzheimer's disease. *Journal of Gerontology: Psychological Sciences and Social Sciences*, 52B, 63-72.

McDermott, M.R. (2001). Redefining health psychology: Matarazzo revisited. *The Health Psychology Update*, 10, 3–10.

Macdonald, G. (2000). A new evidence framework for health promotion practice. *Health Education Journal*, 59, 3–11.

McDowell, I. & Newell, I. (1987). *Measuring health: a guide to rating scales and questionnaires*. New York: Oxford University Press.

Maines, D.R. (1993). Narrative's moment and sociology's phenomena: Toward a narrative sociology. *Sociological Quarterly*, 34, 17–38.

Manyande, A., Berg, S., Gettins, D., Mazhero, S., Marks, D.F. & Salmon, P. (1995).

Preoperative rehearsal of active coping imagery influences subjective and hormonal responses to abdominal surgery. *Psychosomatic Medicine*, 57, 177–82.

Manyande, A., Chayen, S., Priyakumar, P. et al. (1992). Anxiety and endocrine responses to surgery: Paradoxical effects of preoperative relaxation training. *Psychosomatic Medicine*, 54, 275–87.

Marks, D.F. (1990). On the relationship between imagery, body and mind. In P.J. Hampson, D.F. Marks & J.T.E. Richardson (eds) *Imagery: current developments*. London: Routledge, pp. 1–38.

Marks, D.F. (1995). Biased ratings invalidate the 1992 research assessment of UK psychology departments. *The Psychologist*, 8, 315–19.

Marks, D.F. (1996). Health psychology in context. *Journal of Health Psychology*, 1, 7–21.

Marks, D.F. (2001). Supplement on smoking cessation incompletely discloses conflicts of interest, duplicates prior publication and advocates the pharmaceutical products of the sponsoring company in a potentially misleading manner. *European Journal of Public Health*.

Marks, D.F. (2002a). Freedom, responsibility and power: contrasting approaches to health psychology. *Journal of Health Psychology*, 7, 5–14.

Marks, D.F. (2002b). *The health psychology reader*. London: Sage.

Marks, D.F. (2003). Preference analysis: a method for synthesising evidence on effectiveness, efficiency and acceptability. In preparation.

Marks, D.F. & Chipperfield, B.G.A. (1993). A health and lifestyle survey of Londoners. Preliminary data from the Bloomsbury and Islington Health & Lifestyle Survey. In H. Schroder, K. Reschke, M. Johnston, & S. Maes (eds) *Health psychology. Potential in diversity*. Regensburg: S. Roderer Verlag.

Marks, D.F., Murray, M., Evans, B. & Willig, C. (2000). *Health psychology. Theory, research and practice*. London: Sage.

Marks, D.F. & Sykes, C.M. (2002). Randomized controlled trial of cognitive behavioural therapy for smokers living in a deprived area of London: outcome at one-year follow-up. *Psychology, Health & Medicine*, 7, 17–24.

Marteau, T. & Lerman, C. (2001). Genetic risk and behavioural change. *British Medical Journal*, 7293, 1056–9.

Mason, J. (1996). Generating qualitative data: observation, documents and visual data. In *Qualitative researching*. London: Sage.

Matarazzo, J. (1982). Behavioral health's challenge to academic, scientific and professional psychology. *American Psychologist*, 37, 1–14.

Mays, N. & Pope, C. (1995). Observational methods in health care settings. *British Medical Journal*, 311, 182–4.

Mead, N. & Bower, P. (2000). Measuring patient-centredness: a comparison of three observation-based instruments. *Patient Education and Counseling*, 39, 71–80.

Merrill, J. (2000). Ambiguity: exploring the complexity of roles and boundaries when working with volunteers in well woman clinics. *Social Science and Medicine*, 51, 93–102.

Meyer, J. (2000). Using qualitative methods in health related action research. *British Medical Journal*, 320, 178–81.

Mishler, E.G. (1994). *The discourse of medicine*. New Jersey: Ablex Publishing.

Mishler, E.G. (1986). *Research interviewing: context and narrative*. Cambridge, MA: Harvard University Press.

Morgan, D.L. (1993). *Successful focus groups: advancing the state of the art*. London: Sage.

Morse, J.M. (1998). The contracted relationship: ensuring protection of anonymity and confidentiality. *Qualitative Health Research*, 8, 301–3.

Moser, C. & Kalton, G. (1971). *Survey methods in social investigation* (2nd edn). London: Heinemann.

Mothersill, K.J., McDowell, I., & Rosser, W. (1988). Subject characteristics and long-term post-program smoking cessation. *Addictive Behaviour*, 13, 29–36.

Moulding, N. & Hepworth, J. (2001). Understanding body image disturbance in the promotion of mental health: a discourse analytic study. *Journal of Community and Applied Social Psychology*, 11, 305–17.

Mulrow, C.D. (1987). The medical review article: state of the science. *Annals of Internal Medicine*, 106, 485–8.

Mulrow, C.D. (1995). Systematic reviews: rationale for systematic reviews. *British Medical Journal*, 309, 597–9.

Munro, J. (2000). *Globalisation and health* (pamphlet). Sheffield & London: Health Matters & Medact.

Murray, M. (2000). Special issue: reconstructing health psychology. *Journal of Health Psychology*, 5 (3).

Murray, M. (2003). Narrative psychology and narrative research. In P. Camic, J.E. Rhodes & L. Yardley (eds) *Qualitative research in psychology: expanding perspectives in methodology and design*. Washington, DC: American Psychological Association.

Myers, J.L. & Well, A.D. (1991). *Research design and statistical analysis*. New York: HarperCollins.

Napier, B. (1995). Clinical psychology. In *Professional Psychology Handbook*. Leicester: BPS Books.

Nelson, G., Prilleltensky, I. & MacGillivary, H. (2001). Building value-based partnerships: towards solidarity. *American Journal of Community Psychology*, 29, 649–77.

Neyman, J. & Pearson, E.S. (1928). On the use and interpretation of certain test criteria for purposes of statistical inference. Parts I and II. *Biometrika*, 20, 174–240 & 263–94.

Nightingale, D.J. & Cromby, J. (1999). *Social constructionist psychology: a critical analysis of theory and practice*. Buckingham: Open University Press.

Nuffield Institute for Health and NHS Centre for Reviews and Dissemination (1996). Preventing falls and subsequent injury in older people. *Effective Health Care*, 2, 1–16.

Nutbeam, D. & Harris, E. (1999). Theories which explain health behaviour change by focusing on individual characteristics. In D. Nutbeam & E. Harris (eds) *Theory in a nutshell. A guide to health promotion*. Roseville: McGraw Hill.

Ogden, J. (1997). The rhetoric and reality of psychosocial theories: a challenge to biomedicine. *Journal of Health Psychology*, 2, 21–9.

Osborn, M. & Smith, J.A. (1998). The personal experience of chronic benign lower back pain: an interpretative phenomenological analysis. *British Journal of Health Psychology*, 3, 65–83.

Owens, N., Ewins, A.-L. & Lee, C. (1989). Smoking cessation by mail: a comparison of standard and personalized correspondence course formats. *Addictive Behaviours*, 14, 355–63.

Oxman, A.D. & Guyatt, (1988). Guidelines for reading literature reviews. *Canadian Medical Association*, 138, 697–703.

Parker, I. (1992). *Discourse dynamics: critical analysis for social and individual psychology.* London: Routledge.

Parker, I. & the Bolton Discourse Network (1999). *Critical textwork: an introduction to varieties of discourse and analysis.* Buckingham: Open University Press.

Parry, G. & Watts, F. (eds) *Behavioural and mental health research: A handbook of skills and methods.* London: Psychology Press.

Parsons, T. (1950). *The social system.* New York: Free Press.

Patton, M.Q. (2002). *Qualitative research and evaluation methods* (3rd edn). Thousand Oaks, CA & London: Sage.

Pollock, K. (1993). Attitude of mind as a means of resisting illness. In A. Radley (ed.) *Worlds of illness.* London: Routledge, pp. 49–70.

Pope, C. (1991). Trouble in store: some thoughts on the management of waiting lists. *Sociology of Health and Illness,* 13, 193–212.

Potter, J. (1996). Discourse analysis and constructionist approaches: theoretical background. In J.T.E. Richardson (ed.) *Handbook of qualitative research methods for psychology and the social sciences.* Leicester: BPS.

Potter, J. (2003). Discourse analysis and discursive psychology. In P. Camic, J.E. Rhodes & L. Yardley (eds) *Qualitative research in psychology: expanding perspectives in methodology and design.* Washington, DC: American Psychological Association.

Potter, J. & Wetherell, M. (1987). *Discourse and social psychology: beyond attitudes and behaviour.* London: Sage.

Potter, W.J. (1996). *An analysis of thinking and research about qualitative methods.* Mahwah, NJ: Lawrence Erlbaum.

Prilleltensky, I. (2001). Value-based praxis in community psychology: moving towards social justice and social action. *American Journal of Community Psychology,* 29, 747–78.

Putnam, R.D. (1993). *Making democracy work. Civic traditions in modern Italy.* Princeton: Princeton University Press.

Rapport, F. & Maggs, C. (1997). Measuring care: the case of district nursing. *Journal of Advanced Nursing,* 25, 673–80.

Ratcliff, D. (2003). Video methods in qualitative research. In P. Camic, J.E. Rhodes & L. Yardley (eds) *Qualitative research in psychology: expanding perspectives in methodology and design.* Washington, DC: American Psychological Association.

Ratzan, S.C. (2001). Health literacy: communication for the public good. *Health Promotion International,* 16, 207–14.

Raw, M. & Russell, M.A.H. (1980). Rapid smoking, cue exposure and support in the modification of smoking. *Behaviour Research and Therapy,* 18, 363–72.

Richmond, R.L., Makinson, R.J., Kehoe, L.A., Giugni, A.A. & Webster, I.W. (1993). One-year evaluation of three smoking cessation interventions administered by general practitioners. *Addictive Behaviours,* 18, 187–99.

Ricoeur, P. (1984). *Time and narrative.* Chicago: University of Chicago Press.

Riessman, C. (1993). *Narrative analysis.* London: Sage.

Robson, C. (2002). *Real world research: a resource for social scientists and practitioner-researchers.* (2nd edn, 2002). Oxford: Blackwell.

Roethlisberger, F.J. & Dickson, W.J. (1939). *Management and the worker.* Cambridge, MA: Harvard University Press.

Rosenthal, R. (1979). The 'file drawer problem' and tolerance for null results. *Psychological Bulletin,* 86, 638–41.

Rosser, W.W. (1984). The role of the family physician in smoking cessation. *Canadian Family Physician,* 30, 160–5.

Rothenbuhler, K. (1991). The process of community involvement. *Communication Monographs*, 58, 63–78.

Rubin, H.J. & Rubin, I.S. (1995). *Qualitative interviewing: the art of hearing data.* Thousand Oaks, CA & London: Sage.

Schofield, J.W. (1990). Increasing the generalizability of qualitative research. In E.W. Eisner & A. Pehskin (eds), *Qualitative inquiry in education: the continuing debate.* New York: Teachers College Press.

Secretary of State (1997). *The new NHS. Modern. Dependable.* London: Department of Health.

Seedhouse, D. (1998). *Ethics. The heart of health care* (2nd edn). Chichester: Wiley.

Shweder, R.A. (1996). Quanta and qualia: what is the 'object' of the ethnographic method? In R. Jessor, A. Colby and R.A. Shweder (eds) *Ethnography and human development.* Chicago: University of Chicago Press.

Silverman, D. (1993). *Interpreting qualitative data.* London: Sage.

Simmons, S.F. & Reuben, D. (2000). Nutritional intake monitoring for nursing home residents: a comparison of staff documentation, direct observation, and photography methods. *Journal of the American Geriatrics Society*, 48, 209–13.

Simpson, M. & Tuson, J. (1995). *Using observations in small-scale research: a beginner's guide.* Scottish Council for Research in Education.

Smith, C.P. (2000). Content analysis and narrative analysis. In H.T. Reis & C.M. Judd (eds) *Handbook of research methods in social and personality psychology.* Cambridge: Cambridge University Press.

Smith, J.A., Jarman, M. & Osborn, M. (1999). Doing interpretative phenomenological analysis. In M. Murray & K. Chamberlain (eds) *Qualitative health psychology: theories and methods.* London: Sage, pp. 218–40.

Smith, L.T. (1999). *Decolonizing methodologies. Research and indigenous peoples.* London: Zed Books & Dunedin: University of Otago Press.

Society for Community Research and Action (2001). www.apa.org/divisions/div27.

St Leger, L. (2001). Schools, health literacy and public health: possibilities and challenges. *Health Promotion International*, 16, 197–205.

Stainton-Rogers, W. (1996). Critical approaches to health psychology. *Journal of Health Psychology*, 1, 65–77.

Stake, R.E. (1995). *The art of case study research.* Thousand Oaks, CA: Sage.

Stake, R.E. (1998). Case studies. In N.K. Denzin & Y.S. Lincoln (eds) *Strategies of qualitative enquiry.* London: Sage, pp. 86–109.

Stake, R.E. (2000). Case studies. In N.K. Denzin & Y.S. Lincoln (eds), *Handbook of qualitative research* (2nd edn). Thousand Oaks, CA: Sage, pp. 435–54.

Sterling, T.D. (1959). Publication decisions and their possible effects on inferences drawn from tests of significance – or vice versa. *Journal of the American Statistical Association*, 54, 30–4.

Sterling, T.D., Rosenbaum, W.L. & & Weinkam, J.L. (1995). Publication decisions revisited: the effect of the outcome of statistical tests on the decision to publish and vice versa. *American Statistician*, 49, 108–12.

Stern, P.N. (1994). Eroding grounded theory. In J.M. Morse (ed.) *Critical issues in qualitative research methods.* Thousand Oaks, CA: Sage, pp. 212–23.

Sterne, J.A.C., Egger, M. & Sutton, A.J. (2001). Meta-analysis software. In M. Egger et al. (eds) *Systematic reviews in health care.* London: BMJ Books, pp. 336–46.

Stevens, S.S. (1951). *Handbook of experimental psychology.* New York: Wiley.

Stewart, R. & Bhagwanjee, A. (1999). Promoting group empowerment and self-reliance through participatory research: a case study of people with physical disability. *Disability and Rehabilitation*, 21, 338–45.

Stone, G.C. (1979). Patient compliance and the role of the expert. *Journal of Social Issues*, 35, 34–59.

Stone, G.C., Cohen, F., & Adler, N.E. (eds) (1979). *Health psychology – a handbook: theories, applications and challenges of a psychological approach to the health care system.* San Francisco: Jossey-Bass.

Stoppard, J.M. (1998). Dis-ordering depression in women: towards a materialist-discursive account. *Theory and Psychology*, 8, 79–99.

Strauss, A. & Corbin, J. (1990). *Basics of qualitative research: grounded theory procedures and techniques.* Newbury Park, CA: Sage.

Strauss, A. & Corbin, J. (1994). Grounded theory methodology: an overview. In N.K. Denzin & Y.S. Lincoln (eds) *Handbook of qualitative research.* Thousand Oaks, CA: Sage, pp. 273–85.

Swisher, S.N. (1980). The biopsychosocial model: its future for the internist. *Psychosomatic Medicine*, 42, 113–21.

Sykes, C.M. & Marks, D.F. (2002). A re-analysis of a systematic review on smoking cessation. In preparation.

Tabachnick, B.G. & Fidell, L.S. (2001). *Using multivariate statistics* (4th edn). New York: Allyn and Bacon.

Tashakkori, A. & Teddie, C. (1998). *Mixed methodology: combining qualitative and quantitative approaches.* London: Sage.

Taylor, J. (1999). Empowerment, identity and participatory research: using social action research to challenge isolation for deaf and hard of hearing people from minority ethnic communities. *Disability and Society*, 14, 369–84.

Taylor, S. (2001). Locating and conducting discourse analytic research. In M. Wetherell, S. Taylor & S. Yates (eds) *Discourse as data: a guide for analysis.* London: Sage.

Temkin, K. & Rohe, W. (1998). Social capital and neighbourhood stability: An empirical investigation. *Housing Policy Debate*, 9, xx–xx.

ten Have, P. (1999). *Doing conversation analysis.* London: Sage.

Thompson, R.S., Michnich, M.E., Friedlander, L., Gilson, B., Grothaus, L.C. & Storer, B. (1988). Effectiveness of smoking cessation interventions integrated into primary care practice. *Medical Care*, 26, 62–76.

Tsey, K. (1997) Traditional medicine in contemporary Ghana: a public policy analysis. *Social Science and Medicine*, 45, 1065–74.

Tukey, J.W. (1977). *Exploratory data analysis.* Reading, MA: Addison-Wesley.

Vale, L., Donaldson, C., Daly, C., Campbell, Cody, J., Grant, A., Khan, I., Lawrence, P., Wallace, S. & MacLeod, A. (2000). Evidence-based medicine and health economics: a case study of end stage renal disease. *Health Economics*, 9, 337–51.

van Dijk, T.A. (1997). Discourse as interaction in society. In T.A. van Djjk (ed.) *Discourse studies: a multidisciplinary introduction Vol 2: discourse as social interaction.* London: Sage.

Ville, I., Ravaud, J.-F., Diard, C. & Paicheler, H. (1994). Self-representations and physical impairment: a social constructionist approach. *Sociology of Health and Illness*, 16, 301–21.

Ward, C. (1995). Consenting to surgery. In C. Ward (ed.) *Essays on ethics relating to the practice of plastic surgery.* London: Churchill Livingstone.

Wardle, J. (2000). Editorial. Public health psychology: expanding the horizons of health psychology. *British Journal of Health Psychology*, 5, 329–36.

Ware, J.E., Snow, M., Kosinski, B. & Gandeck, B.(1993). *SF-36 health survey: manual and interpretation guide*. Boston: The Health Institute, New England Medical Center.

Wetherell, M. (1998). Positioning and interpretative repertoires: conversation analysis and post-structuralism in dialogue. *Discourse and Society*, 9, 387–412.

Wetherell, M., Taylor, S. & Yates, S.J. (2001). Introduction. In M. Wetherell, S. Taylor & S. Yates (eds) *Discourse theory and practice: a reader*. London: Sage.

White, M. & Epston, D. (1990). *Narrative means to therapeutic ends*. New York: Norton.

WHOQOL Group (1993). *Measuring quality of life: the development of the World Health Organization Quality of Life Instrument (WHOQOL)*. Geneva: WHO.

Whyte, W.F. (1955) *Street corner society: the social structure of an Italian slum* (2nd edn). Chicago: University of Chicago Press.

Wiljhuizen, G.J. & Ooijendijk, W. (1999). Measuring disability, the agreement between self-evaluation and observation of performance. *Disability and Rehabilitation*, 21, 61–7.

Wilkin, D., Hallam, L. & Doggett, M. (1993). *Measures of need and outcome for primary health care*. Oxford: Oxford University Press.

Wilkinson, L. (1999). Statistical methods in psychology journals: guidelines and explanations. *American Psychologist*, 54 (8), 594–604.

Wilkinson, S. (1998a). Focus groups in health research: exploring the meanings of health and illness. *Journal of Health Psychology*, 3 (3): 329–48.

Wilkinson, S. (1998b). Focus group methodology: a review. *International Journal of Social Research Methodology*, 1 (3): 181–203.

Wilkinson, S. & Kitzinger, C. (2000). Thinking differently about thinking positive: a discursive approach to cancer patients' talk. *Social Science and Medicine*, 50, 797–811.

Willig, C. (1999). *Applied discourse analysis: social and psychological interventions*. Buckingham: Open University Press.

Willig, C. (2001). *Introducing qualitative research in psychology*. Buckingham: Open University Press.

Wilson, H.S. & Hutchinson, S.A. (1996). Methodological mistakes in grounded theory. *Nursing Research*, 45, 122–4.

Windsor, R.A., Lowe, J.B. & Bartlett (1988). The effectiveness of a worksite self-help smoking cessation program: a randomized trial. *Journal of Behavioral Medicine*, 11, 407–21.

Winett, R.A., King, A.C. & Altman, D.G. (1989). *Health psychology and public health*. New York: Pergamon.

Wing, J.K. (1992). *SCAN: Schedules for clinical assessment in neuropsychiatry*. Geneva: WHO.

Wood, L.A. & Kroger, R.O. (2000). *Doing discourse analysis*. London: Sage.

Yardley, L. (1997). Introducing material-discursive approaches to health and illness. In L. Yardley (ed.) *Material discourses of health and illness*. London: Routledge.

Yardley, L. (1999). Understanding embodied experience: beyond mind body dualism in health research. In M. Murray & K. Chamberlain (eds) *Qualitative health research: theories and methods*. London: Sage.

Yardley, L. (2000). Dilemmas in qualitative health research. *Psychology and Health*, 15, 215–28.

Yardley, L. & Beech, S. (1998). 'I'm not a doctor': deconstructing accounts of coping, causes and control of dizziness. *Journal of Health Psychology*, 3, 313–27.

Yardley, L., Sharples, K., Beech, S. & Lewith, G. (2001). Developing a dynamic model of treatment perceptions. *Journal of Health Psychology*, 6, 269–82.

Yin, R.K. (1982). Studying the implementation of public programs. In W. Williams et al. (eds) *Studying implementation: methodological and administrative issues*. Chatham, NJ: Chatham House, pp. 36–72.

Yin, R.K. (1994). *Case study research: design and methods* (2nd edn). Thousand Oaks, CA: Sage.

Yin, R.K. & Heald, K.A. (1975). Using the case survey method to analyze policy studies. *Administrative Science Quarterly*, 20, 371–81.

INDEX